The Archaeology of Shamanism

The meaning of 'shamanism' has been debated for almost three centuries, ever since the term was coined to describe the activities of those who attained altered states of consciousness in order to mediate between human beings and the supernatural world. The ritual practices that characterised these perceived contacts with other realities have left highly physical traces in the archaeological record of prehistoric peoples, and the potential for the recognition of shamanic belief systems in the past is now being realised as never before.

In this timely collection, Neil Price provides a general introduction to the archaeology of shamanism by bringing together recent work on the subject. Blending theoretical discussion with detailed case studies, the issues addressed include shamanic material culture, responses to dying and the dead, shamanic soundscapes, the use of ritual architecture and shamanism in the context of other belief systems. Following an initial orientation reviewing shamanism as an anthropological construct, the volume focuses on the Northern hemisphere with case studies from Greenland to Nepal, Siberia to Kazakhstan. The chapters span a chronological range from the Upper Palaeolithic to the present and explore such cross-cutting themes as gender and the body, identity, landscape, the social perception of animals, prehistoric 'art', and shamanism in the heritage and cultural identity of indigenous peoples. The volume also addresses the interpretation of shamanic beliefs in terms of cognitive neuroscience and the modern public perception of shamanism in the past.

This book is an essential study of ancient shamanism through its material remains. It serves as a source of front-line case studies for specialists, while making these discussions accessible to a broader public. Archaeologists, anthropologists, historians of religion and psychologists will find the volume a valuable work of reference, as will those interested in alternative religions and spiritual philosophies.

Neil S. Price is a Lecturer in Archaeology at the University of Uppsala, Sweden. He has written extensively on the Viking Age, and has conducted research projects in France, Iceland, Russia and Sápmi (Lappland).

Frontispiece. Ivory maskette, 500–1 BC, Tyara, northern Québec. (Photo: Canadian Museum of Civilization; KbFk-7:308).

The Archaeology
of Shamanism

Edited by Neil S. Price

London and New York

First published 2001 by Routledge
11 New Fetter Lane, London EC4P 4EE

Simultaneously published in the USA and Canada
by Routledge
29 West 35th Street, New York, NY 10001

Routledge is an imprint of the Taylor & Francis Group

Typeset in Italian Garamond by Exe Valley Dataset Ltd
Printed and bound in Great Britain by TJ International, Padstow, Cornwall

British Library Cataloguing in Publication Data
A catalogue record for this book is available from the British Library

Library of Congress Cataloging in Publication Data
The archaeology of Shamanism/edited by Neil Price.
    p. cm.
  Includes bibliographical references and index.
  1. Shamanism. 2. Ethnoarchaeology. 3. Material culture. I. Price, Neil S.

  GN475.8.A73 2001
  306.6′91144–dc21   2001031750

ISBN 0-415-25254-7 (hbk)
ISBN 0-415-25255-5 (pbk)

Contents

Figures

Contributors

Martin Appelt is a Research Fellow in Archaeology at the National Museum of Denmark's Greenland Research Centre. His recent work and writings have focused on the Palaeo-Eskimo cultures of the Eastern Arctic, and since 1985 he has conducted archaeological fieldwork in Greenland, Denmark, Canada and Tunisia. Among his recent books are *Late Dorset in High Arctic Greenland* (co-author, 1999) and *Identities and Cultural Contacts in the Arctic* (co-editor, 2000).

Ekaterina Devlet is a Senior Researcher at the Institute of Archaeology, Russian Academy of Sciences in Moscow, and Assistant Professor at the Russian State University for the Humanities. She has published over 50 papers on prehistoric art and shamanism, while her books include *Pre-Columbian Art of the Central American Indians* (2000) and *Spiritual Life of the Ancient Peoples of Northern and Central Asia: the World of the Rock Art* (with Marianna Devlet, 2001).

Thomas A. Dowson is a Lecturer in the School of Art History and Archaeology at the University of Manchester. He has published extensively on various rock art traditions, with research focusing on shamanism, archaeological approaches to artistic traditions and their popular representation, and the impact of sexual politics on archaeology. His publications include *Rock Engravings of Southern Africa* (1992), *Images of Power: Understanding San Rock Art* (with David Lewis-Williams, 2000) and *Queer Archaeologies* (editor, 2000).

Natalia Fedorova is a Research Fellow at the Institute of History and Archaeology (Ural Division, Russian Academy of Sciences) in Ekaterinberg. Her research focuses on the Iron Age of western Siberia, ancient art and cultural communication. Among her recent books are *Ugrian Heritage* (1994), *Gone into the Hills: Iron Age Cultures of the Northwestern Yamal* (1998), and *Cholmogor Treasure: Antiquities of the 3rd–4th Centuries AD from the Surgut Arts Museum Collection* (2001).

Hans Christian Gulløv holds a professorship in Greenland's Cultural History at the National Museum of Denmark's Department of Research. He is a former senior scholar at the Institute of Eskimology and Danish Polar Center, visiting lecturer at the University of Greenland and curator of Inuit Collections at the National Museum. He is the scientific editor of *Monographs on Greenland, Man & Society Series*, and has conducted anthropological and archaeological fieldwork in Greenland and Siberia.

Sandra E. Hollimon is Lecturer in Anthropology at Sonoma State University, California. She is also Senior Prehistoric Archaeologist at Sonoma State's Anthropological Studies Center. Her publications include "Archaeology of the 'Aqi: gender and sexuality in prehistoric Chumash society", in *Archaeologies of Sexuality* (Routledge), and "Death, gender and the Chumash peoples: Mourning ceremonialism as an integrative mechanism" (American Anthropological Association).

Peter Jordan is a Research Fellow at the Institute of Archaeology, University College London. He has conducted research into the material culture of hunter fisher gatherers in western Siberia and recently received his doctorate from the University of Sheffield.

J. D. Lewis-Williams is Professor emeritus in the Rock Art Research Institute, University of the Witwatersrand, Johannesburg, South Africa. He has published extensively on southern African San and west European Upper Palaeolithic art, and his many books include *Shamans of Prehistory* (with Jean Clottes, 1998) and *Stories that Float from Afar: Ancestral San Folklore* (2000).

Martin Porr is currently a PhD student at the University of Southampton, preparing a thesis on Early Upper Palaeolithic mobiliary art. He has published several works on hunter-gatherer anthropology, social theory and Palaeolithic archaeology. Together with Linda R. Owen, he is co-editor of *Ethno-Analogy and the Reconstruction of Prehistoric Artefact Use and Production* (1999).

Neil S. Price is a Lecturer in Archaeology at the University of Uppsala, Sweden. He has written extensively on the Viking Age, and has conducted research projects in France, Iceland, Russia and Sápmi (Lappland). His books include *The Vikings in Brittany* (1989), *Cultural Atlas of the Viking World* (co-author, 1994), and *The Viking Way: Religion and War in Late Iron Age Scandinavia* (in press).

Andrzej Rozwadowski is a Lecturer at the Institute of Eastern Studies of the Adam Mickiewicz University in Poznań, Poland, where he completed his doctorate. His research focuses on the ancient art of Central Asia and Siberia and its relations to local cultural traditions, particularly that of shamanism. He has undertaken fieldwork in Uzbekistan, Kazakhstan, and Yakutia, and is co-editor of *Rock Art and Shamanism of Central Asia* (in Polish, 1999).

Patricia D. Sutherland is a Curator of Archaeology at the Canadian Museum of Civilization. Since 1975 she has worked extensively throughout Arctic Canada, where her research has focussed on the Palaeo-Eskimo cultural tradition. She co-curated the museum exhibit *Lost Visions, Forgotten Dreams: Life and Art of an Ancient Arctic People*, and is currently preparing a book on Palaeo-Eskimo art.

Robert J. Wallis is a Lecturer in the Department of Archaeology and Co-ordinator of Archaeology at New College, University of Southampton, where he received an MA (Archaeology and Anthropology of Rock Art) and PhD. Research interests include the archaeology of shamanism and neo-Shamanism, art and society, the politics of the past, and the Neolithic and Germanic communities of north-western Europe.

Damian Walter completed his doctorate in the Department of Anthropology and Sociology at the School of Oriental and African Studies, University of London in 2001. He currently works as a teaching assistant in the same department.

Aaron Watson, University of Reading, UK, specialises in the Neolithic and Bronze Age of the British Isles, and has recently completed a doctorate examining stone circles and henges. He has a particular interest in exploring how people might have experienced monumental buildings in prehistory, and seeks to reintegrate elements such as sound into archaeological interpretations.

Howard Williams is a Lecturer in Archaeology at Trinity College, Carmarthen, Wales. He has published a series of articles on early medieval cemeteries, social memory and burial archaeology, and has recently completed a doctorate on early Anglo-Saxon cremation practices. He is currently editing a book entitled *Death, Memory and Material Culture*, and co-directing a research project on Roundway Down, Wiltshire.

Acknowledgements

The core of *The Archaeology of Shamanism* is formed by a series of papers presented in a session of the same name which I organised for the 5th Annual Meeting of the European Association of Archaeologists (EAA), held at Bournemouth in September 1999. However, the idea of the book in fact pre-dated the conference, and several of the contributors who did not attend the session had already agreed to write for this volume: rather than a collection of conference proceedings, it should instead be seen as a structured work of which certain parts were aired in preliminary form at a meeting along the way. As organiser, I would like to thank Tim Darvill and Eileen Wilkes whose administrative work made the EAA session possible; as both organiser and editor, I would like to thank all the contributors for their hard work and commitment to this project, which began life as a long series of emails sent out from Uppsala to various corners of the globe in late 1998.

One participant in the EAA session did not contribute to the book, one non-participant who had originally agreed to contribute had to pull out at a later stage due to other commitments, and two would-be contributors patiently remained on my 'stand-by list' until it was clear that the session and/or book were full. All of them nonetheless made their mark on the project, and I would therefore like to thank Tim Bayliss-Smith, Robert Layton, Inga-Maria Mulk and David Whitley for their understanding and encouragement.

An important part of this book developed during the spring of 2000 on a combined conference and field-trip visiting sites of shamanic rock art in the Drakensberg, Waterberg and Magaliesberg of South Africa, under the guidance of David Lewis-Williams and his colleagues from the Rock Art Research Institute (RARI) at the University of the Witwatersrand. The experience of discussing the shamanic world-view with some of its most brilliant interpreters is always invigorating under any circumstances, but the memory of these conversations in the specific context of the rock shelters, as the sun set on the Berg, or around the fire as the constellations of the southern sky appeared overhead, will remain long in my mind. My thanks to all at RARI, and to all the friends and colleagues who were there.

The project of bringing this volume to fruition has run parallel with the latter stages of producing my book on the belief systems of the early medieval North, and the academic advice and assistance that I have received for the latter has inevitably affected the former: I therefore refer the reader to the more extensive acknowledgements given in *The Viking Way: Religion and War in Late Iron Age Scandinavia* (Price in press). However, for very specific contributions to the present work, bestowed in various forms from a kind word to long nights of conversation, I would like to thank Amanda Chadburn, David Miles, Adrian Olivier and Andrew Sherratt. I am also grateful to my colleagues and students at the Department of Archaeology and Ancient History at the University of Uppsala, whose lively engagement with the ancient mind has been a constant source of inspiration. I would especially like to thank my wife, Linda Qviström, for her unswerving support, cheerfully provided despite my early imposition of a moratorium on shaman jokes in our home.

For permission to reproduce photographs and figures, I thank the Canadian Museum of Civilisation; Norfolk Museums and Archaeology Service; and the Institut für Ur- und Frühgeschichte, Abteilung Ältere Urgeschichte und Quartärökologie, Universität Tübingen.

For early encouragement at Routledge I would like to thank a number of enthusiastic referees, and former commissioning editor of archaeology Vicky Peters. My editor has been Julene Barnes, who, together with editorial assistant Polly Osborn and the members of the design team, has my heartfelt thanks for all the hard work and good humour (far better than I deserved) that has gone into the preparation of this book. Its gestation has been accompanied by an exchange of emails and conversations on subjects ranging from theatrical criticism to Cajun food, and I hope that some of the fun that we had shows in these pages.

Neil Price
Uppsala, at the turn of winter, March 2001

Part One

The Archaeology of Shamanism
Cognition, Cosmology and World-View

Chapter One

An archaeology of altered states: Shamanism and material culture studies

Neil S. Price

INTRODUCTION: ŠAMAN/SAMA:N/SHAMAN

When a dissident priest called Avvakum arrived in the lands of the nomadic, reindeer-herding Evenki in the early 1650s, having been exiled to central Siberia by the patriarch of the Russian Orthodox Church, no outsider had ever heard of a *šaman*, let alone written the word down or explored the cosmological understandings that underpinned its meaning. By the time of his execution for heresy in 1682, Avvakum's descriptions communicated during his sojourn among the Evenki had already laid the foundations for what anthropologists would later term the study of shamanism.

Over the following 150 years, as Siberia was traversed by missionaries, political exiles (often highly educated intellectuals), Tsarist agents and European travellers, more and more stories were recorded of the intriguing beliefs and practices to be found among the tribal peoples there: from the Nenets, Mansi, Khanty, Ngansan and Enets of the Uralic group around the Yamal peninsula, the Ob and Yenisei river basins and the north Siberian coast; the Turkic-speaking Yakut and Dolgan on the lower Lena; the Tungusic–Mandchurian peoples of central Siberia, including the Even and the Evenki themselves; and the Yukaghir, Chukchi, Koryak and Itelmen of eastern Siberia and the Pacific coast, amongst many others.

The tales told by these early voyagers were startling, and aroused intense interest in Russia and Europe. A fragmentary picture emerged of an 'ensouled world' in which everything was alive, and filled with spirits – animals, natural features, even what to Western eyes were inanimate objects. To such beings could be linked almost every aspect of material life: sickness and health, the provision of food and shelter, success in hunting, and the well-being of the community. The maintenance of good relationships with these spirits was thus of crucial importance, and the most striking of the travellers' stories concerned the special individuals who attained states of trance and ecstasy in order to send out their souls to communicate with these beings, to enlist their aid or bind them to their will, sometimes even to engage them in combat. The operative sphere of these people, whom the Evenki called *šaman*, was revealed as a world of mediation, of negotiation between the realm of human beings and the adjacent, occasionally coincident, planes of existence in which dwelt the gods, the spirits of nature, and the souls of the dead. The complex variety of equipment used in these ceremonies was also described: the strange headgear and jackets hung with jingling amulets, the fur and feathers of animals, metal images; the masks and veils; the effigies and figurines; and above all, the drums.

Some of this data was published and widely discussed in scholarly circles, and during the eighteenth century the Evenk concept of the *šaman* was taken up in Russian as a useful collective for the similar figures that were encountered from one tribe to another across the region. From the phonetic constructions used to record these concepts (the indigenous Siberians had no written language), *šaman* or *sama:n* was soon normalised via Russian to the western European languages, creating the more conventional 'shaman' (the Evenki pronounced the word with the accent on the second syllable, 'sha-márn', but the alternative forms of 'shár-man' or 'sháy-man' are now more common). At first, there were few that associated these individuals, and the role that they played within their communities, with 'religion' in the sense of an organised system of worship. The notion of a collective pattern of belief – shaman*ism* – arose first when the Christian missions began to seriously target the Siberian peoples for conversion, and thus sought to identify a pagan religion towards the overthrow of which they could concentrate their efforts (see Thomas and Humphrey 1994, and Znamenski 1999, for recent studies of church/state perceptions of indigenous belief).

SHAMANIC RESEARCH IN RUSSIA AND BEYOND

This interpretation of exactly what shamanism was/is has been central to shamanic studies from the very beginning. Already in 1853, the Finnish scholar Castrén challenged the idea that shamanism could be described as a religion rather than as a pattern of behaviour, and this debate continued throughout the late 1800s when the first major Russian works on the subject appeared. By the beginning of the twentieth century, this social, psychological and (arguably) religious phenomenon was already the subject of an established body of literature (see, for example, Shashkov 1864; Potanin 1881–3; Agapitov and Khangalov 1883; Radloff 1884; Pripuzov 1885; Mikhailovski 1895; Shimkevich 1896; Sieroszewski 1993 [1896], 1902; this period of early research is summarised in Hultkrantz 1998).

Similar practices had earlier been described from other parts of the northern hemisphere, for example in Schefferus' influential book *Lapponia* (1673) on the Sámi of Fenno-Scandia, but it was not until the early 1900s when the American Museum in New York launched the Jesup North Pacific Expedition that the beliefs of other circumpolar arctic and sub-arctic cultures began to be specifically – though tentatively – described in terms of shamanism. The link to Siberia was eased by the widespread accessibility of English-language publications such as Bogoras' (1911) and Jochelson's (1908) reports from the Jesup Expedition, Czaplicka's 1914 survey of the region, and Shirokogorov's classic *Psychomental Complex of the Tungus* (1935). Through the early twentieth century the notion of shamanism spread slowly in North America, being applied to the 'medicine-men' of First Nations peoples, but even here the definitions common in Siberia were being adapted to local circumstances (e.g. Dixon 1908).

Although shamanism was widely adopted as a psychological and psychiatric concept in the years between the world wars, as Hultkrantz has noted, 'it is difficult to find surveys of [non-Russian] shamanism before 1950' (1998: 61). There were, however, many foreigners working on the Siberian material. Finnish researchers were particularly active (e.g. Holmberg [Harva] 1915, 1922, 1927, 1938; Granö 1919–21; Donner 1922; Lehtisalo 1924, 1937; other significant Western works include Stadling 1912 and Nioradze 1925), and post-Revolutionary Russian research continued within the strict ideological frameworks of Marxist interpretations (see Hultkrantz 1998: 65–7 and Balzer 1990). Until the fall of the Soviet Union, or at least the late 1980s, the division between Western and Eastern studies of shamanism was almost total.

Soviet writers such as Zelenin (1936, 1937, 1952) and Anisimov (1963) sought to explain shamanism in terms of a particular concentration of power and shifting control of production, with an additional emphasis on medical interpretations often based on notions of mental illness. The explanation of shamanism as due to a kind of 'arctic hysteria' induced by cold and deprivation was raised by Ohlmarks in 1939 – significantly in the political climate of Nazi Germany – and together with the idea of the shaman as mentally unbalanced psychopath this was adopted with enthusiasm in Soviet Russia, where it became fundamental in the policies of suppressing this perceived threat of independent thought and spiritual allegiance. Ethnocentric 'explanations' were also given prominence, while other Russian scholars sought refuge in collecting raw data which did not need to be forced into an ideologically inspired interpretative straitjacket (the research from this period is summarised in Popov's bibliography from 1932, listing some 650 Russian works on shamanism; a German-language version appeared in 1990). The scholars who maintained a most strictly empirical line, and thus avoided the regime's appropriation of their work, are now bearers of the tradition of Russian research in the post-Soviet era (e.g. Vajnstein and Basilov – see Hultkrantz, 1998: 66, for an assessment of these writers' significance).

At the socio-political 'border' of Russian scholarship, another major block of work developed, again building on research from the late 1800s and focusing on shamanism among the Nordic and Sámi populations of Scandinavia. More than 300 publications have appeared on the shamanic complex of *seiðr* and related rituals in Old Norse belief (collected and discussed in Price in press, with further treatment in Price 2000a and b, 2001b; see also DuBois 1999 for a recent cross-cultural study of Scandinavian religion). An even greater number of publications, over 800, deal with Sámi religion (collected in Rydving 1993b; the works of Bäckman, Hultkrantz, Manker, Mebius, Pentikäinen, and Rydving himself are especially central). Case studies of the Norse and Sámi demonstrate particularly clearly the use of specialised shamanic practices for aggressive ends, and also the prominence of sexual elements in shamanic rituals; importantly, both of these traits are relatively common among the arctic and sub-arctic peoples, a fact that belies the common association of shamanism almost exclusively with healing that has characterised Western perceptions in the wake of Eliade's classic work from 1964.

The research history of shamanism in Western anthropology, comparative theology and related disciplines has been charted many times, and this is not the place for yet another introductory essay on the 'meaning' of this phenomenon (useful texts in this regard include Eliade 1964, into the orbit of which most subsequent works have been drawn; Lessa and Vogt 1965; Wallace 1966; Edsman 1967; Motzki 1971; Furst 1974; Hultkrantz 1973, 1979, 1993, 1998; Humphrey 1980; Lewis 1981, 1989; Atkinson 1992; Ripinsky-Naxon 1993; Vitebsky 1995; Pentikäinen 1998; Pentikäinen *et al.* 1998; Bowie 2000: 190–218; Larsson 2000). We may, however, note the importance of two key themes of relevance to the archaeological interpretations of the present book. The first of these concerns the relationship of shamanic belief systems to their environmental setting (e.g. Hultkrantz 1965; Pentikäinen 1996; Bowie 2000: 118–50), explored further below in a landscape context. The second focuses on the links that are sometimes postulated between shamanism and another, equally hotly debated anthropological construct: totemism (the classic introduction can be found in Lévi-Strauss 1962; see Layton 2000 for a recent review of this discussion). As the study of northern shamanism has ebbed and flowed in popularity during the last century, three main forms of interpretation have predominated. The Nivkh ethnographer Chuner Taksami, himself an ethnic Siberian and acquainted with several shamans, has perhaps stated it best (1998: 14):

Shamanism is an historical phenomenon within a system of traditional faiths distinctive of nearly all Siberian peoples. Some people consider shamanism as a variety of primitive religion; others tend to think of it as a set of beliefs and customs centred on the shaman's personality; and others still associate shamanism with witchcraft and magical spells.

Retrospective reviews of these changing fashions of interpretation, and more recent responses to them, can be found in the international journal of shamanic research, *Shaman*, and in a series of influential conference publications from the last three decades (e.g. Diószegi and Hóppal 1978; Hóppal 1984; Hóppal and von Sadovszky 1989; Hóppal and Pentikäinen 1992; Siikala and Hóppal 1992; Hóppal and Howard 1993).

One major trend however continues to polarise shamanic studies: the question of geographic frames of reference. Even now, echoing the debates of the early twentieth century, some historians of religion strongly resist the use of the term 'shamanism' beyond certain regions of central Siberia. In one sense these objections seem baffling, given that – as we have seen – the concept of shaman*ism* has always been an externally imposed construction, and does not exist anywhere at all other than in the minds of its students. Not even the Evenki have an overall word for what the *šaman* does, though like several other Siberian peoples they have a broad vocabulary for the different components of the shamanic complex. As both a term and a notion, shamanism is entirely an academic creation, and as such it is certainly a useful tool serving to describe a pattern of ritual behaviour and belief found in strikingly similar form across much of the arctic and sub-arctic regions of the world. Even within this broad understanding, the meaning of shamanism is entirely a matter of consensus, discussion and continuing redefinition; this extends to terminology, many scholars now preferring to write of 'shamanhood' or 'shamanship'. The essential question is to whether we can truly speak of shamanism beyond the circumpolar sphere.

It is here that we enter a broader framework of interpretation, which moves outward from Siberia and the circumpolar region on a sliding scale of inclusion to embrace shamanistic traits in the ritual practices of South America, Oceania, Africa (particularly controversially), and ultimately the globe – an approach recently typified by the work of Piers Vitebsky (1995). In many cases this is still rooted in scholarly discussion, but in the broadest and most popular understanding 'shamanism' has latterly come to cover virtually any kind of belief in 'spirits' and the existence of other worlds, states of being or planes of consciousness – a definition that of course encompasses the majority of the world's religions, organised or otherwise, ancient and modern. In this context the term 'shaman' has similarly been used to refer to almost any kind of mediator, in any kind of medium, between one perception of the world and another. As a result, those popularly described as shamans have included an astonishing variety of individuals ranging from Jesus to Jim Morrison.

These are not the shamanisms of this book. Instead we follow the general direction taken by related academic disciplines, as summarised by Mathias Guenther: 'the view held generally by scholars in the anthropology of religion and in comparative religion . . . [is] . . . that shamanism is a religious phenomenon that can be formally delineated and differentiated from other, more complex religions' (1999: 426). Considering Taksami's identification of shamanism as an *historical* phenomenon (1998: 14), how far is it reasonable to talk of shamanism in the prehistoric past? The answer, of course, can only be sought in studies of material culture, and thus archaeology.

SHAMANISM AND MATERIAL CULTURE STUDIES

The inclusion of shamanism in archaeological interpretations has in general run parallel with its adoption in anthropological and comparative theological circles, as discussed above. Until relatively recently, however, such work was largely confined to the study of prehistoric 'art', especially in the context of the Palaeolithic painted caves and the early identification of their images as artefacts of 'hunting magic' (see Bahn and Vertut 1988; cf. Lommel 1967). In the 1960s and 70s, a concern for the material culture of consciousness received new impetus with explorations of narcotics and hallucinogens in the archaeological record (in later years the work of Andrew Sherratt has been particularly important here, e.g. 1987, 1991). From the 1980s onwards, shamanism has reappeared in archaeological interpretations with some regularity, mostly in the context of the post-processual concern for ancient symbolism and the meaning-content of material culture. Latterly, the emphasis on cognitive archaeology has increased this trend. Individually, the 'shamanically relevant' publications of recent years run well into treble figures, making separate citation meaningless here: what has been missing in this work is an overview of the field as a whole – the stated purpose of this book.

There are, of necessity, many omissions. We do not discuss the rich shamanic heritage of the Classical world, the ecstatic cults of the Greeks and Romans; to an extent, some aspects of early Christianity and the desert religions of the Middle East may also be viewed in this light. In many parts of Europe even down to relatively recent times, there were traces of shamanism in the agrarian cults and local folkloric observances of the rural population (see Ginzburg 1983, 1990 and Klaniczay 1990: 129–50 for examples from the Mediterranean, the Baltic and the Balkans). Similarly, available space sadly did not permit a discussion of African and Pacific cultures, nor do we touch upon the belief systems of the central and southern Americas. The 'shamanic world', in all its diversity, is vast, and is impossible to cover comprehensively in a volume of this kind – nor is this our aim. The shamanic traditions of all of the regions represented here, and those that are not, could and do form the subject of book-length studies in their own right.

Instead, this volume has been conceived as an introduction to the field, focusing deliberately on the northern hemisphere while taking occasional diversions to follow specific lines of enquiry and interpretation. We begin with Siberia and Central Asia, the 'cradle of shamanism' discussed above, which has been curiously neglected in recent archaeological works on this aspect of early belief. We then move eastwards to North America, Canada and Greenland, and conclude by moving out of the arctic and sub-artic territories to Northern Europe and a group of papers that explore new dimensions, even new definitions, of shamanism outside this circumpolar sphere.

The geographical organisation has been chosen advisedly, because all of shamanic research is characterised by cross-cutting themes that would soon render redundant any attempt to draw them out in individual sections. In allowing the regional variations of northern shamanism to emerge, we hope to simultaneously provide the reader with a comprehensive survey of archaeological approaches to specific shamanistic themes through studies of prehistoric 'art', both portable and parietal; constructions of gender, identity and the body, including their articulation in dress and costume; landscape; architecture; mortuary behaviour; and human–animal relationships. We also address issues such as the interpretation of shamanic beliefs in terms of cognitive neuroscience, and the response to ancient shamanism among modern Pagans.

Shamanism and rock art

The field of rock art research is a special case, as it is here that the archaeological employment of shamanic interpretations has undoubtedly been most prominent in the last two decades. Perhaps as a result of the considerable influence that this exciting work has exerted on shamanic studies in a broader sense (see Price 2001a), the application of shamanic metaphors to parietal art has also aroused surprisingly vitriolic reactions from a small minority of researchers. However, such Pavlovian responses have earned little sympathy in the wider profession, and most recent collections exploring the current state of rock art research have included appropriately detailed reviews of shamanic approaches (e.g. Helskog and Olsen 1995; Chippindale and Taçon 1998). For this reason we shall not concentrate on this material here.

However, the very significant prominence that rock art interpetations have assumed in the archaeology of shamanism does require an overview of this work, here provided in chapter 2 by David Lewis-Williams, the pioneer of these approaches in southern Africa and one of the most internationally influential scholars in shamanic research. We here go back to the source for explanatory models that have been much imitated in the subsequent work of others, tracing the development of ideas that have set the pattern for this branch of shamanic interpetation in archaeology: from entoptic phenomena and altered states of consciousness, dreams, transformation and spirit animals, to the crucial concept of the rock surface as a membrane between the worlds, through to recent work emphasising the past and present political context of the art; Lewis-Williams' paper also includes a bibliography of the major literature within this field.

The first of the papers on Siberia and Central Asia, by Katja Devlet (chapter 3), also considers rock art, but from a quite different perspective to the 'southern African School' by putting forward an empirical discussion of imagery related to ritual costume and the shamanic coat. Western readers in particular may be astonished by the detail of the motifs presented, in many cases for the first time in an English-language publication: there surely cannot be a closer correlation between recent, ethnographically recorded data and archaeological finds from the distant past, though the exact (causal?) nature of their relationship is intriguing. Andrzej Rozwadowski takes a different approach in chapter 5 by reviewing the above-mentioned discussion of entoptic phenomena 'ten years on', presenting a critically-aware reappraisal of images in the rock art of Kazakhstan, focusing not on individual motifs but on their combination and landscape context.

Shamanism and portable art

The focus on shamanic interpretations of rock art has tended to obscure the role played by images on portable objects, and by material culture related to shamanic practices but not directly part of the shaman's 'equipment'. In chapter 11 Thomas Dowson and Martin Porr move directly on from discussions of Upper Palaeolithic cave art to the plastic decoration of sculpted anthropomorphic figurines found in Germany, arguing that they must be seen in a similar shamanic context to the paintings that have received more attention. Their detailed analysis of markings on the carvings, and their themes of human-animal transformation, suggest new interpretations of early Stone Age beliefs. Patricia Sutherland analyses a different, and far more extensive, repertoire of shamanic artefacts, from the Palaeo-Eskimo cultures of northern Canada. In chapter 9 she reviews a wide range of objects, some puzzling, all beautifully carved, that chart the arctic hunters' relationship to their prey and the other beings (both real and in spirit form) that seem to have populated their environment. Again, themes of transformation and trance visions recur in this material, and we can trace a dim ancestry between the 'X-ray' depictions of animals and similar motifs in Siberian shamanism. Our third example of portable shamanic 'art' comes from Siberia itself, where in chapter 4 Natalia Fedorova surveys a century of interpretations that have been applied to the cast bronze figures of warriors, birds and bears that emerged in the first century BC. She examines the case for shamanic iconography in the metalwork in the light of changing ideologies and social stratification during the Iron Age, and presents a new conclusion.

Shamanism and landscape

In chapters 6 and 7 we take a long step back from the individual, and examine respectively the shamanic landscapes of the modern-day Siberian Khanty and the hill tribes of the Nepal Himalayas. Peter Jordan and Damian Walter examine shamanic ritual and its practitioners in relation to space, both of performance and of perception: Jordan traces the significance of different zones within the landscape, decoding their combined association with shamanic belief and the seasonal procurement round; Walter contrasts two different types of ritual practitioners – shamans and lineage mediums – and examines how their respective spheres of influence are linked to spatial perceptions.

Both authors focus on the role played by material culture in articulating and expressing these ideas, and confront the archaeological implications. Like Håkan Rydving's innovative studies of Sámi religion (e.g. 1987, 1993a), these works look further to the reconstruction of a partly lost shamanic perspective from the memories that it has left behind, working within a 'post-shamanistic' thought-world in which the old ideas are still potent but obscurely transformed. This can even involve a kind of shamanism without shamans, which can perhaps best be formulated as a 'shamanic approach to life' (Willerslev In press, on Yukaghir hunters in Siberia; additional examples of the same phenomenon can be found in other accounts of recent fieldwork among Siberian groups, such as Humphrey 1983 and Pentikäinen 1998).

Shamanic architecture

Leading on from the broad canvas of landscape and 'shamanic space' we come to essays on architectural constructions specifically built in connection with shamanic practices. In chapter 10, Hans Christian Gulløv and Martin Appelt provide one of our most extraordinary case studies with their report of excavations in High Arctic Greenland, more than 1,000 km north of the arctic circle at the point where the first immigrants are believed to have crossed over from northern Canada. Referring to detailed ethnographies and archaeological data on the ancestral Inuit and their predecessors, they discuss the construction of a megalithic stone structure used for collective shamanic rituals, preserved largely intact by the freezing conditions for over a millenium. In chapter 12, Aaron Watson similarly breaks new, though utterly different, ground in considering the aural dimensions of shamanic practice. His sonic experiments inside megalithic structures from the British Neolithic suggest that their design incorporated elements that caused sound to behave in unusual ways, and that altered states of consciousness – even trance – could be induced through drumming and other percussive practices. His demonstration of how the movement of the drummer affected the sonic patterns and thus the neuropsychological responses of the listeners is startling, as is the realisation that sounds made inside one structure could be heard inside another nearby, while nothing could be heard by those standing outside. What was the role of sonic performance in the function of megalithic architecture in the Neolithic and early Bronze Age?

Shamanism and identity

From the earliest observations, scholars of shamanic practice have focused on the highly complex gender constructions that are associated with almost all such rituals (see Schmidt and Voss 2000 for recent overviews). The so-called 'soft-men' of Siberia and the 'berdaches' of the Native Americans are well-known, if somewhat misleading, archetypes in this context, and the sexual elements touched on above in relation to Scandinavian shamanism are of vital importance here. These have formed the primary focus of attention for generations of Russian researchers, as well as for more recent scholars such as Bernard Saladin d'Anglure and Sabine Lang. This material is reviewed here by Sandra Hollimon in chapter 8, who argues that the systems of multiple gender that characterise(d) many First Nations peoples in North America should be accepted as the rule rather than the exception when examining the earlier prehistory of the continent.

The theme of social identity and the deliberate construction of shamanic experience is echoed by Howard Williams, who in chapter 13 discusses the evidence for an 'ideology of transformation' manifested in the mortuary behaviour of the early Anglo-Saxons. Using shamanic metaphors, he argues that the social identity of the dead was renegotiated through their cremation together with specially selected – perhaps even specially bred – animals, merging different aspects of their natures in the transformative medium of fire.

Variation and change in shamanism and its sources

Another theme running throughout the book is the dynamic nature of shamanic practice and belief – in all the examples presented these patterns of behaviour are never static, but instead both change over time and vary from one region to the next. The common elements that empower a shamanic interpretation are discussed alongside the individual traits that distinguish its culturally specific expressions. We hope that this variation is also emphasised in the range of contributions here, from the remote prehistory of the Upper Palaeolithic to fieldwork among modern peoples. The use of anthropological analogy to bridge sometimes immense gaps of time and location is a great temptation in shamanic research, and the scholars whose studies are presented here all work with a deliberate concern for the distinctions between ethnographic data and archaeological sources.

Many definitions for shamanism are offered in these pages, but all are individually outlined by reference to the long tradition of shamanic research sketched above and ultimately dating to the ill-fated Avvakum's first observations among the Evenki in the seventeenth century. At all times, this archaeology of shamanism remains sharply aware of its human sources: the indigenous peoples on whom virtually all our understanding of shamanism is based. This is important, as is the observation that the current resurgence of shamanic interpretation among archaeologists is firmly a part of this tradition, and is unrelated to the growing popular interest in shamanism in the context of alternative spiritual philosophies.

In this volume we have deliberately sought not to avoid this aspect of shamanic perceptions, but wish instead to promote dialogue, believing that a willingness to meet – in a balanced way – the challenges brought by these new perspectives on the past is a fundamental prerequisite for archaeologists working in this field. For this reason, considerable space is devoted here to a discussion of these issues, linking to a more extensive review later in the book.

MODERN PAGANISM AND THE ARCHAEOLOGY OF (NEO-)SHAMANISM

Several scholarly works have appeared in recent years treating the emergence of neo-shamanic movements in the Western world (a selection are reviewed by Bowie 2000: 209–13; see also Vitebsky forthcoming). However, modern Pagans of all persuasions have themselves been active in publicising their beliefs, and some of these works, such as the monumental alternative survey of prehistoric Britain produced by the musician and poet Julian Cope (1998), are certainly worthy of serious consideration by archaeologists: a close reading makes it clear that the latter share a surprising majority of concerns – if not approaches – with Pagans (see Darvill 1999). An offhand academic rejection of differently-framed perspectives ironically risks alienating a part of archaeology's public which is actively interpreting, using and experiencing the past in precisely the way that many theorists have long been advocating. It should also be noted that a promotion of dialogue in no way obstructs archaeologists' critical evaluation of different views of the past (the spectre of ultimately empty relativism conjured up by many opponents of post-processualism has long since been laid to rest).

Many academics react with alarm to any association of their work with alternative religious beliefs and the perceived professional ridicule that can attach to them, while others strive for increasing dialogue and collaboration with groups of 'neo-shamans' and others working within the broad traditions of modern Paganism. The contributors to this volume fall into both camps, and the balance of papers is intended to reflect this ongoing debate and tension in archaeological shamanic research. The majority of academic archaeologists probably see themselves as somewhat astride this division, being generally materialists maintaining a deliberately wide distance between their own work and the beliefs of modern Pagans, while hopefully remaining open to dialogue. Clearly, mutual respect must form the foundation of any effective reciprocity, but beyond this three distinct issues – often wrongly conflated – emerge in the relationship between neo-shamanists and archaeologists.

First, there are debates centring on the right of open interpretation and access (in every sense) to the past, especially as physically represented by ancient monuments. This is the area of broadest archaeological agreement with the position taken by many neo-shamanists, who request a proportionate level of consultation on heritage management policies relating to the public interpretation, and perhaps excavation, of places seen as spiritually significant. Unfortunately polarised positions have occasionally been adopted on both sides here, but there are indications of increasing mutual comprehension and sympathy. There are clearly also questions of balance to consider, remembering that this does nevertheless concern a minority interest – if 16 per cent of visitors to Avebury outside the periods of Pagan festivals come there for spiritual reasons (Wallis, this volume), presumably 84 per cent do not – but this viewpoint could perhaps be equally applied to sites associated with other faiths. Particularly in the wake of the controversial excavations at 'Seahenge', the Bronze Age timber structure discovered in 1999 at Holme-Next-The-Sea on the east coast of England and discussed by Wallis below, there are signs that archaeologists and Pagan groups are moving into more productive positions in their relationship.

The second main issue in this context concerns the specific interpretative contribution of neo-shamanist groups. Many Pagans argue that their beliefs, and particularly the ways in which these are put into practice, provide them with a unique insight into the nature of what they perceive as similar beliefs in the past. It is here that many archaeologists differ sharply from neo-shamanist opinion, finding it hard to credit any link (beyond basic inspiration) between ancient practices and modern neo-shamanic rituals often given the same names by their adherents. This is not in any way an expression of doubt as to the sincerity of modern Pagans, but merely to question the privileging of their understandings of ancient religion above those of anyone else. From a purely academic viewpoint, with all its inherent biases and limitations, it is almost always impossible to 'reconstruct' ancient shamanic rituals; the claim that this can be achieved by other means – operative and spiritually empowered – remains to most archaeologists an article of faith, with all its inherent biases and limitations. Here, too, there are those who argue for greater common ground than is readily perceived, but there is little doubt that any progress (as defined variously by the different parties involved) will be slow.

This question of shamanism as a *living* belief system lies at the heart of the third area of concern, namely the relationship between the traditional cultures from which almost all our knowledge of shamanism derives, and those who transform this knowledge into new practices firmly rooted in the developed nations of the West. Many indigenous peoples regard neo-shamanism as little more than an expression of 'consumer religion', an essentially familiar process of cultural imperialism and carefully selective appropriation played out in a new form by spiritually jaded Westerners, and exclusively on their terms. Harsh though this assessment sounds, it is worth stating clearly, as there is a widespread sense of frustration among indigenous groups who feel that archaeologists prefer to play down such differences in the cause of a liberal pluralism within the discipline. The multitude of stresses placed upon indigenous cultures around the globe, very many of which are the inheritors of shamanic traditions in various manifestations, frequently threaten the very continuation of their lifestyle in its most fundamental form. In this context, the depth of bitterness felt towards neo-shamanists, who are seen as collaborative agents of this process of cultural oppression, truly has to be seen to be understood. As noted above, archaeologists in general have usually been bystanders in this conflict, perhaps unjustifiably, as material culture studies has long been implicated in many aspects of the debate on indigenous rights; however, those archaeologists who work closely with indigenous groups almost exclusively take their part in these discussions – a further dimension of the tensions between academics and neo-shamanists.

In this as in other aspects of these issues, we should of course note the difficulties of generalising about 'indigenous peoples', 'neo-shamanists' or, indeed, 'archaeologists'. All these terms naturally cover a multitude of organisations and individuals, and here it should be emphasised that the vast majority of neo-shamanists clearly have nothing but respect for the indigenous groups who accuse them of stealing their spiritual heritage. They are profoundly saddened by what they feel to be a misunderstanding of intent, and indeed regard their embracing of neo-shamanism as a sign of even deeper commitment to the values of what they often see as more psychologically healthy cultures, a way to greater harmony with the environment and their fellow humans that is in active opposition to the very agenda with which they are often identified by traditional peoples.

However, indigenous spokespeople have been quick to point out that 'good intentions' also abounded among the European empires that had the most devastating impact on their way of life. There are, furthermore, darker sides to a small minority of neo-shamanic groups, who take their beliefs into the realm of explicitly political appropriations of archaeology, especially on the far right of the political spectrum. The activities of such groups, particularly in North America, further complicate the relationship between modern Pagans (the vast majority of whom abhor such extremism) and archaeologists. Another factor also arises here, as Piers Vitebsky (1995: 151) has noted when he describes how the values commonly found as a fundamental part of neo-shamanic lifestyles – though by no means exclusive to them (such as vegetarianism) – are frequently at odds with those prevailing in traditional shamanic cultures. He warns of a worrying trend in which, because of this, a few neo-shamanic groups are beginning to look unfavourably on the practices of indigenous peoples, and to find them wanting. This is clearly a problem, and one which again goes to the core of related concerns in modern archaeology, as articulated in the growing awareness of post-colonial context and the necessity of acknowledging the indigenous voices of the Third and Fourth worlds.

In the final chapter of this volume, Robert Wallis addresses all these questions, arguing persuasively from his dual position as both an academic archaeologist and active neo-shaman. Clearly, modern Paganism can no longer be ignored by archaeologists working in this field, any more than we can disassociate ourselves from other political issues of race, sexuality and gender. Wallis claims that the archaeology of shamanism must in some way begin with the archaeology of neo-shamanism: few archaeologists may agree with this controversial assessment, but many are coming to see that such perspectives must at least be recognised and included in their work.

CONCLUSION

The research history of shamanic studies, in any discipline, has always followed a cyclical pattern of definition and redefinition: the archaeology of shamanism is no exception to this. However, as with the development of theoretical perspectives in archaeology, the incorporation of ideas that originated in anthropology, comparative theology and related areas of research inevitably involves their transformation into something new, and uniquely related to material culture studies.

Much has been written in recent years about an 'archaeology of mind', with various permutations of cognitive approaches on offer, and the search for ancient thought patterns, 'world-views' and 'mind-sets' is now part of the archaeological mainstream. However, there can be few areas of archaeology so intimately bound up with these aspirations as the study of shamanism, itself definable as a view of the world, a particular perception of the nature of reality. We should not forget that in the shamanic societies contacted and documented through early modern ethnography (and still existing under cultural siege in many parts of the globe), the understanding of 'shamanism' that the community shared with the 'shaman' provided the ultimate basis for the continuation of existence: the essential pattern of what it was to be a human being in those cultures. There can be little doubt that this kind of perception – and above all its impact on the material traces that constitute our research base – is fundamental for our own comprehension of prehistoric peoples and the worlds in which they understood themselves to move.

Through an archaeological examination of shamanism we necessarily draw nearer these intangibles that are so important a part of our research but yet so difficult to close with. The papers in this book demonstrate a variety of avenues by which to approach these elusive mentalities, and it is hoped that they may serve as a introduction for others wishing to pursue a similar goal – a true archaeology of altered states.

REFERENCES

Agapitov, N.N. and Khangalov, M.N. (1883) *Materiali dlja izuchenija shamanstva v Siberi*, Irkutsk: no publisher credited.

Anisimov, A.F. (1963) 'The shaman's tent of the Evenks and the origin of the shamanistic rite', in H.N. Michael (ed.) *Studies in Siberian Shamanism*. Toronto: University of Toronto Press.

Atkinson, J.H. (1992) 'Shamanisms today', *Annual Review of Anthropology* 21: 307–30.

Bahn, P. and Vertut, J. (1988) *Images of the Ice Age*, London: Windward.

Balzer, M.M. (1990) *Shamanism: Soviet Studies of Traditional Religion in Siberia and Central Asia*, New York: Sharpe.

Bogoras, V.G. (1911) *The Chukchee*, Publications of the Jesup North Pacific Expedition vol. XI, New York: American Museum of Natural History.

Bowie, F. (2000) *The Anthropology of Religion*, Oxford: Blackwell.

Castrén, M.A. (1853) *Vorlesungen über die finnische Mythologie*, Nordische Reisen und Forschungen vol. 3, St Petersburg: Kaiserlichen Akademie der Wissenschaften.

Chippindale, C. and Taçon, P. (eds) (1998) *The Archaeology of Rock-art*. Cambridge: Cambridge University Press.

Cope, J. (1998) *The Modern Antiquarian: A Pre-millenial Odyssey through Megalithic Britain*, London: Thorsons.

Czaplicka, M.A. (1914) *Aboriginal Siberia: A Study in Social Anthropology*, Oxford: Clarendon Press.

Darvill, T. (1999) 'Music, muses, and the modern antiquarian: a review article', *The Archaeologist* 34: 28–9.

Diószegi, V. and Hóppal, M. (eds) (1978) *Shamanism in Siberia*, Budapest: Akadémiai Kiadó.

Dixon, R.B. (1908) 'Some aspects of the American shaman', *Journal of American Folkore* 21: 1–12.

Donner, K. (1922) *Bland samojeder i Siberien*. Helsinki: Söderström.

DuBois, T.A. (1999) *Nordic Religions in the Viking Age*, Philadelphia: University of Pennsylvania Press.

Edsman, C.-M. (ed.) (1967) *Studies in Shamanism*, Stockholm: Almqvist and Wiksell.

Eliade, M. (1964) *Shamanism: Archaic Techniques of Ecstasy*, New York: Pantheon.

Furst, P. (1974) The roots and continuities of shamanism, *ArtsCanada* 184/7: 33–50.

Ginzburg, C. (1983) [1966] *The Night Battles: Witchcraft and Agrarian Cults in the Sixteenth and Seventeenth Centuries*, London: Routledge and Kegan Paul.

—— (1990) *Ecstasies: Deciphering the Witches' Sabbath*. London: Hutchinson.

Granö, J.G. (1919–21) *Altai: upplevelser och iakttagelser under mina vandringsår*. 2 vols, Helsinki: Söderström.

Guenther, M. (1999) 'From totemism to shamanism: hunter-gatherer contributions to world mythology and spirituality', in R.B. Lee and R. Daly (eds) *The Cambridge Encyclopedia of Hunters and Gatherers*, Cambridge: Cambridge University Press.

Helskog, K. and Olsen, B. (eds) (1995) *Perceiving Rock Art: Social and Political Perspectives*, Oslo: Novus.

Holmberg [Harva], U. (1915) *Lappalaisten uskonto*, Borgå: Poorvoosa.

—— (1922) *The Shaman Costume and its Significance*, Turku: University of Åbo.

—— (1927) *Finno-Ugric, Siberian [mythology]*. The mythology of all races, Vol. 4, Boston: Archaeological Institute of America.

—— (1938) *Die religiösen Vorstellungen der altaischen Völker*, Helsinki: Suomalainen tiedeakatemia.

Hóppal, M. (ed.) (1984) *Shamanism in Eurasia*, Göttingen: Herodot.

Hóppal, M. and Howard, K. (eds) (1993) *Shamans and Cultures*, Budapest: Akadémiai Kiadó.

Hóppal, M. and Pentikäinen, J. (eds) (1992) *Northern Religions and Shamanism*. Budapest: Akadémiai Kiadó.

Hóppal, M. and von Sadovszky, O. (eds) (1989) *Shamanism Past and Present*, 2 vols, Budapest: Ethnographic Institute.

Hultkrantz, Å. (1965) 'Types of religion in the arctic hunting cultures: a religio-ecological approach', in H. Hvarfner (ed.) *Hunting and Fishing*, Luleå: Norrbottens Museum.

—— (1973) 'A definition of shamanism', *Temenos* 9: 25–37.

—— (1979) *The Religions of the American Indians*. Berkeley: UCP.

—— (1993) 'Introductory remarks on the study of shamanism', *Shaman* 1/1: 3–14.

—— (1998) 'On the history of research in shamanism', in J. Pentikäinen, T. Jaatinen, I. Lehtinen and M-R. Saloniemi (eds) *Shamans*, Tampere: Tampere Museum.

Humphrey, C. (1980) 'Theories of North Asian shamanism', in E. Gellner (ed.) *Soviet and Western Anthropology*, London: Duckworth.

—— (1983) *Karl Marx Collective: Economy, Society and Religion in a Siberian Collective Farm*, Cambridge: Cambridge University Press.

Jochelson, W. (1908) *The Koryak*, Publications of the Jesup North Pacific Expedition, Vol. VI, New York: American Museum of Natural History.

Klaniczay, G. (1990) *The Uses of Supernatural Power*, Cambridge: Polity Press.

Larsson, T.P. (ed.) (2000) *Schamaner: essäer om religiösa mästare*, Falun: Nya Doxa.

Layton, R.H. (2000) 'Shamanism, totemism and rock art: 'Les chamanes de la préhistoire' in the context of rock art research', *Cambridge Archaeological Journal* 10/1: 169–86.

Lehtisalo, T. (1924) *Entwurf einer Mythologie der Jurak-Samojeden*, Helsinki: Société Finno-Ougrienne.

—— (1937) 'Der Tod und die Wiedergeburt des künftigen Schamanen', *Journal de la Société Finno-Ougrienne* 48/2: 1–34.

Lessa, W.A. and Vogt, E.Z. (eds) (1965) *Reader in Comparative Religion*, 3rd ed, New York: Harper and Row.

Lévi-Strauss, C. (1962) *Totemism*, London: Merlin.

Lewis, I.M. (1981) 'What is a shaman?' *Folk* 23: 25–35.

—— (1989) *Ecstatic Religion: An Anthropological Study of Spirit Possession and Shamanism*, 2nd ed, London: Routledge.

Lommel, A. (1967) *Shamanism: The Beginnings of Art*, New York: McGraw-Hill.

Mikhailovski, V.M. (1895) 'Shamanism in Siberia and European Russia'. *Journal of the Royal Anthropological Institute* 24: 62–100, 126–58.

Motzki, H. (1971) *Schamanismus als Problem religionswissenschaftlicher Terminologie*, Köln: Brill.

Nioradze, G. (1925) *Der Schamanismus bei den sibirischen Völkern*, Stuttgart: no publisher credited.

Ohlmarks, Å. (1939) *Studien zum Problem des Schamanismus*, Lund: Gleerup.

Pentikäinen, J. (ed.) (1996) *Shamanism and Northern Ecology*, Berlin: Mouton de Gruyer.

—— (1998) *Shamanism and culture*. Helsinki: Etnika.

Pentikäinen, J., Jaatinen, T., Lehtinen, I. and Saloniemi, M-R. (eds) (1998) *Shamans*, Tampere: Tampere Museum.

Popov, A.A. (1932) *Materialy dlja bibliografi russkoj literatury po enija shamanstva*, Leningrad: no publisher credited.

—— (1990) *Materialen zur Bibliographie der russischen Literatur über das Schamanentum der Völker Nordasiens*, Berlin: Schletzer.

Potanin, G.N. (1881–3) *Rocherki severo-zapadnoi Mongolii. Rezul'tati puteshestviya, ispolnennago v 1876–1877 godakh*, St Petersburg: RS.

Price, N.S. (2000a) 'Drum-Time and Viking Age: Sámi-Norse identities in early medieval Scandinavia', in M. Appelt, J., Berglund and H.C. Gulløv (eds) *Identities and Cultural Contacts in the Arctic*, Copenhagen: National Museum of Denmark and Danish Polar Center.

—— (2000b) 'Shamanism and the Vikings?', in W.W. Fitzhugh and E.I. Ward (eds) *Vikings: The North Atlantic Saga*, Washington, DC: Smithsonian Institution.

—— (2001a) 'The archaeology of shamanism: beyond rock-art', in C. Chippindale, B. Smith and G. Blundell (eds) *Seeing and Knowing: Ethnography and Beyond in Understanding Rock-art*.

—— (2001b) 'The archaeology of seiðr: circumpolar traditions in Viking pre-Christian religion', in S. Lewis (ed.) *Proceedings of the Viking Millenium International Symposium*, St John's: Parks Canada.

—— (in press) *The Viking Way: Religion and War in Late Iron Age Scandinavia*, Uppsala: Uppsala University Press.

Pripuzov, N.V. (1885) *Materiali dlja izuchenija shamanstva po Iakuty*, Irkutsk: no publisher credited.

Radloff, W. (1884) *Aus Sibirien*, Leipzig: Weigel.

Ripinsky-Naxon, M. (1993) *The Nature of Shamanism: Substance and Function of a Religious Metaphor*, Albany: SUNY Press.

Rydving, H. (1987) 'Shamanistic and postshamanistic terminologies in Saami (Lappish)', in T. Ahlbäck (ed.) *Saami religion*, Åbo: Donner Institute.

—— (1993a) *The End of Drum-Time: Religious Change Among the Lule Saami, 1670s-1740s*, Uppsala: Uppsala University Press.

—— (1993b) *Samisk religionshistorisk bibliografi*. Uppsala: Uppsala University Press.

Schefferus, J. (1673) *Lapponia*, Frankfurt: no publisher credited.

Schmidt, R.A. and Voss, B.L. (eds) (2000) *Archaeologies of Sexuality*, London: Routledge.

Shashkov, S. (1864) *Shamanstvo v Sibirii*, St Petersburg.

Sherratt. A. (1987) 'Cups that cheered: the introduction of alcohol to prehistoric Europe', in W. Waldren and R. Kennard (eds) *Bell Beakers of the Western Mediterranean: The Oxford International Conference 1986*, Oxford: BAR.

—— (1991) 'Sacred and profane substances: the ritual use of narcotics in later Neolithic Europe', in P. Garwood, D. Jennings, R. Skeates and J. Toms (eds) *Sacred and Profane: Proceedings of a Conference on Archaeology, Ritual and Religion*, Monograph 32, Oxford: Oxford University Committee for Archaeology.

Shimkevich, P.P. (1896) *Materiali dlja izuchenija shamanstva po Goldi*, Khabarovsk: no publisher credited.

Shirokogoroff [sic], S.M. (1935) *Psychomental Complex of the Tungus*, London: Kegan Paul, Trench and Trubner.

Sieroszewski, W. (1902) 'Du chamanisme d'après les croyances Yakoutes', *Revue de l'histoire des religions* 46: 204–33, 299–338.

—— (1993) [1896]. *Iakuty: opyt etnograficheskogo issledovanii*, 2nd ed., Moskva: Rossiiskaia politicheskaia entsiklopediia.

Siikala, A-L. and Hóppal, M. (eds) (1992) *Studies on Shamanism*, Helsinki: Finnish Anthropological Society.

Stadling, J. (1912) *Shamanismen i norra Asien*, Stockholm: Cederquist.

Taksami, C.M. (1998) 'Siberian shamans', in J. Pentikäinen, T. Jaatinen, I. Lehtinen and M-R. Saloniemi (eds) *Shamans*, Tampere: Tampere Museum.

Thomas, N. and Humphrey, C. (eds) (1994) *Shamanism, History and the State*, Ann Arbor: University of Michigan Press.

Vitebsky, P. (1995) *The Shaman*, London: Macmillan.

—— forthcoming. *The New Shamans: Psyche and Environment in an Age of Questing*, New York: Viking Penguin.

Wallace, A.F.C. (1966) *Religion: An Anthropological View*, New York: Random House.

Willerslev, R. (in press) 'The hunter as a human 'kind': hunting and shamanism among the Upper Kolyma Yukaghirs of Siberia', in T.A. Vestergaard (ed.) *Religious Ideas and Practices in the North Atlantic Area*, Moesgård: Centre for North Atlantic Studies.

Zelenin, D. (1936) 'Die animistische Philosophie des sibirischen Schamanismus', *Ethnos* 1/4: 81–5.

—— (1937) 'Zur Frage der Entwicklungeschichte der primitiven Religionen', *Ethnos* 2/3: 74–91.

—— (1952) *Le culte des Idoles en Sibérie*, Paris: Payot.

Znamenski, A.A. (1999) *Shamanism and Christianity: Native Encounters with Russian Orthodox Missions in Siberia and Alaska, 1820–1917*. Westport: Greenwood Press.

Chapter Two

Southern African shamanistic rock art in its social and cognitive contexts

J.D. Lewis-Williams

The images of San (Bushman) rock art[1] are among the most captivating and best understood in the world. This dual claim may read like the rhetoric of a tourist brochure or a chauvinist's hyperbole. It is nevertheless justifiable.

The first part of my claim is supported by the endless variety, delicacy, fine shading, and animation that one finds in the, literally, many thousands of rock shelters scattered throughout the subcontinent. These are the characteristics of the art that account for its popularity and abiding interest. But they are also responsible for an assumption that has bedevilled study of the art since the first researchers started to investigate it in the nineteenth century. It was almost universally assumed that the images that we find so exquisite were made as ends in themselves and that they had no social or symbolic significances; they merely depicted animals and people.

Arising from this notion, the art-for-art's-sake explanation held sway for many decades. Researchers claimed that the San made the images as *objets d'art*, to entertain and be admired by their fellows; the paintings were thought 'to record scenes and events, sometimes the loss of a headman or ruler or some other misfortune, but more often a scene of beauty remembered for its aesthetic qualities' (Cooke 1969: 150). Even today, when we know a great deal about the cognitive and cosmological significances of the images, it is hard to believe that the care that was so obviously taken in shading and depicting tiny details was not admired at the time when the images were made. A possible aesthetic component is, however, insufficient to explain the meanings of the images.

The images were made in socially contingent circumstances that were, of course, very different from those of the researchers who study them and that in all probability did not embrace twentieth-century Western notions of commodified 'art'. The sheer beauty of the images has blinded many a researcher to aspects of San society and belief that may have impinged on the making and meaning of the paintings. Indeed, it was long assumed that researchers could know nothing about the beliefs of the people who made the images and that they should therefore concentrate on elucidating stylistic sequences in the same way that art historians recognise 'schools' of Western art (e.g. Burkitt 1928).

Today we know that such pessimism is unfounded and that there is as much evidence for the second part of my opening claim as there is for the first. The images themselves are not the only category of data that requires explanation; they are not the only life-line that we have to the ancient rock painters. Both nineteenth- and twentieth-century records have preserved a great deal about San beliefs, myths, rituals and general way of life. Like all ethnographies, these records are incomplete and must be seen in the context of the times and manner of their recording. Still, whatever the limitations of the ethnography, the images cannot be explained in isolation from it, any more than a Renaissance painting of the Nativity can be understood in isolation from Christian beliefs, Church history, and the Bible. San image-making must be set in its intellectual and social contexts; the ethnography and the images should be studied in tandem as mutually illuminating corpora of data: the ethnography sends us to the painted rock shelters with more informed ideas about what to look for; and the images return us to the ethnography to seek explanations for their enigmatic features and, moreover, for their apparently 'literal' components.

When researchers direct their attention to the ethnographic record, it soon becomes apparent that the art is not a literal 'narrative' of San life: it does not 'reflect' daily life with its social structures and economy. Nor are the animals depicted a reflection of the range of species that lived alongside of the image-makers (Vinnicombe 1976; Lewis-Williams 1981); even hunting, often taken to be a major theme of the art, is comparatively rarely represented (Pager 1971: 335–6). How, then, did San image-making articulate with the lives and beliefs of the image-makers?

In the first place, it is necessary to recall that material culture, far from passively reflecting daily life, is variously implicated in the construction, reproduction and subversion of beliefs and social relations (Hodder 1982a and b; Shanks and Tilley 1987; Giddens 1984; Bordieu 1977). In daily life, human beings manipulate material culture to achieve ends of which they are often perfectly aware. By manipulating items of material culture they attempt, successfully or unsuccessfully, to shift the locus of power, to exploit social relations, in short, to intervene in their socio-political environment. Now, if rock art images are items of material culture, which they surely are, they can be interrogated as socio-political interventions rather than as passive reflections (cf. Conkey 1993). Moreover, an art as detailed and varied as that of the San holds exceptional promise of success for such an undertaking. In rock arts where the imagery is largely uniform and repetitive it is much more difficult to link notions of human intervention and agency to specific images and features of images. With San rock art, researchers can go beyond generalised, theory-derived assertions about 'the art' to precise demonstration that deals with specific images and their intelligible features; in many other archaeological contexts this is a difficult task indeed (Johnson 1989).

To show that the making of San rock art images was only one part of a concatenation of social events and processes and that they were 'used' in multiple ways after their apparent completion, I begin by sketching in outline the area of San belief and life with which the images were principally concerned. I then show that the production and consumption of the art was situated in a web of social relations that were negotiated and contested at all stages in the production and use of images (cf. Conkey 1993; Dobres and Hoffman 1994; Dobres 2000).

SAN RELIGION IN ITS SOCIAL AND CONCEPTUAL CONTEXTS

Today there is some controversy about the terms that should or should not be used to denote San religion (Lewis-Williams 1992). A century and a half ago, many southern African colonists denied that the San had any religion at all, or indeed were intellectually capable of entertaining religious beliefs. A lone voice of protest against this view was raised in the 1870s by Wilhelm Bleek, the German philologist who was at that time working in Cape Town. He trenchantly declared that San rock art expressed the 'ideas that most deeply moved the Bushman mind, and filled it with religious feelings' (Bleek 1874: 13). In the theological and political tenor of the time, this was a shocking and subversive assertion. Indeed, Bleek made his claim in the context of a theological dispute in which the Anglican Church charged Bishop J.W. Colenso with heresy because he believed that the Zulu people, with whose evangelisation he was charged, had sincere and genuine beliefs in God and evinced Christian virtues (Spohr 1962; Eberhard 1996; Lewis-Williams 2000). Bleek represented Colenso at the heresy trial because the cleric himself refused to recognise the authority of the Archbishop of Cape Town. In such a prejudiced climate it is not surprising that Bleek's insights were ignored, and it was many decades before the existence of 'San religion' came to be recognised.

Bleek and his sister-in-law, Lucy Lloyd, worked largely in the 1870s, before anthropology was a widely accepted discipline and before much was known about the religions of small-scale societies. Devotedly, they took down verbatim what their informants told them about their beliefs, but they evidently understood very little of it; nor did the Bleek family publish the key texts concerned with San religion until the 1930s (Bleek 1933, 1935, 1936). There was, therefore, no debate in the nineteenth century and the first decades of the twentieth about what their informants' religion should be called. Today, in the much more informed anthropological climate of our time, a suitable label for San religion is sometimes disputed. This is no idle logomachy for, as we shall see, the essence of San religion and what it has in common with religions in other small-scale societies impact on our understanding of southern African rock art. To grasp something of that, admittedly elusive, essence, I draw on the Bleek and Lloyd records, which were contemporary with the making of the last images, and also on twentieth-century records of San religion in the Kalahari Desert some 1,400 km to the north of where the Bleek informants lived (Figure 2.1). Researchers have demonstrated marked parallels between these two San groups, despite their considerable linguistic differences (Vinnicombe 1972a; Lewis-Williams and Biesele 1978; Lewis-Williams 1981, 1988a, 1992; Guenther 1999); the framework, if not all the details, of San religion was widespread.

The people whom the Bleek family studied were known as the /Xam-ka !kwe, or simply the /Xam (for a series of articles on the /Xam San see Deacon and Dowson 1996; Deacon 1986, 1988; for verbatim /Xam texts see Bleek and Lloyd 1911; Bleek 1924; Guenther 1989; Lewis-Williams 2000). They lived in the semi-arid interior of the southern African plateau (Figure 2.1), a region characterised by hot summers with scattered thunderstorms, and cold, dry winters. They lived in bands, or camps, of on average about twenty-five people and moved seasonally to exploit the scarce plant foods and waterholes that were liable to dry up or turn bitter in the winter (see /Xam texts in Bleek and Lloyd 1911; Lewis-Williams 2000). They hunted with bows and poisoned arrows. Farther to the east, a similar life-style prevailed in the much better watered Drakensberg mountains, though with due regard to perennial streams and more prolific plant foods. This is a densely painted area on the eastern and southern fringes of the south-eastern mountain massif of South Africa and Lesotho.

Both in the land of the /Xam and in the Drakensberg, the San believed in a trickster-deity known as /Kaggen, a word often translated as 'the Mantis' (Bleek 1924). The San did not, however, 'worship' the preying mantis insect, as the colonists came to believe; the insect was but one of /Kaggen's many avatars, which included eland, eagles and snakes (for more on /Kaggen see Schmidt 1973; Lewis-Williams 1981:117–26 and 1997; Hewitt 1986). The cosmos which /Kaggen and the /Xam inhabited was three-tiered: there were spiritual realms above and below the level on which people lived. The spiritual realms nevertheless constantly impinged on the lives of people, and the San conception of the cosmos was less clearly formulated than 'tiered' and an anthropological description may suggest (Silberbauer 1981: 52, 95; Lewis-Williams 1996, 1997; Guenther 1999).

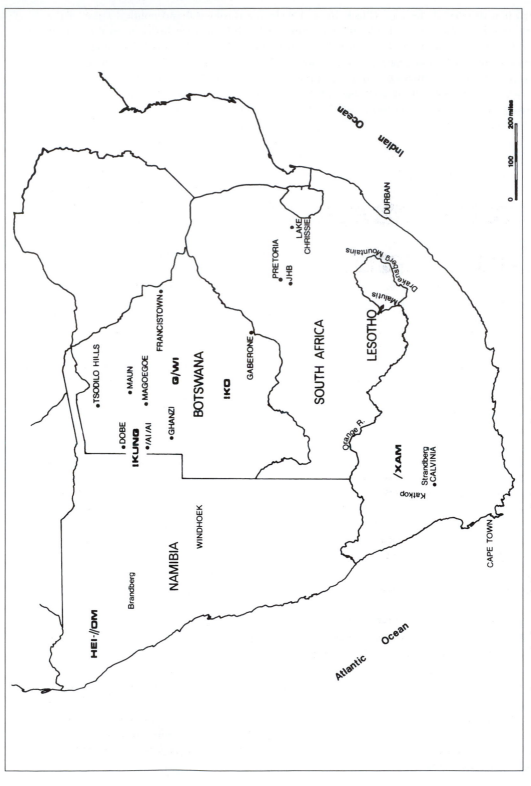

Figure 2.1 Map showing the locations of San groups and places mentioned in the text.

Ritual specialists moved between these realms. They accomplished this kind of trans-cendence by entering an altered state of consciousness in a large 'medicine' dance, in more solitary circumstances, or in dreams. Trance was induced not through the ingestion of psychotropic substances but by intense concentration, prolonged rhythmic dancing, audio-driving and hyperventilation (but see Winkelman and Dobkin de Rios 1989). In the spirit world, they healed the sick of ailments often sent by malevolent spirits of the dead, caused rain to fall, and guided the movements of antelope so that they ran into the hunters' ambush (Bleek 1933, 1935, 1936; Marshall 1969, 1999; Biesele 1978, 1993; Katz 1982; Katz *et al.* 1997). In the 1950s researchers in the Kalahari found that up to half of the men and a third of the women in a San camp were ritual specialists of this kind, and the nineteenth-century texts suggest that similar proportions obtained amongst the /Xam. These specialists did not enjoy any political privileges and very few, if any, material benefits. Today those living in the Kalahari still say that they brave the terrors of the spirit world for the benefit of the people whom they represent and not for personal gain (e.g. Katz *et al.* 1997; but see Wilmsen 1989; Gulbrandsen 1991).

The /Xam called these ritual specialists *!gi:ten* (sing. *!gi:xa*). A *!gi:xa* is a person who is full of *!gi:*, a supernatural potency, or energy, that /Kaggen created and put in many 'strong' things, chief of which was the eland, the largest and fattest of all African antelope. *!gi:ten* activated this potency and caused it to 'boil' up their spines and to 'explode' in their heads, thus catapulting them into the spirit world (an altered state of consciousness). In the language of the !Kung San of the northern Kalahari such ritual specialists are called *n/om k"ausi* (sing. *n/om k"au*). *N/om* is the equivalent of *!gi:*, and *k"au* means 'owner'. Other San languages have their own words for potency and those who manipulate it. There is thus no indigenous word to denote ritual specialists in all San communities. In the absence of such a term, I use the now-universal Tungus (central Asia) word 'shaman' and refer to San religion as 'shamanism'. (For more on San shamanism see Marshall 1969, 1999; Katz 1982; Biesele 1978, 1993; Katz *et al.* 1997; Lewis-Williams 1981, 1987; Hewitt 1986; Lewis-Williams and Dowson 1999; Guenther 1999; Keeney 1999.)

Shamanism is today a disputed category (Atkinson 1992). Some researchers feel that the word has been used to cover too wide a range of beliefs and rituals (for definitions of 'shamanism' see, among others, Shirokogoroff 1935; Eliade 1964; Lommel 1967; Hultkrantz 1973; Bourguignon 1974; Vitebsky 1995). On the other hand, it usefully points to worldwide phenomena. The many varieties of shamanism should come as no surprise: Christianity, too, has widely different churches, ranging from Eastern Orthodox, to Roman Catholic, to charismatic fundamentalist groups, but there is no reasonable objection to referring to all of them as 'Christian'. Similarly, there are sufficient commonalties between central Asian shamanism, the so-called 'classic' shamanism, and that practised in North America and elsewhere. San religious beliefs and rituals fall comfortably into this category, and the general word 'shamanism' is therefore appropriate (Lewis-Williams 1992).

/Xam San myths show that /Kaggen was the original shaman (Lewis-Williams 1997). He created potency and imbued the eland with it (Bleek 1924). When he created the eland, he was in fact creating the foundation of San shamanism (Lewis-Williams 1997). Together with the eland, /Kaggen protected other large antelope and tried to outwit San hunters and cause the animals to escape from them (Bleek 1924, 1935). He was thus also a 'Lord of the Animals', a figure common in shamanistic communities. To outwit /Kaggen, hunters observed a series of ritual avoidances. Most importantly, 'shamans of the game', as the /Xam called them, entered the spirit world to trick the trickster and to guide antelope herds into the hunters' ambush.

San rock art

Whatever other meanings San rock art may have conveyed, it was in large measure concerned with the *n/om*, rituals and experiences of shamans (Lewis-Williams 1981, 1982, 1987, 1990; Lewis-Williams and Blundell 1998; Lewis-Williams and Dowson 1999; Yates *et al.* 1985; Dowson 1992; Deacon 1988; Walker 1996). The shamanistic images include: depictions of trance dances in which the men dance with flywhisks and suffer nasal haemorrhages (an indication in San rock art of altered states) while the women, depicted peripherally, sing and clap the rhythm of potency-filled songs (Figs 2.2, 2.3, 2.4). The eland, the most *n/om*-filled animal, is in many regions of southern Africa also the most frequently depicted and the one on which the painters expended most care and energy. In addition, there are images depicting shamanistic activities and hallucinatory percepts, such as out-of-body travel, transformation into an animal, and fantastic rain-animals that were killed in the spirit world so that their blood and milk would fall as rain.

Figure 2.2 Rock painting of a shamanistic dance. In the centre, two or more figures dance and hold what appears to be a rope studded with white dots; to the right, another figure holds the line above its head. This line represents the mystical 'threads of light' that San shamans climbed to reach God's realm in the sky where they pleaded for the lives of the sick and for rain (Lewis-Williams *et al.* 2000). These 'threads' can be seen by shamans only; the viewers of this painting thus see what ordinary people at a dance cannot see. To the left, five seated figures clap the rhythm of a powerful 'medicine song' that will enable the shamans to climb the 'threads of light'. Above the dance is a line of conical men's hunting bags, oblong women's carrying bags, quivers, bows and other objects. Bags were symbols of transition to the spirit world (Lewis-Williams 1996). Below the dance are numerous arrows. Men do not leave dangerous poisoned arrows lying around; these painted arrows may therefore represent the invisible 'arrows of sickness' that spirits of the dead shoot at people (Bleek 1935: 5) and that are seen by shamans only. To both the left and the right are women's digging-sticks, weighted with round bored stones. Women beat on the ground with these stones to contact the spirit world (Bleek 1935: 35–7). Colours: dark red and white. KwaZulu-Natal Drakensberg.
Copy by Harald Pager.

Figure 2.3 In this painted shamanistic dance scene, a number of men dance towards a group of seated, clapping women, some of whom have babies on their backs. Marshall (1969: fig. 2) illustrates "Young men dancing their strong approach steps" as they advance to seated, clapping women; a comparison between Marshall's 1950s photograph and this rock painting is striking. In the painting, the men hold flywhisks and what may be arrows. Flywhisks are closely associated with the trance dance and are not used in everyday life. Some of the men are wearing eared caps. These caps were made from the scalps of small antelope and sewn so that the ears stood up. Game was believed to follow the wearer of such a cap and thus be enticed into the hunters' ambush. A curious therianthropic figure wearing dancing rattles is in the centre of the group. Unusually, its antelope head is at the rear, not the head, of the figure. It represents transformation in the context of the shamanistic dance. Colours: dark red and white. KwaZulu-Natal Drakensberg.
Copy by Harald Pager.

It is unlikely that every shamanistic vision was depicted; the circumstances of the experience probably determined whether it should be 'fixed' or not. Nor is it possible to say that all apparently shamanistic images were made by shamans, for we have very few records of the identities of the painters. It does, however, seem likely that the images that depict visions were made by those who actually experienced them. If ordinary people did paint, the images that they produced are today indistinguishable from those done by shamans; if there were any non-shaman painters, they drew on the same vocabulary of images as did the shamans, and their images were thoroughly integrated into panels of shamanistic paintings. Similarly, images of eland, though delicately shaded, exquisitely delineated and lacking any non-real features and,

Figure 2.4 In this shamanistic dance group standing and seated women are shown surrounding a single dancing figure. They are clapping the rhythm of a medicine song. The dancer holds flywhisks and a large number of them are next to him. As in Figure 2.2, there are bags and weighted digging-sticks. One of the women to the left has a hand raised to her nose in a frequently painted posture. The nose was believed to be the seat of potency, and it was from here that blood flowed when a trancer entered an altered state of consciousness (Lewis-Williams 1981). Colour: dark red. KwaZulu-Natal Drakensberg.
Copy by Harald Pager.

moreover, that may or may not have been made by shamans, are frequently shown in contexts that are clearly shamanistic (Figure 2.5). Indeed, there is evidence, to which I shall come in a moment, that suggests strongly that eland depictions were 'reservoirs of *n/o*' to which people, perhaps not shamans alone, turned when they felt a need for transcendent support (Lewis-Williams and Dowson 1990). It is therefore an error to believe that each and every image originated in a specific vision. Some images may be a blending of numerous visits to the spiritual realm or, such as in the case of eland, a fixing of *n/om* for various purposes.

At this point a further word of caution is necessary. Rather than being a one-dimensional, monolithic shamanistic statement, San rock art deals in subtle and oblique ways with a broad diversity of (nevertheless interrelated) referents, including girls' puberty rituals, boys' first-kill observances, marriage rites and diverse social relations (Lewis-Williams 1981, 1998, 1999). It would, however, be wrong to suppose that these additional meanings are present in equal proportion to the aspects and implications of shamanism and that they impacted equally on the original San viewers. The context of an image focuses attention on one segment of its semantic spectrum (Lewis-Williams 1990, 1998). In San rock art, the rock face (Lewis-Williams and

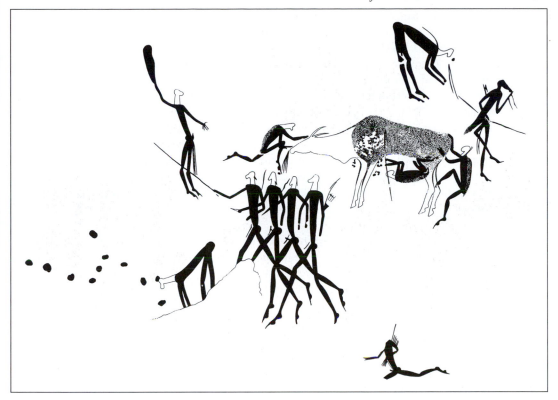

Figure 2.5 One of many rock paintings that show 'non-real' relationships between human beings and eland. The emanations of blood and/or foam from the eland's nose indicate that it is dying; the 'hanging' positions of its hoofs suggest that it may be lying on its side or 'floating' in the spirit world. One figure attends to the eland's head, a common occurrence in the art, while two others hold the eland's body. Above the eland, a man is depicted in the typical bending-forward posture that shamans adopt when their *n/om* causes their stomach muscles to contract painfully (Lewis-Williams 1981). This figure also bleeds from the nose, an indication that he is 'dying' in trance as his spirit leaves his body on extracorporeal travel. This figure conceptually parallels the dying eland, the source of his *n/om.* Above and to the right of the eland is a figure that may be therianthropic and that has a hand raised to its nose (cf. Fig. 2.4). It is in a crossed-legged position that is frequently associated with shamanistic groups (Vinnicombe 1976; Lewis-Williams 1981). Four figures walk towards the left. Each is 'infibulated', that is, each has an enigmatic line drawn across the penis (cf. Fig. 2.4). In front of them is another figure in an acute bending-forward posture and a number of dots made with the tip of a finger. Such dots, which appear in many paintings, may represent *n/om* (Dowson 1989; see also Lewis-Williams and Blundell 1997). Colours: dark red and white. KwaZulu-Natal. Copy by Harald Pager.

Dowson 1990) and associated paintings focus on the shamanistic associations of images (Lewis-Williams 1998). This claim for the primacy of shamanistic concerns may, perhaps, be contested because we have no direct access to the original viewers and because, as some researchers have it, meaning is created at the moment of interaction between viewer and image. I doubt the usefulness of these reservations in the study of San rock art. Whatever the variations in personal apprehension of the images may have been, there was, I argue, a notion in the mind of the painter before he or she began to fashion the image, and that shared beliefs made it possible for this notion to be accessed by the majority of viewers.

In any event, San shamanism is not an 'optional extra' for a few people; it was and still is the very framework of San thought and society (Biesele 1978, 1993). Its pervasive and persuasive power is founded largely on altered states of consciousness that everyone has the potential to access, even if only in dreams. Later, I describe an instance in which a woman who was not a shaman received a revelation from the spirit world. Indeed, the shared human nervous system is universally a powerful foundation that can be exploited in socio-political contexts. As Bourguignon (1974: 234) points out, visions acquired in altered states are 'raw materials for potential cultural utilisation'. Making a similar point, Rappaport (1999: 219) notes:

> Trance and less profound alterations of consciousness are frequent concomitants of ritual participation . . . The relationship between alterations of the social condition and alterations of consciousness is not a simple one, but it is safe to say that they augment and abet each other.

To understand how rock art effected socio-political interventions within the framework of the San shamanistic cosmos and how alterations of consciousness can 'augment and abet', as Rappaport puts it, alterations of the 'social condition', I distinguish four stages in the production and consumption of rock art images (Lewis-Williams 1995); to focus exclusively on the act of making of the images would be to miss an important part of their influence. I show that at all stages, shamanistic beliefs and experiences were directly or obliquely implicated. The four stages that I consider are: (1) the acquisition of imagery; (2) the manufacture of paint; (3) the making of the images; and (4) the subsequent use of the images.

THE ACQUISITION OF IMAGERY

The making of a San rock art image must have begun with an idea, or spiritual insight, and an impulse to 'fix' that idea on the rock surface. There were at least four contexts in which San shamans acquired insights into the spiritual world: the trance dance; special curing rituals that did not entail a full dance; viewing rock art; and dreams. I deal with each of these in turn.

During the course of a present-day dance in the Kalahari, when a number of shamans are in trance, a couple may draw the others' attention to what they believe they can see, perhaps a number of spirit-eland standing in the semi-darkness beyond the light of the central fire. The others look in the direction indicated, and then they too see the same visions. There is thus, at the very moment of revelation, a sharing of insights that makes for commonality of visions. Moreover, the describing of visions after everyone has returned to a normal state of consciousness is a further powerful influence on what people 'see' in future trance experiences. Everyone, not just shamans, listens avidly to the shamans' reports from the spirit world, and such circumstances contribute to the construction and reinforcement of the community's concepts of supernatural entities. Then, when shamans or novices next enter trance, they tend to hallucinate what they expect to hallucinate.

Reinforcement is, however, only part of the matter. There are, at the same time, forces pulling in the opposite direction. Irrespective of how powerful the informing social influence may be, the human brain in an altered state of consciousness is liable to produce novel, or aberrant, hallucinations. There is an inescapable tension between, on the one hand, ideally desired religious experience and, on the other, the untamed brain/mind with the unpredictable experiences that it sometimes generates and that, in altered states, are liable to spin out of control and transmute ecstasy into terror. It is out of that tension that religious travail is fashioned; it is a site of personal and social contestation.

In all societies, most people ignore these sports of the human nervous system because they are seeking specific kinds of visions that they can understand and that will make them feel part of a social group. But some people do seize upon hallucinatory novelties and then present them to others as specially privileged insights that set them above others or, more forcefully, challenge the whole power structure of the community. In some circumstances, the individual visionary thus opposes rather than conforms to social constraints. Both these attitudes to the mental imagery of altered states of consciousness are found among the San. In the past, the tension between socialised and idiosyncratic mental imagery presented shaman-artists with an opportunity to negotiate their social positions by manipulating, within socially accepted parameters, certain classes of imagery and their associated painted images (Dowson 1994).

The physical choreography of the dance is one of the factors that focus the attention of the community on the shamans and their visions. The configuration of the dance thus provides a context for the generation and negotiation of different kinds of mental imagery. The trance, or healing, dance is the one San ritual that brings together all people, no matter what their age or gender. In the Kalahari today these dances are circular (Marshall 1969: Figures 1, 3, 4). In the 1870s, J.M. Orpen (1874: 10) recorded a similar circular choreography of the dance in the south-eastern mountains:

> It is a circular dance of men and women following each other, and it is danced all night. Some fall down; some become as if mad and sick; blood runs from the noses of others whose charms are weak, and they eat charm medicine, in which there is burnt snake powder.

The form of the dance was, however, open to manipulation, even as the visions themselves were. Rock paintings show what appear to be a number of ways in which participants arranged their relative positions (Figures 2.2, 2.3, 2.4), though we should not accept too readily that San conventions of depicted perspective were the same as ours. One trend observable in the painted record of the southern Drakensberg seems to have been a development from a dance form that placed a number of shamans on an equal footing to one in which a single prominent shaman was surrounded by smaller figures. As Dowson (1994) argues, these different kinds of paintings project different conceptions of social reality and are evidence for the manipulation of rock art imagery by groups and by individuals.

In all types of painted choreography, dancers are sometimes shown with lines emanating from their noses. As we have seen, Orpen's informant, Qing, told him that dancers fell down 'as if mad and sick' and that blood ran from the noses of some whose 'charms are weak' (Orpen 1874: 10). Bleek and Lloyd found that /Xam shamans also suffered nasal haemorrhages and that they rubbed their blood on those whom they wished to heal; they believed that its odour would keep evil spirits of the dead at bay (Bleek 1935, 1936). Twentieth-century researchers in the Kalahari did not encounter much nasal bleeding among shamans, but they were told that a shaman may bleed in especially challenging or dangerous circumstances (Marshall 1960: 374, 1999: 87; Lewis-Williams 1981: 81). The wider importance of blood will become apparent as I proceed.

In a 'special curing', the second context in which shamans achieve insights into spiritual things, one or two shamans may enter trance without the women's supportive clapping and singing (Marshall 1999: 58–60). This happens when a person is deemed to be particularly ill. Under these circumstances, a shaman may 'see' into the body of a patient and discern the cause of the illness. The cause is then removed by the laying on of hands. First, it is drawn into a shaman's body; then it is expelled through a 'hole' in the back of the neck, a supernatural event that is visible to shamans only and that appears in some rock paintings (e.g. Lewis-Williams and

Dowson 1999: Figure 32d). Some shamans become renowned for their curing ability and may be summoned from afar to perform a special curing if someone is gravely ill. San people seem always to believe that the really powerful shamans live in areas other than their own, and a certain amount of respect accrues from being summoned to heal at a distant place. Special curings are thus a particularly fertile context for social differentiation and for sustaining communication between distant camps.

The viewing of rock art, the third context, may be dealt with more briefly. The painted visions and experiences of shamans that accumulated over time in the rock shelters probably also provided insights that could become part of other shamans' experiences when they entered altered states. As we shall see, panels of images were long-term 'reservoirs' that could be tapped for power and insight. There was, therefore, probably a recursivity between rock art images and shamans' visions. This two-way interaction sustained the parameters, though not all the idiosyncratic details, of San spiritual experience. The constraining effect of painted images may not have been as tight as that exercised by written and printed texts in other societies, but their influence should not be underestimated.

Dreaming is the fourth context that we need to consider. Bleek and Lloyd recorded the ways in which nineteenth-century/Xam shamans made rain and went on out-of-body journeys whilst in a dream (Lewis-Williams 1987). In a particularly striking and well documented twentieth-century instance, Beh, a Kalahari !Kung woman, dreamed of galloping giraffes (Biesele 1993; Marshall 1999: 75–6). When she awoke, she was able to sense in the rhythm of their pounding hoofs the metre of a song. She was not herself a shaman, but when she sang the song to her husband, who was a shaman, he instantly recognised it as a new, god-given source of animal-potency. He, in turn, passed the song on to other shamans, and in a comparatively short time, the giraffe 'medicine song' had spread across the Kalahari and was being sung alongside older songs, such as eland and gemsbok. Beh and her husband became well-known people, though not politically powerful. For Beh, the dream of galloping giraffe confirmed the reality of the spirit world, but she nevertheless passed her revelation on to her husband who, being a shaman, was able to harness it. As I have said, all people may experience unusual visions and dreams and thus have their belief in the supernatural realm reinforced, but only a few seize upon them and develop their potential.

This tension between personal revelations and socially sanctioned visions is evident in the rock art (Dowson 1988; Dowson and Holliday 1989). Many rock art motifs are widespread. The eland, for instance, is the most frequently depicted animal in most regions of southern Africa (Maggs 1967; Pager 1971; Smits 1971; Lewis-Williams 1972, 1974; Vinnicombe 1972a and b, 1976). Yet, idiosyncratic motifs do occur. For these motifs to have been intelligible to other people they must have fallen within the broad, general framework of San symbolism and experience. An apparently unique painting of crabs (Figure 2.6), for example, develops an existing San metaphor of being under water, as a way of expressing some of the sensations of trance experience: subjects in deep trance feel weightless and experience difficulty in breathing and impaired, blurred vision (Dowson 1988; see also Biesele 1993: 71). Numerous painters expressed these sensations by juxtaposing images of shamans in trance with depictions of fish (Lewis-Williams 1988b). For whatever reasons, crabs, as a painted 'underwater' motif, did not become accepted by other painters as images of fish did. So we can probably conclude that the person who painted the unique images of crabs retained a special insight into 'underwater' experience and that this insight was not dissipated amongst shamans in general, as was Beh's giraffe song. Whether any prestige accrued from this insight and whether it developed into political power are questions that we cannot now answer, though we can speculate that the painting was made in a comparatively recent historical period when the egalitarian ethos of San shamanism was being undermined and prominent individual shamans were beginning to emerge (Dowson 1988; cf. Guenther 1986).

So far I have considered only imagery that derives from visions and the experiences of altered states of consciousness. Much other rock art is concerned with ways in which the spirit world interpenetrates the material world. Some paintings, such as those of shamanistic dances, combine observable reality (such as dancers wearing ankle rattles) and spiritual reality that was 'seen' by shamans only (such as expelled sickness, supernatural potency [Figure 2.7] , physical transformations into part-animal, part-human therianthropes [Figure 2.3], and the 'threads of light' that lead to the spirit world [Figure 2.2]); these paintings present the privileged views of shamans who can 'see' both their material surroundings and the presence of spiritual entities. Indeed, even some images that appear at first glance to be realistic are in fact problematic. Apparently realistic depictions of eland, for instance, that could easily be taken to be *objets d'art* representing real, individual animals sometimes have features that

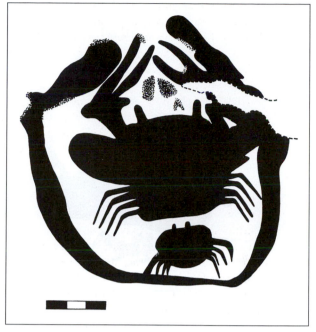

Figure 2.6 A unique painting of two fresh-water crabs surrounded by a thick black line. The smaller crab has no pincers. These crabs are territorial, and they sometimes lose their pincers in battles over territory. The painting may be a metaphorical representation of a combat between shamans in the spirit world. At the top right, there are two bags (cf. Fig. 2.2). Colour: black. Eastern Free State.
Copy by T. A. Dowson.

suggest that another, non-real, element is present (Figure 2.7; cf. Lewis-Williams 1987: Figure 5). It seems that too rigid a distinction between purely visionary images and purely realistic ones is a Western imposition and unhelpful. If southern African rock art teaches us anything, it is that, for the San, reality was a shifting, elusive notion that differed from the Western idea of reality. It was this mercurial property that was so open to manipulation by individuals and groups.

THE MANUFACTURE OF PAINT

Little is recorded about the ways in which San rock painters prepared their paint. Perhaps early writers who had an opportunity to investigate this considered it too prosaic a matter to warrant their attention. There is, however, an important account that strongly suggests that the making of paint was far from prosaic.

In the early 1930s Marion Walsham How arranged an interview with a 74-year-old southern Sotho man, Mapote. How was at this time living in Qacha's Nek, a small town in southern Lesotho. As a young man, Mapote had learned to paint with San in their caves. He was a son of Chief Moorosi, and had half-San stepbrothers, the sons of Moorosi's San wives (How 1962: 33). According to Mapote, the 'true' San painted at one end of a cave, while he and his half-San stepbrothers painted at the other end. Researchers have not observed a distinction between

Figure 2.7 A rock painting that shows an upside-down eland, a convention for indicating death. The white lines that radiate from it probably represent the *n/om* that is released when an eland dies; this *n/om* can be seen by shamans only. The red and white line on its throat may be related to the line studded with white dots (Fig. 2.2). Below the dead eland is an eland calf. Colours: dark red and white. KwaZulu-Natal Drakensberg. Copy by Harald Pager.

paintings at opposite ends of rock shelters, so we do not know how general this separation may have been, or, indeed, how many southern Sotho people were taught how to paint. It may have been something that happened very seldom, though, as Mapote implied, the relationship between the San and the southern Sotho was clearly close (Wright 1971; Vinnicombe 1976). Either way, Mapote's statement suggests that the San whom he knew maintained a distinction between their own paintings and paintings made by other people: painting, as they saw it, was an essentially San activity, even though others could, at least in the time of social disintegration of which Mapote was speaking, learn some of the skills.

When How produced a piece of red pigment that a friend had given her some time before she met Mapote, he was excited and declared it to be an authentic San pigment known as *qhang qhang*; it 'glistened and sparkled' in contrast to commercially available ochre which was dull by comparison. Mapote said that *qhang qhang* was dug out of the high basalt capping of the south-eastern mountains. Many southern Sotho people regarded it as a 'powerful medicine' that would ward off lightning and hail (How 1962: 34). Not only the San themselves but also neighbouring peoples thus believed one of the pigments to have supernatural powers (Lewis-Williams 1981: 116). This is one of numerous shared beliefs of a kind that neighbouring agriculturalists took over, and in the process transmuted (Hammond-Tooke 1997, 1998, 1999; *contra* Jolly 1995).

The transformation of this highly prised pigment into paint was, according to Mapote, accompanied by ritual procedures. He said that a woman had to heat the *qhang qhang* out of doors at full moon until it was red hot. It was then ground between two stones until it was a fine powder. The production of red pigment was, therefore, at least in certain circumstances, a collective enterprise in which people exercised different kinds of technical expertise. The control of this expertise was probably implicated in the negotiation of social power (cf. Dobres 1988, 2000); although there was a strong element of synergy, there was also potential for the privileging of one component of the paint-making process above others.

The role of a woman in the preparation of pigment parallels the part played by women at a trance dance. They generally sit in a circle around a central fire. It is all the women together who supply the vital, and vitalising, 'medicine' songs and the complex rhythmic clapping that helps the dancing shamans to enter trance and thus perform curings and acquire visions. Within the contexts of both the dance and the making of rock paintings men and women co-operated. So constituted, the dance and the preparation of paint were both potential synergistic ritual arenas for the negotiation of gender roles: the contribution of women to shamanistic rituals was crucial and defined, in part, what the San understood by 'woman' and 'man'. At the same time, individual women may have manipulated these gender relations and their participatory technical acts to their own advantage (Parkington 1989; Solomon 1992, 1999; Stevenson 1995; see also Dobres and Hoffman 1994; Dobres 2000). Indeed, in the Kalahari in recent times women's trance rituals have begun to emerge (Katz and Biesele 1986; Katz *et al.* 1997), and similar movements may have taken place in the past as well. If women were also painters, researchers have not been able to identify a distinctive category of imagery as having been made by them. Still, the making of rock art may have been a site of gender contestation in the time of social stress, though we should not make the error that many researchers do when they impose largely Western 'gender lines' on San communities. Katz *et al.* (1997: 119) found that, for the !Kung of the northern Kalahari,

> crossing 'gender lines' in working with *n!om* . . . just is not problematic – the 'lines' we thought we saw didn't exist! We had wondered about this remarkable fluidity earlier, and it applied not only to gender roles in dancing but to each individual's creativity in many areas, including the receiving or composing of songs, story-telling, and beadwork.

Be that as it may, we can now return to How's account of the way in which Mapote prepared his paint. After some commercial ochre (How deemed her piece of *qhang qhang* too precious to be used) had been obtained from a local store and ground to a powder, Mapote asked for another highly significant ingredient for his paint: 'the blood of a freshly killed eland' (How 1962: 37). *Qhang qhang*, that highly desired substance, was, he said, the only pigment that the San mixed with eland blood; other pigments were mixed with other media. If the blood were not fresh, it would coagulate and not mix with the pigment and soak into the rock. As How observes, the need for fresh blood implies that painting took place after an eland kill (Vinnicombe 1976). Significantly, a large kill is one of the occasions that trigger a communal trance dance (Marshall 1969). No eland blood was available, and Mapote made do with fresh ox blood that How obtained from the local butcher who had just slaughtered an ox. Mapote then set about painting an eland because, as he put it, 'the Bushmen of that part of the country were of the eland' (How 1962: 38). Perceptively, Vinnicombe (1976) took the title of her book from Mapote's observation (for more on the San phrase 'of the eland' and its shamanistic origin and connotations, see Lewis-Williams 1988a).

The importance of eland blood as an ingredient in the manufacture of red paint was confirmed and enlarged upon in the early 1980s by an old woman of partial San descent, known as 'M', who was living just south of the Drakensberg (Jolly 1986; Lewis-Williams 1986; Prins 1990). Her father had been a shaman-artist, and she pointed to paintings that he had made in a rock shelter. Her elder sister, who had died a few years before M was interviewed, had been taught her father's shamanistic, though not artistic, skills and had been known locally as a rain-maker. According to M, the act of painting an image was not a single, isolated event. On the contrary, a whole sequence of events started with a ritualised eland hunt. She explained that a young girl accompanied a group of hunters who went out after an eland. This girl 'hypnotised' the eland by pointing an arrow at it; on the arrow was 'medicine' that had been prepared by shamans. The participation of a young girl in a hunt, essentially a male activity, again recalls the participation of both men and women in trance dances and suggests a further arena for the negotiation of gender as well as other social and political relations. Although M did not specify the age of the young girl, it is worth noting that the /Xam people spoke of a girl at puberty as having supernatural power (Lewis-Williams 1981: 52); she could use this power to transform men at whom she looked into pillars of stone or trees (Deacon 1988; Lewis-Williams

2000). The preparation of ochre by a 'woman' and participation in the hunt of a 'young girl' may suggest differential participation by females in the production of rock art imagery at this particular juncture in San history.

When the girl had exercised her power, people led the dazed eland back, again by supernatural means (though the movements of exhausted or wounded eland can be fairly easily controlled), to a place near the rock shelter, a sandbank that M pointed out in the adjacent river (Jolly 1986). This is where they killed the eland. The people then prepared a mixture of its blood and fat. M explained that eland blood contained supernatural potency (Jolly 1986: 6); she used the Xhosa word *amandla*. In San scarification rituals, M said, this mixture of blood and fat imbued the recipient with eland potency. She went on to explain that eland blood was also used in the preparation of paint, and thus confirmed Mapote's statement. Her words and actions in the rock shelter to which she took us suggested that a painting made with eland blood was a kind of storehouse of potency.

Further, it should be noted that a dying eland bleeds from the nose and foams at the mouth, even as a shaman who, in the San's own phrase, is 'dying' in trance bleeds from the nose (Figure 2.6). Qing implied this parallel when he told Orpen (1874: 2) that the therianthropic figures in the art (shamans partially transformed into animals; Lewis-Williams 1981) had been 'spoilt [entered trance; Biesele pers. comm.] at the same time as the elands and by the dances of which you have seen paintings' (for a fuller explanation and interpretation of Qing's complex statement see Lewis-Williams 1980).

Two kinds of blood were thus involved in the production of rock paintings. First, shamans bled from the nose when they entered trance to obtain visions of the spirit world, some of which would find their way into rock paintings. At this time, their 'dying' in trance and bleeding paralleled the nasal bleeding of a dying eland. Second, the potent blood of an eland was, at least sometimes, used in the making of rock art images.

The whole process of manufacturing paint was thus socially situated and open to manipulation. Different individuals could be differentially involved in the process, and this variability could be used to contain or challenge the circle of power (cf. Dobres and Hoffman 1994; Dobres 2000). At the same time, it appears that different kinds of paint were recognised, some with blood and some without, and, possibly, other kinds about which we now know nothing. Clearly, for the San, rock paintings were far from any Western notion of *objets d'art*, and the processing of pigments was more than just material technique.

THE MAKING OF ROCK PAINTINGS

The delicate workmanship and sureness of line that are evident everywhere in southern Africa suggest that it is unlikely that all shamans painted; it seems more likely that only some acquired this special skill. This inference is in accordance with /Xam overlapping categories of shamans (Lewis-Williams 1981, 1992). Even as there were shamans of the game, shamans of the rain, and healers, there may well have been 'shamans of the images' whose special skill was the manifesting of the spirit world in the rock shelters. At some times and in some places, the making of rock paintings may have bestowed a privileged status on those who acquired the necessary skills (cf. Riddington 1988; Ingold 1993). As renowned healers are summoned to distant camps, respected painters may have been requested to journey to a rock shelter and to embellish it with images of power and insight.

If it is unlikely that all shamans painted, it seems even less likely that San shamans painted while in deep trance. If not actually unconscious, they tremble violently and would be unable to hold a brush and achieve the sure, delicate lines of the art. More probably, they painted while in a normal state of consciousness, recalling their vivid glimpses of the spirit world and making *n/om*-impregnated images of those visions and of the animals that were their principal sources of potency. Probably, the very act of painting assisted in the recall, recreation and reification of otherwise transient glimpses of spiritual things. When painting, they were working with, and in some sense reconciling, mental images that, in some instances, derived from hallucinations of the spirit world and the depictive images that they emblazoned on the walls of rock shelters. Like Wordsworth's observation on poetry, San rock art should be seen as powerful emotion recollected in (at least comparative) tranquillity.

The status of many San rock art images not as *objets d'art* but as 'fixed' visions is further seen in the way in which some of them enter or leave cracks, steps or other inequalities in the rock surface (Lewis-Williams and Dowson 1990). Sometimes an antelope, a snake or a rain-animal is painted in such a way as to suggest that it is emerging from behind, or passing into, the rock surface. This feature of the art is probably related to the San belief that the spirit world is reached, in the first instance, by means of an underground journey. For some nineteenth-century /Xam shamans this journey started by diving (in their trance experience) into waterholes (Bleek 1935; cf. Biesele 1978). It seems probable that rock shelters were also sometimes seen as potential entrances to the spirit world and that the rock face was a kind of 'veil' suspended between this world and the other world (Lewis-Williams and Dowson 1990). Shaman-artists used both their technical and their esoteric spiritual skills to coax the animals and other inhabitants of the spirit world from behind the 'veil' and then, using ritually prepared, potent paint, to fix these visions on the rock face for all to see and share.

Unfortunately, we do not know if this fixing of mediating visions was accompanied by rituals or how a shaman-artist prepared him- or herself for the task. For instance, was the fixing of visions considered as dangerous as spiritual journeys to the other world? Perhaps, like the dance in which they were acquired, the fixing of visions was also considered an appropriate occasion for the singing of 'medicine' songs to strengthen shamans in their work. If the task of 'materialising' visions on the 'veil' was considered hazardous and in need of communal support in varying degrees, this was another circumstance in which social relations could be challenged or reinforced. Whatever the case, it seems unlikely that San painters were anything like the detached ascetics of the Western Romantic fiction. On the contrary, San image-makers were working with powerful substances, visions of the supernatural, and the 'veil' that thinly separated them from the realm of spiritual power and terror.

THE USE OF ROCK PAINTINGS

Once made, many San images continued to perform significant functions; they were not made for one occasion only and then ignored. The rock shelters were not simply 'galleries' packed with *objets d'art*. As I have already argued, many paintings were things-in-themselves, not just pictures of things that existed elsewhere, perhaps out in the countryside or around a camp-fire.

Again, there is, unfortunately, little ethnographic information on precisely what happened to these potent images after they had been made. Given the three stages that I have so far described, it seems unlikely that paintings would simply have dropped out of the ambit of San ritual and belief. On the contrary, such evidence as we do have suggests that they continued to play an important function.

In the first place, M's statements suggest that the images were important visually, but in a specific, non-Western way. She demonstrated how, long ago, San people danced in the painted rock shelter to which she took Peter Jolly and me and how they raised their arms and turned to the paintings when they wished to intensify their potency (*amandla*). As they danced and looked at the paintings, power flowed from the images and entered into them. This was, I believe, her way of saying that the sight of the paintings deepened the dancers' trance experience. The images were reservoirs of *n/om*.

M then expanded on this notion that the images themselves contained potency. She said that if a 'good' person placed his or her hand on a depiction of an eland, the potency in the painting would flow into the person, thus giving him or her special powers. To demonstrate how this was done, she held my wrist and arranged my fingers so that my entire hand was on a depiction of an eland. As she did so, she unnervingly cautioned that, if a 'bad' person did this, his or her hand would adhere to the rock and the person would eventually waste away and die. Her actions recalled the 'laying on of hands' during a San curing dance: shamans place their hands on people and draw sickness out of them and into their own bodies; they then expel the sickness through a 'hole' in the back of the neck, and it flies back to the spirit world from whence it came. A comparable process of transference of supernatural essence, it seems, could take place between a person and a painted image imbued with power. In the case of paintings, the images were thus mediators between the material world and spiritual realms and entities.

The importance of touching, and not merely looking at, rock paintings is supported by evidence from various parts of southern Africa. In the Western Cape Province patches of paint have been rubbed smooth (Yates and Manhire 1991). It is not entirely clear with what the patches were rubbed, but the smoothness of the rock, particularly in the centre of the patches, is easily discerned. In addition, some Western Cape images were rubbed, possibly both before and after the paint dried; their outlines are characteristically blurred and smeared. Rubbed images have also been recorded in the Waterberg in Northern Province (Laue 2000; Peters 2000). Similarly, the making of positive handprints that are common in parts of the Western Cape Province and some other regions was probably closely associated with ritual touching of the rock rather than (exclusively) with the making of 'pictures' of hands (Lewis-Williams and Dowson 1999: 108; Lewis-Williams and Blundell 1997).

There is thus evidence that some of the paintings were not made merely to be viewed. After they had been made, they continued to be involved in rituals, and physical contact with some images facilitated the acquisition of potency. M's remarks suggest that the touching of paintings was not open to everyone and that for some people it could be hazardous. Significantly, she was implying differential access to the art and concomitant social differentiation.

More than that, the fixed visions already on the rock face probably contributed, as I have suggested, to the dancers' hallucinations, informing and constraining the stream of mental images that the human nervous system produces in deep altered states of consciousness. All in all, the painted images did not merely record events and experiences. They became sources of potency and active components in a complex ritual of dancing, singing and clapping that controlled the spiritual, or hallucinatory, experiences of shamans and, possibly other people's as well. Painted rock shelters were nodes on the landscape where the spirit realm was especially immanent (Ouzman 1996).

There was, then, probably a recursivity in the ritual sequence of making and using rock paintings: the paintings impacted on the formation of mental images, some of which were destined to be 'fixed' on the rock face. Yet the recursivity loop was not ineluctable. Rather, the recursivity was mediated and manipulated by shamans in specific historical circumstances. The 'distance' between new painted images and older ones was crucial in establishing the social position of the makers. Similarities said one thing, differences another.

As time went by, certain rock shelters acquired more and more of these spiritual images. In some shelters paintings were done one on top of another, thus building up multiple layers of images, the oldest ones fading into a blurred red background. In some instances, paintings were carefully overpainted, apparently in an effort to renew them visually and spiritually (Vinnicombe 1976: 141, 161, 164, 170, 180, 185, 187, 236, 329, 330; Yates and Manhire 1991). Exactly which paintings were chosen for renewal and which were not probably had social significance, and the most densely and 'renewed' rock shelters were probably regarded as places of exceptional personal or group power (Dowson 1988, 1994; cf. Ouzman 1996 on rock engravings).

The roles played by these places and images no doubt varied according to the social circumstances of their viewing. For example, when viewed from within a San community, images would have reinforced or challenged social relations between San individuals and various interest groups. When people from outside the San community, such as neighbouring Bantu-speaking agriculturists, were present, for whatever reasons, images that would otherwise have been divisive may, for the San, have performed a unifying role in the face of the contestation implied by the presence of others. That is why it is necessary always to situate the production–consumption trajectory as precisely as possible.

SAN SHAMANISM: AN OVERALL FRAMEWORK

I have argued that the constitutive role of San rock art images and their making need not be merely assumed, or asserted, in the light of current material culture theory. Because of, first, the variety and intricacy of the art and, second, the availability of detailed records of San belief and society, the mechanisms and processes whereby the images achieved social and political ends can be identified. Establishing exactly what those social and political ends were is a task that has still has a long way to go, but, with at least some of the mechanisms now established, there is every chance of success.

Overall, it is essential to recognise the centrality and formative power of San shamanism and the cosmos in which it operated. As with image-making, so too in myth-telling: the tiered shamanistic cosmos, the shamanistic mode of transcending the levels, and the metaphors of transcendence need to be understood if the myths are to make sense (Lewis-Williams 1996, 1997). It is all too easy to read San myths as if they were simple tales concocted for the entertainment of children, and indeed it is as 'children' that the San have often been seen, a view extending to their intellectual abilities and gaining spurious 'support' from their comparatively short stature. This racist notion has been tragically formative in conceptions of southern African history, and has undermined our understanding of the San's complex rock art.

San shamanism may therefore be thought of as a dual framework. In the past, it provided a cognitive datum line for San life as it was lived from day to day; at the same time, it was a malleable set of concepts and relationships that was at the heart of the reproduction and contestation of San society. Today, it affords a framework for research: an understanding of how San shamanism functioned and how the images of San rock art were socio-political interventions gives researchers some purchase on what would otherwise be an exceedingly slippery southern African past.

ACKNOWLEDGEMENTS

I am grateful to numerous colleagues who read and usefully commented on drafts of this article. Over the years, Megan Biesele has been an inexhaustible source of information about the Ju/'hoan San of the Kalahari. Ghilraen Laue drew the map in Figure 2.1 and assisted with the preparation of the manuscript. Figure 6 was traced and redrawn by Thomas Dowson. Figures 2.2–2.5 are from the Harald Pager Collection in the archives of the Rock Art Research Institute at the University of the Witwatersrand. They were originally published in his book *Stone Age Myth and Magic* (1975). Shirley-Anne Pager, Harald's widow, generously donated a collection of his work to the Institute. The illustrations were prepared for publication by Siyakha Mguni, research officer in the Rock Art Research Institute. The Rock Art Research Institute is funded by the University of the Witwatersrand and the National Research Foundation; the Institute also acknowledges grants from Anglo-American, Anglo-Gold and De Beers.

NOTE

1 San rock art comprises both paintings and engravings. The paintings are found on the walls of rock shelters across the subcontinent, though they are densely clustered in regions such as the Drakensberg and the Cederberg. The engravings are found on open rocks on the plains of the central plateau, where there are fewer rock shelters. It is with rock paintings that I am concerned in this paper; for more on rock engravings, see Dowson (1992).

REFERENCES

Atkinson, J. (1992). 'Shamanisms today', *Annual Review of Anthropology* 21: 307–37.
Biesele, M. (1978) 'Sapience and scarce resources: communication systems of the !Kung and other foragers', *Social Science Information* 17: 921–47.
—— (1993) *'Women like Meat': The Folklore and Foraging Ideology of the Kalahari Ju/'hoan*, Johannesburg: Witwatersrand University Press.
Bleek, D.F. (1924) *The Mantis and his Friends*, Cape Town: Maskew Miller.
—— (1933) 'Beliefs and customs of the /Xam Bushmen, Part VI: Rain-making', *Bantu Studies* 7: 375–92.
—— (1935) 'Beliefs and customs of the /Xam Bushmen, Part VII: Sorcerors', *Bantu Studies* 9: 1–47.
—— (1936) 'Beliefs and customs of the /Xam Bushmen, Part VIII: More about sorcerors and charms', *Bantu Studies* 10: 131–62.
Bleek, W. H. I. (1874) 'Remarks on J.M. Orpen's "Mythology of the Maluti Bushmen" ', *Cape Monthly Magazine* (N.S.) 9: 10–13.
Bleek, W.H.I. and Lloyd, L.C. (1911) *Specimens of Bushman Folklore*, London: George Allen.
Bourdieu, P. (1977) *Outline of a Theory of Practice*, Cambridge: Cambridge University Press.
Bourguignon, E. (1974) 'Cross-cultural perspectives on the religious uses of altered states of consciousness', in I.I. Zaretsky and M. Leone (eds) *Religious Movements in Contemporary America*, Princeton: Princeton University Press.
Burkitt, M.C. (1928) *South Africa's Past in Stone and Paint*, Cambridge: Cambridge University Press.
Conkey, M.W. (1993) 'Humans as materialists: image making in the Upper Palaeolithic', in D.T. Rasmussen (ed.) *The Origin of Humans and Humanness*. Boston: Jones & Bartlett.
Cooke, C.K. (1969) *Rock Art of Southern Africa*, Cape Town: Books of Africa.
Deacon, J. (1986) ' "My place is the Bitterpits": the home territory of Bleek and Lloyd's /Xam San informants', *African Studies* 45: 135–55.
—— (1988) 'The power of a place in understanding southern San rock engravings', *World Archaeology* 20: 129–40.
Deacon, J. and Dowson, T.A. (eds) (1996) *Voices from the Past: /Xam Bushmen and the Bleek and Lloyd Collection*, Johannesburg: Witwatersrand University Press.
Dobres, M.-A. (1988) 'The underground world of the Upper Paleolithic on the central Russian plain: social organization, ideology and style', unpublished MA thesis, State University of New York, Binghamton.
—— (2000) *Technology and Social Agency: Outlining a Practice Framework for Archaeology*, Oxford: Blackwell.
Dobres, M.-A. and Hoffman, C.R. (1994) 'Social agency and the dynamics of prehistoric technology', *Journal of Archaeological Method and Theory* 1(3): 211–58.
Dowson, T.A. (1988) 'Revelations of religious reality: the individual in San rock art', *World Archaeology* 20: 116–28.
—— (1989) 'Dots and dashes: cracking the entoptic code in Bushman rock paintings', *South African Archaeological Society Goodwin Series* 6: 84–94.

—— (1992) *Rock Engravings of Southern Africa*, Johannesburg: Witwatersrand University Press.

—— (1994) 'Reading art, writing history: rock art and social change in southern Africa', *World Archaeology* 25: 332–44.

Dowson, T. A. and Holliday, A.L. (1989) Zigzags and eland: an interpretation of an idiosyncratic combination. *South African Archaeological Bulletin* 45: 17–27.

Eberhard, E. (1996) 'Wilhelm Bleek and the founding of Khoisan research', in J. Deacon and T.A. Dowson (eds) *Voices from the Past: /Xam Bushmen and the Bleek and Lloyd Collection*, Johannesburg: Witwatersrand University Press.

Eliade, M. (1964) *Shamanism: Archaic Techniques of Ecstasy*, New York: Bollingen Foundation.

Giddens, A. (1984) *The Constitution of Society: Outline of the Theory of Structuration*, Berkeley: University of California Press.

Guenther, M.G. (1986) *The Nharo Bushmen of Botswana: Tradition and Change*, Hamburg: Helmut Buske Verlag.

—— (1989) *Bushman Folktales*, Studien zur Kulturkunde, 93, Wiesbaden: Franz Steiner Verlag.

—— (1999) *Tricksters and Trancers: Bushman Religion and Society*, Bloomington: Indiana University Press.

Gulbrandsen, O. (1991) 'On the problem of egalitarianism: the Kalahari San', in R. Gronhaug, G. Haaland and G. Henriksen (eds) *The ecology of choice and symbol: essays in honour of Fredrik Barth*, Bergen: Alma Mater Forlag.

Hammond-Tooke, W.D. (1997) 'Whatever happened to /Kaggen?: a note on Khoisan/Cape Nguni borrowing', *South African Archaeological Bulletin* 52: 122–4.

—— (1998) 'Selective borrowing? The possibility of San shamanistic influence on Southern Bantu divination and healing practices', *South African Archaeological Bulletin* 53: 9–15.

—— (1999) 'Divinatory animals: further evidence of San/Nguni borrowing?', *South African Archaeological Bulletin* 54: 128–32.

Hewitt, R.L. (1986) *Structure, Meaning and Ritual in the Narratives of the Southern San*, Hamburg: Helmut Buske Verlag.

Hodder, I. (1982a) 'Theoretical archaeology: a reactionary view', in I. Hodder (ed.) *Symbolic and Structural Archaeology*, Cambridge: Cambridge University Press.

—— (1982b) *Symbols in action*, Cambridge: Cambridge University Press.

How, M.W. (1962) *The Mountain Bushmen of Basutoland*, Pretoria: Van Schaik.

Hultkrantz, Å. (1973) 'A definition of shamanism', *Tenemos* 9: 25–37.

Ingold, T. (1993) 'Technology, language and intelligence: a consideration of basic concepts', in K. Gibson and T. Ingold (eds) *Tools, Language and Cognition in Human Evolution*, Cambridge: Cambridge University Press.

Johnson, M.H. (1989) 'Conceptions of agency in archaeological interpretation', *Journal of Anthropological Archaeology* 8: 189–211.

Jolly, P. (1986) 'A first generation descendant of the Transkei San', *South African Archaeological Bulletin* 41: 6–9.

—— (1995) 'Melikane and Upper Mangolong revisited: the possible effects on San art of symbiotic contact between south-eastern San and southern Sotho and Nguni communities', *South African Archaeological Bulletin* 50: 68–80.

Katz, R. (1982) *Boiling Energy: Community-healing Among the Kalahari !Kung*. Cambridge, Mass.: Harvard University Press.

Katz, R. and Biesele, M. (1986) '!Kung healing: the symbolism of sex roles and culture change', in M. Biesele, R. Gordon and R. Lee (eds) *The Past and Future of !Kung Ethnography: Critical Reflections and Symbolic Perspectives. Essays in Honour of Lorna Marshall*, Hamburg: Helmut Buske Verlag.

Katz, R., Biesele, M. and St. Denis, V. (1997) *Healing Makes Our Hearts Happy: Spirituality and Cultural Transformation Among the Kalahari Ju/'hoansi*, Rochester: Inner Traditions.

Keeney, B. (1999) *Kalahari Bushmen Healers*, Philadelphia: Ringing Rocks Press.

Laue, G.B. (2000) *Taking a Stance: Posture and Meaning in the Rock Art of the Waterberg, Northern Province, South Africa*, unpublished MSc. thesis, University of the Witwatersrand, Johannesburg.

Lewis-Williams, J.D. (1972) 'The syntax and function of Giant's Castle rock-paintings', *South African Archaeological Bulletin* 27: 49–65.

—— (1974) 'Superpositioning in a sample of rock-paintings from Barkly East District', *South African Archaeological Bulletin* 29: 49–65.

—— (1980) 'Ethnography and iconography: aspects of southern San thought and art', *Man* 15: 467–82.

—— (1981) *Believing and Seeing: Symbolic Meanings in Southern San Rock Art*, London: Academic Press.

—— (1982) 'The economic and social context of southern San rock art', *Current Anthropology* 23: 429–49.

—— (1986) 'The last testament to the southern San', *South African Archaeological Bulletin* 41:10–11.

—— (1987) 'A dream of eland: an unexplored component of San shamanism and rock art', *World Archaeology* 19: 165–77.

—— (1988a) '"People of the eland": an archaeo-linguistic crux', in T. Ingold, D. Riches and J. Woodburn (eds) *Hunters and Gatherers 2: Property, Power and Ideology*, Oxford: Berg.

—— (1988b) *The World of Man and the World of Spirit: An Interpretation of the Linton Rock Paintings*, Margaret Shaw Lecture 2, Cape Town: South African Museum.

—— (1990) *Discovering Southern African Rock Art*, Cape Town: David Philip.

—— (1992) 'Ethnographic evidence relating to "trance" and "shamans" among northern and southern Bushmen', *South African Archaeological Bulletin* 47: 56–60.

—— (1995) 'Modelling the production and consumption of rock art', *South African Archaeological Bulletin* 50: 143–54.

—— (1996) ' "A visit to the Lion's house": the structure, metaphors and socio-political significance of a nineteenth-century Bushman myth', in J. Deacon and T.A. Dowson (eds) *Voices from the Past: /Xam Bushmen and the Bleek and Lloyd Collection*, Johannesburg: Witwatersrand University Press.

—— (1997) 'The Mantis, the Eland and the Meerkats: conflict and mediation in a nineteenth-century San myth', in P. McAllister (ed.) *Culture and the Commonplace: Anthropological Essays in Honour of David Hammond-Tooke*, African Studies Special Issue 56 (2), Johannesburg: University of the Witwatersrand Press.

—— (1998) 'Quanto?: the issue of "many meanings" in southern African San rock art research', *South African Archaeological Bulletin* 53: 86–97.

—— (1999) ' "Meaning" in southern African San rock art: another impasse?', *South African Archaeological Bulletin* 54: 141–5.

—— (2000) *Stories that Float from Afar: Ancestral Folklore of the /Xam San of Southern Africa*, Cape Town: David Philip Publishers.

Lewis-Williams, J.D. and Biesele, M. (1978) 'Eland hunting rituals among northern and southern groups: striking similarities', *Africa* 48: 117–34.

Lewis-Williams, J.D. and Blundell, G. (1997) 'New light on finger-dots in southern African rock art: synesthesia, transformation and technique', *South African Journal of Science* 93: 51–4.

—— (1998) *Fragile Heritage: A Rock Art Fieldguide*, Johannesburg: Witwatersrand University Press.

Lewis-Williams, J.D., Blundell, G., Challis, W., and Hampson, J. (2000) 'Threads of light: re-examining a motif in southern African San rock art', *South African Archaeological Bulletin* (in press).

Lewis-Williams, J.D. and T.A. Dowson. (1990) 'Through the veil: San rock paintings and the rock face', *South African Archaeological Bulletin* 45: 5–16.

—— (1999) *Images of Power: Understanding Bushman Rock Art*, 2nd edition. Johannesburg: Southern Book Publishers.

Lommel, A. (1967) *Shamanism: The Beginnings of Art*, New York: McGraw-Hill.

Maggs, T.M. O'C. (1967) 'A quantitative analysis of the rock art from a sample area in the Western Cape', *South African Journal of Science* 63: 100–4.

Marshall, L. (1960) '!Kung Bushman bands', *Africa* 30: 325–55.

—— (1969) The medicine dance of the !Kung Bushmen. *Africa* 39: 347–81.

—— (1999) *Nyae Nyae !Kung: Beliefs and Rites*, Cambridge, Mass.: Peabody Museum.

Orpen, J.M. (1874) 'A glimpse into the mythology of the Maluti Bushmen', *Cape Monthly Magazine* (N.S.) 9 (49): 1–13.

Ouzman, S. (1996) 'Thaba Sione: place of rhinoceroses and rock art', *African Studies* 55 (1): 31–59.

Pager, H. (1971) *Ndedema*, Graz: Akademische Druck.

—— (1975) *Stone Age Myth and Magic*, Graz: Akademische Druck.

Parkington, J. (1989) 'Interpreting paintings without a commentary', *Antiquity* 63: 13–26.

Peters, M. (2000) *The Power Brokers: Potency Collection in the Spirit Realm, with Special Reference to Site X'*, unpublished MSc. thesis, University of the Witwatersrand, Johannesburg.

Prins, F.E. (1990) 'Southern Bushman descendants in the Transkei rock-art and rain-making', *South African Journal of Ethnology* 13: 110–16.

Rappaport, R.A. (1999) *Ritual and Religion in the Making of Humanity*, Cambridge: Cambridge University Press.

Riddington, R. (1988) 'Knowledge, power and the individual in subarctic hunting societies', *American Anthropologist* 90: 98–110.

Schmidt, S. (1973) 'Die Mantis religiosa in den Glaubensvorstellungen der Khoesan-Völker', *Zeitschrift für Ethnologie* 98 (1): 102–27.

Shanks, M. and Tilley, C. (1987) *Reconstructing Archaeology: Theory and Practice*, Cambridge: Cambridge University Press.

Shirokogoroff, S.M. (1935) *Psychomental Complex of the Tungus*, London: Kegan Paul, Trench and Trubner.

Silberbauer, G.B. (1981) *Hunter and Habitat in the Kalahari Desert*, Cambridge: Cambridge University Press.

Smits, L.G.A. (1971) 'The rock paintings of Lesotho, their content and characteristics', *South African Journal of Science Special Publication* 2: 14–19.

Solomon, A. C. (1992) 'Gender, representation, and power in San ethnography and rock art', *Journal of Anthropological Archaeology* 11: 291–329.

—— (1999) ' "Mythic Woman": a study in variability in San rock art and narrative', in T.A. Dowson and J.D. Lewis-Williams (eds) *Contested Images: Diversity in Southern African Rock Art*, Johannesburg: University of the Witwatersrand Press.

Spohr, O.H. (1962) *Wilhelm Heinrich Emmanuel Bleek: A Bibliographical Sketch*, Varia Series 6, Cape Town: University of Cape Town Libraries.

Stevenson, J. (1995) *Man-the-shaman: is it the Whole Story? A Feminist Perspective on the San Rock Art of South Africa*, unpublished MA thesis, University of the Witwatersrand, Johannesburg.

Vinnicombe, P. (1972a) 'Myth, motive and selection in southern African rock art', *Africa* 42: 192–204.

—— (1972b) 'Motivation in African rock art', *Antiquity* 46: 124–33.

—— (1976) *People of the Eland: Rock Paintings of the Drakensberg Bushmen as a Reflection of their Life and Thought*, Pietermaritzburg: University of Natal Press.

Vitebsky, P. (1995) *The Shaman*, London: Macmillan.

Walker, N. (1996) *The Painted Hills: Rock Art of the Matopos*, Gweru, Zimbabwe: Mambo Press.

Wilmsen, E.N. (1989) *Land Filled with Flies*, Chicago: Chicago University Press.

Winkelman, M. and Dobkin de Rios, M. (1989) 'Psychoactive properties of !Kung Bushman medicine plants', *Journal of Psychoactive Drugs* 21: 51–9.

Wright, J.B. (1971) *Bushman Raiders of the Drakensberg: 1840–1870*, Pietermaritzburg: University of Natal Press.

Yates, R., Golson, J. and Hall, M. (1985) 'Trance performance: the rock art of Boontjies Kloof and Sevilla', *South African Archaeological Bulletin* 40: 70–80.

Yates, R. and Manhire, A. (1991) 'Shamanism and rock paintings: aspects of the use of rock art in the south-west Cape, South Africa', *South African Archaeological Bulletin* 46: 3–11.

Part Two

Siberia and Central Asia
The 'Cradle of Shamanism'

Chapter Three

Rock art and the material culture of Siberian and Central Asian shamanism

Ekaterina Devlet

INTRODUCTION

In Siberia and Central Asia – the 'homelands' of shamanism – there is no ancient tradition of written language, and consequently no direct descriptive data on the lifestyle and belief systems of the prehistoric population. Valuable insights can be however gained from the comparison of rock art images with ethnographic material, which indicate that a shamanic world-view was fundamental for the complex symbolism of the Siberians. Indeed, some of the rock art panels can be understood solely in the context of shamanic ideas.

In this chapter I would like to focus on two chronologically separated rock art motifs: first historical petroglyphs, which probably date to the last two or three centuries, and second their probable ancient prototypes – images that have been claimed to date from the Bronze Age and even earlier periods. I shall then compare images of both periods with the distinctive coats worn by shamans, and with their various accoutrements and ethnographically recorded items of equipment such as so-called spirit-containers.

SHAMANIC COSTUME AND ITS ICONOGRAPHY IN ROCK ART

In some of the Asian and American cultures with shamanic belief systems we find no special ritual costume worn by the shamans, but among those who had such apparel it is clear that these marvellous coats were always in some way embodiments of a shamanic world-view. The cosmological iconography of these jackets – with pendants, breastplates and other attached details – often depicts the tripartite division of the universe, and these associations may be reinforced by the materials chosen for the coats' component parts, for example the hides of reindeer, elk or bear. The shaman's costume was also invested with several additional layers of meaning and complex symbolism.

One example of this is the depiction of skeletons on the breast-piece or on the back as a prominent feature of Siberian shamanic coats (Ivanov 1954). They may be explained as representing the bones of the wearer's shaman-ancestor, serving as the shaman's shield, protection and armour, and as the guarantee of his or her survival (Alexeev 1975: 152). Another interpretation of these skeletal costume elements explains them as representations of a shaman brought back to life after the dismemberment that occurs during the initiation process: the depicted bones thus refer to the wearer's own skeleton.

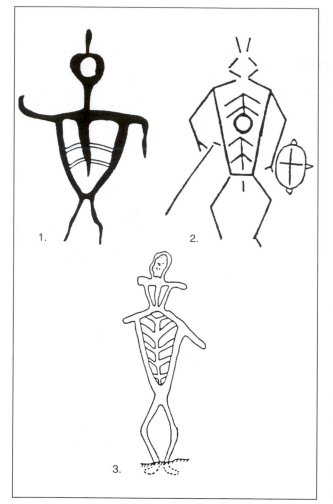

Figure 3.1 Rock art anthropomorphs in the 'X-ray style'.
1. Aya Bay, Lake Baikal (after Okladnikov 1974); 2. Mount Ukir (after Khoroshih, cited in Mikhailov 1987); 3. Bolshaja Kada (after Okladnikov and Martinov 1972);

The same concept may be traced in Siberian rock art anthropomorphs in the so-called 'X-ray style', representing a shamanic perspective on an intermediate condition between death and revival (see Devlet 2000). Figure 3.1 shows examples from the Lake Baikal region, Mount Ukir and Bolshaja Kada.

In the rock art of relatively recent periods it is possible to identify images of shamans, depicted as engaged in their ritual activities. Being quite schematic in form, these figures are nonetheless dynamic. Some of the anthropomorphs shown in these images are wearing fringed coats and are engaged in a shamanic performance with a drum. A range of such images from the historical period in the Altai region are shown in Figures 3.2 and 3.3 (see also Ivanov 1954; Okladnikov and Zaporozhskaja 1972; Kyzlasov and Leontiev 1980; Martinov 1985; Kubarev 1988; Okladnikova 1989). Such images are known in the rock art of different regions, and in addition they are found pecked or engraved on stone plaques recovered from barrows. Those shown with extended arms resemble the anthropomorphic figures which in time replaced the cross-handles on drums of the kind shown in their hands (see below, p. 49).

Bands of lines hanging from the hands and arms are common details of such anthropomorphs, and sometimes a similar fringe is shown in the form of lines or triangular marks on the profile of the figure's back. Similar fringes may be seen on the coats of recent Siberian shamans. The fringe of a shaman's coat is an important element, which marks his or her ornithomorphic nature (i.e. the ability to transform into a bird or to gain its abilities such as the capacity for flight). By means of the latter, the shaman is able to penetrate into the upper sphere of the universe and make contact with divine powers. This ornithomorphic essence appears to have been the most ancient characteristic of the shamanic coat, and by extension its fringe was the most crucial symbolic element in its decoration. It may be suggested that the textile fringe represented and replaced the natural feathers of a bird's wings, an effect reinforced by the attachment of real feathers, tied so as to hang loose from the elbows and shoulders of the coat. According to ethnological records, for some of the Siberian peoples the fringe along the bottom of the coat symbolised a connection with the underworld, and was intended to represent snakes; in some cases bears' paws were also attached to the hem.

A common belief throughout Siberia is that in the mythical, timeless period 'before' the remembered time of human beings (a concept somewhat akin to the so-called Dreamtime of Australian aborigines) there were no distinctions in form or essence between people, animals and birds. Shamans could cross these boundaries of time and space to change their essence and appearance, and it is this idea that is reflected by the symbolism of the shamanic coat.

At the Niukzha rock art site in the Olekma River basin, the idea of shamanic flight is graphically depicted (Figure 3.4; Okladnikov and Mazin 1976). Here we see the shaman, represented with a drum and hammer, and a very clearly depicted jacket with fringes that spread out around him as he moves, flying among the stars and other celestial bodies. The exaggerated details of the fringe attached to the bottom and sleeves of the shaman's coat stand here for the above-mentioned ability to fly, and as a symbol for the shaman's role as a mediator between the celestial and terrestrial parts of the universe. The rock art images thus confirm the very ancient roots not only of these garments, but also of the complex cosmological symbolism that they represent.

Among the anthropomorphic personages depicted in the pre-Bronze and Bronze Age rock art from the Altai region, Tuva and Mongolia, there are frontal images of male and female figures wearing long, fringed coats with bands hanging down from the hands, arms, and sometimes from the sides, chest and hem (for examples see Novgorodova 1984; Okladnikova 1990; Kubarev 1988; Kubarev and Jacobson 1996; Jacobson 1997). Most of these figures are shown with raised hands, suggesting that they are 'praying', perhaps appealing to celestial realms or supernatural powers; others are shown with extended hands, as if they are flying. This, in combination with the

Figure 3.2 Rock art images of shamans from the Altai region. 1. Karakol (after Martinov 1985); 2. Altai (after Gurkin, cited in Ivanov 1954); 3–4. Shalkoby (after Okladnikova 1989).

Figure 3.3 Fine line engraving of a shaman on a stone plaque from the Altai. (after Grichan 1987).

Figure 3.6 Paintings on shamans' drums (after Ivanov 1954).

being that it had once been: this ritual confirmed the drum as a living entity, and it was following this act that images were created on it. The painting of the drum-skin with different motifs was thus the final action in the process of drum creation (Lvova *et al.* 1988: 168–71). The drum and drumstick together thereafter became personal attributes of the shaman, gaining the ability to change the essence of things and to transform themselves into anything that the shaman might need in the course of his or her activities. These needs might arise during a journey to another world, or during a struggle with the shaman's enemies.

Some of the imagery used on drums can be explained through reference to the ethnological sources, and from there it is possible to extrapolate to the images depicted in the rock art; from this material it is in turn possible to suggest that similar petroglyphs and paintings may also have been sacral images (Ivanov 1954). In the rock art one can see several interesting variants of drums, in some of which the contours of the drum itself enclose an anthropomorphic figure with extended arms from which apparently hang suspensions of some kind (Fig 3.2). In their real prototypes, schematic anthropomorphic figures with extended arms and hands sometimes replaced the cross-handle by which the drum was held (Funk 1995). These anthropomorphs could also be decorated with features referring, as before, to various shamanic functions. Examples of this include pendants that hung from the cross-handles, which resemble the fringes along the sleeves and sides of the shamanic coat. In some examples of rock art images, and drum-skin paintings depicting shamans holding such drums with anthropomorphic cross-handles, there is a striking similarity between the anthropomorphs, as if they are duplicates of one another. It may be that this symbolises the isomorphic nature of the shaman and the drum. Some Siberian natives (for example, the aboriginal inhabitants of the southern Altai) believed in complete identification between a shaman and his or her drum: the destruction of the drum was equivalent to the shaman's death (Lvova *et al.* 1988: 170–1).

According to the shamanic belief systems of Siberia and central Asia, spirits and souls were considered as material objects. The rules and customs that regulated communication with these spirits contained a number of restrictions that may be explained by the perception of their material nature. Relationships between the world of spirits and the world of human beings were in many ways conventional. Siberian aboriginal people sometimes constructed physical representations of a dead shaman if his or her soul began to worry their living relatives (Ivanov 1979). Known as *chalu*, these objects frequently took the form of a small drum with an anthropomorphic figure in the centre. The hands were formed by a string with suspended conical metal pendants or bands. The same function could also be served by anthropomorphic images of shaman-ancestors attached to a piece of fabric cut into vertical bands. There are further cases from the Siberian ethnographies in which these anthropomorphic representations of shamanic spirits were completely replaced by simple rectangular pieces of fabric, again cut into coloured bands: these items had the same function and meaning as the figurines. Feathers were frequently attached to such bands, symbolizing the shaman's ability to fly. For example, according to explanations recorded by Ivanov among the people of the Altai, a piece of fabric with thirteen dark blue bands and a bird's tail attached to it represented 'a winged woman-shaman' (Ivanov 1979: 164). The same source notes that fabrics with bands could designate both male and female shamans, in addition to 'celestial maidens, the winged spirits of hunters, those spirits possessing the ability to interfere with terrestrial life, and those capable of flight' (Ivanov 1979: 164).

The exact timing of the drum's appearance as a shamanic attribute is still a matter of discussion. Researchers have established that shamans could once perform their offices with the help of a bow. From the evidence of a rock art panel at Yelanka on the Middle Lena River, it is possible to suggest that these two shamanic attributes originally co-existed, as alongside anthropomorphic figures in jackets with ovoid and circular drums a figure with a bow is also depicted (Okladnikov and Zaporozhskaja 1972: Figure 119). Anthropomorphic figures holding bows on the rock art panel at Oglakhty on the Middle Yenisei may also be interpreted as shamans or proto-shamans (Devlet 1966: Fig. 24). We can suggest that this dynamic pair of figures may be engaged in some sort of shamanic activity because of their head-gear – one wears a hat topped with two horns and from the other emerge four rays.

The Siberian ethnological sources make it clear that many other items could replace the drum for use in shamanic rituals. During the period when shamanic activity was suppressed by the state it was actively dangerous to keep drums in the house, and at this time practising shamans used frying-pans as drums (Balser 1995). Ethnologists have recorded how, depending on circumstances, different tools could take on the qualities of shamanic equipment and be used instead of the drum. For example, during burial ceremonies an axe could be used in the rituals for a dead man while a tool for digging up roots was used in the services for a dead woman. After the ceremonies were over, these items were placed in a special location near a birch tree; there are records of many such objects being visible there at any one time, despite which they were never taken by anyone (Lvova *et al.* 1988: 193).

Drum-sticks are also depicted in the rock art. They may be quite schematic, but in some cases it is possible to recognise types known from existing examples in the ethnological collections – usually a curved stick or a stick with three points.

SHAMANIC HEAD-GEAR

Head-gear was a particularly important element of a shaman's garments, and often decorated with horns or antlers, and with bird feathers or other ornithomorphic features. The complex symbolism of the antlers resembles that of the shaman's jacket and attached details. As we have seen, some details of the coat symbolised the bones of the wearer's ancestor, which protected the shaman in the course of his or her activities. In the same way, the antlers also represented a link with a shaman-ancestor, it is thought through their resemblance to a plant's roots in the context of a metaphorical 'family tree'. According to information recorded among the Nanai people, a great shaman was buried in a special head-dress with antlers which were taken from the head-gear that he used for shamanizing. The antlers were tied by a rope to a pole erected on the surface of the grave. The Nanai believed that after some time the antlers left the grave and moved themselves to their new owner (Smoliak 1991: 231).

When they were placed on shamanic head-gear, antlers lost their animal nature and gained a new, symbolic meaning. This operated at several levels, as the antlers also represented the number of helping spirits that the shaman could command, each tine of the antlers being a container for a single spirit (Smoliak 1991: 227–33). Again, in this context the antlers were perceived as the roots of a mythical tree, with different aspects of the shaman's power represented by, or 'growing on', its branches.

In the Altai, shamans who wore bands decorated with feathers and shells were called 'birds' (Lvova *et al.* 1988: 175). The inhabitants of the Lower Amur also put real antlers or iron copies of them on their ritual head-gear, but they were often finished off with a bird figure. As in the case of the shamanic jacket, the most important elements were artistically enhanced, and it is these features that were the most long-lived, surviving predominantly unchanged over the centuries as a conscious link with ancient traditions.

Shamanic head-gear furnished with rays or horns is also recognizable in the rock art. Recent engravings of rayed head-gear from the historical period can be paralleled with similar carvings from Neolithic and Bronze Age panels from the Upper and Lower Lena, Aldan, Olekma, and Angara rivers' basin (Figure 3.7; Ivanov 1954; Okladnikov and Zaporozhskaja 1972; Okladnikov 1977; Sunshugashev 1990). Schematic, anthropomorphic figures with rays on their heads are a particular feature of Siberian and Central Asian rock art (see Rozwadowski, this volume). Their bodies may be curvilinear, and some of them are missing legs or hands, but they are always depicted with rays either on the head or even replacing it. The differential treatment of these figures in relation to others on the rock surface strengthens the impression that they represent some supernatural being, and in this context we should recall the use of hallucinogens and other mind-altering substances in shamanic practices.

The highly decorated jacket and other items of equipment formed the material manifestations of a shaman's special status. In tandem with the ethnological records, the presence of these or similar items in excavated contexts or in rock art depictions lends support

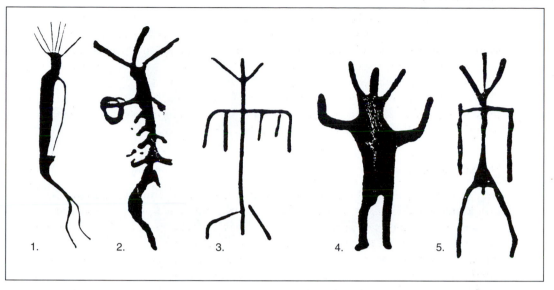

Figure 3.7 Rock art anthropomorphs in head-gear with rays. 1. Painting from Shishkino, Upper Lena River (after Okladnikov 1977); 2. Lake Maloye, Middle Yenisei River (after Sunchugashev 1990); 3. Chasovnya, Middle Lena River (after Okladnikov and Zaporozhskaja 1972); 4. Kozlovo, Upper Lena River (after Okladnikov 1977); 5. Suruktakh-Khaya, Yakutia (after Ivanov 1954).

to the interpretation of the image or buried person as a shaman, or at least as someone who had been involved in ritual activity.

In addition to the above-mentioned items, other grave-goods such as zoomorphic and anthropomorphic amulets, certain bones of fish and birds, and assemblages of small sticks have also been interpreted as items of shamanic equipment. Some of the better-preserved Neolithic and Bronze Age burials have even enabled reconstructions to be made of early shamanic clothing (Figure 3.8 shows one such woman's grave from Ust'-Uda; Okladnikov 1955: Fig. 175). The reconstructions made from archaeological evidence accord well with the material gathered by later ethnographers.

There is little consensus in the debate as to when shamanic practices first appeared in Siberia. The crucial problem has always been the limitations of our data, and in this context it may be seen that rock art motifs provide a unique opportunity for tracing the early roots of shamanic concepts. Nevertheless, there are clearly difficulties in interpreting which images are 'shamanic' and which are not.

As the native Asian peoples became more culturally assimilated, the sacral motifs lost their symbolism. The formerly sacred images and associated material culture moved to the profane sphere, and were incorporated into daily life as objects of everyday use. The penetration into Siberia of new religious beliefs gradually transformed most of these sacred features, which had once been the property of a very restricted number of owners, into items of common knowledge.

On the decorated domestic utensils of the Siberian peoples in historical times one can find images which have their roots in the ancient, traditional beliefs, and which retain the characteristic features of sacral motifs. On tobacco containers made from birch bark, for example, one can recognise shamans amongst figures from more recent traditions. Figure 3.9 shows three Yakut examples, which contain a variety of elements that clearly demonstrate the

Figure 3.8 Burial from Ust'-Uda and a reconstruction of the ritual coat of a female shaman (after Okladnikov 1955).

co-existence of traditional shamanic beliefs alongside the new Christian teachings. These containers were made during the period when the latter were gaining more and more followers. In the upper example a sick person is shown lying in bed, with a cross on the shelf above. In addition to the Christian protection afforded by the cross, a shaman is also trying to help the ill person by means of a ritual which he performs in the opposite corner near a table with sacred bowls. A similar scene takes place in the middle example, and on the third, lower tobacco container we see a two-headed bird that was a recognized form of helping spirit for Yakut

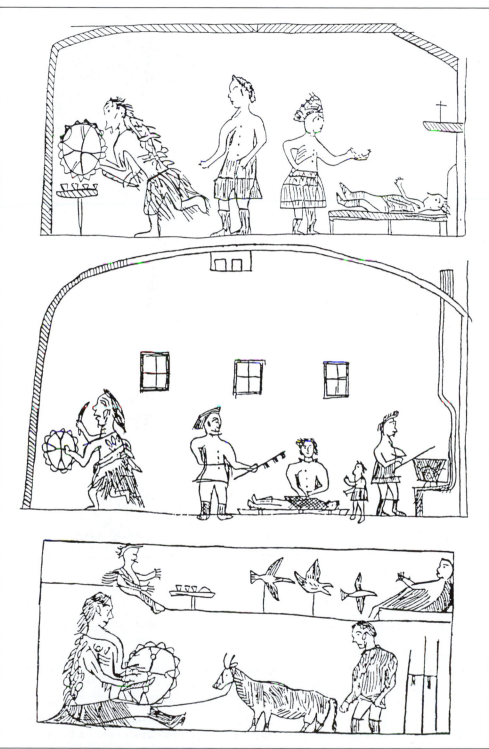

Figure 3.9 Shamans depicted on Yakut birch-bark tobacco containers (after Ivanov 1954).

Figure 3.10 Shamanizing in a yurt. Rock art panels from the historical period, Shalkoby, Altai (after Okladnikova 1989).

shamans (Ivanov 1954). The ethnological sources show clearly how new saints were incorporated into the pantheons of the native Siberian peoples (Basilov 1998). People appealed to them for help, and even asked priests to pray for their intervention for good luck (Smoliak 1991). The composition of the images on the Yakut tobacco containers resembles that of some rock art panels with recent engravings from the Altai, which depict shamanic rituals in a *yurt*, the traditional dwelling of the nomads (Figure 3.10 shows two examples from Shalkoby; Okladnikova 1989).

Through the centuries the iconography of shamanic images retained its important basic features. As the technology of armour, tools and other items improved, cultic and ritual practice remained conservative and preserved its ancient roots. Until very recent times, only a very few members of the community were competent in the performance of these rites. Their symbolic frame of reference was passed on from generation to generation, and was retained in the material culture of sacral objects, equipment and images.

REFERENCES

Alexeev, N. (1975) *Traditsionniye religiozniye verovania yakutov v XIX – nachale XX v*, Novosibirsk: Nauka.

Balser, M.M. (1995) 'Ot bubnov k skovorodam: paradoksalniye izmenenia shamanisma v istorii sakha (yakutov)', in D. Funk (ed.) *Shamanism y ranniye religioznoje predstavlenia*. Moscow: Institute of Ethnology and Anthropology, Russian Academy of Sciences.

Basilov, V. (1998) 'Shamanism in Central Asia in the XVI-XIX centuries', *Bulletin of the International Association for the Study of the Cultures of Central Asia*. 21: 37–47.

Bokovenko, V. (1996) 'Problema rekonstruktsii religioznikh system nomadov Tsentralnoy Azii v skyphskuyu epokhu', in A. Alexeev, N. Bokovenko, V. Zuev and V. Semenov (eds) *Priesthood and Shamanism in the Skythian Period. Proceedings of an international conference*, St Petersburg: Russian Humanitarian Scientific Fund.

Devlet, E. (2000) 'X-ray style anthropomorphic rock art images and the mythological subject of obtaining the gift of shamanizing', *Archaeology, Ethnology and Anthropology of Eurasia*. 2(2): 88–95.

Devlet, M. (1966) 'Bronzovie bliashky v forme slozhnogo luka iz Khakasii', *Kratkie soobshenia Instituta Archeologii* 107: 70–4.

Funk, D. (1995) 'Materialy A.V. Anokhina po shaorskomu shamanismu', *Ethnological Studies of Shamanism and other Indigenous Spiritual Beliefs and Practices* 1: 180–206.

Grichan, Y. (1987) 'Novie materialy po izobrazitelnomu iskusstvu Gornogo Altaja', in I. Gemuev and A. Sagalaev (eds) *Traditsionie verovanja i byt narodov Sibiri (XIX-nachalo XX v)*, Novosibirsk: Nauka.

Ivanov, S. (1954) *Materialy po izobrazitelnomu iskusstvu narodov Sibiry XIX-nachale XX v*, Novaja seria 22, Moscow-Leningrad: Trudy Instituta Ethnographii.

—— (1979 *Skulptura altaytsev, Khakassov y sibirskikh tatar* (*XVIII-pervaja chetvet' XX v.*) Leningrad: Nauka.

Jacobson, E. (1997) 'The "bird woman", the "birthing woman", and the "woman of the animal": a consideration of the female image in petroglyphs of Ancient Central Asia', *Annales du musée Guimet et du musée Cernuschi* 52: 37–59.

Kubarev, V. (1988) *Drevniye rospisi Karakola*, Novosibirsk: Nauka.

Kubarev, V. and Jacobson, E. (1996) *Sibérie du Sud: Kalbak-Tash I (République de l'Altai)*, Répertoire des Pétroglyphes de l'Asie Centrale, Fasc. 3. Paris: de Boccard.

Kyzlasov, L. and Leontiev, N. (1980) *Narodniye risunky khakassov*. Moscow: Nauka.

Lvova, E., Oktyabrskaya, I., Sagalaev, A. and Usmanova, M. (1988) *Prostranstvo y vremia. Veshniy myr. Traditsionnoie mirovozrenie tiurkov Yuznoi Sibiri*. Novosibirsk: Nauka.

Martinov, A. (1985) 'O drevnikh izobrazenijach Karakola', in A. Martinov (ed.) *Archeologiya Yuznoi Sibiri*, Kemerovo: State University.

Mikhailov, T. (1987) *Buryatskii shamanism: istoria, struktura y sotsialnie funktsii*, Novosibirsk: Nauka.

Miklashevich, E. (1998) 'Exkursii', *Vestnik SAIPI*. V.1: 12–14.

Novgorodova, E. (1984) *Myr petroglyphov Mongolii*. Moscow: Nauka.

Okladnikov, A. (1955) *Neolit y bronzovij vek Pribaykalia*. Part III. Moscow-Leningrad: Nauka.

—— (1974) *Petroglyphi Baikala – pamiatniki drevney kultury narodov Sibiri*, Novosibirsk: Nauka.

—— (1977) *Petroglyphi verkhnei Leny*, Leningrad: Nauka.

Okladnikov, A. and Martinov, A. (1972) *Sokrovisha Tomskikh pisanits*, Moscow: Iskusstvo.

Okladnikov, A. and Mazin, A. (1976) *Pisaniti reky Olekmy y Verkhnego Priamurja*. Novosibirsk: Nauka.

Okladnikov, A. and Zaporozhskaja, V. (1972) *Petroglyphi srednei Leny*, Leningrad: Nauka.

Okladnikova, E. (1989) 'Petroglyphy urochishia Shalkoby (Gornii Altay)', in S. Vainshtein (ed.) *Novoye v ethnographii*. Moscow: Nauka.

—— (1990) *Tropoiu Koguldeia*. Leningrad: Lenizdat.

Prokofieva, E. (1961) 'Shamanskie bubni', in M. Levin and L. Potapov (eds) *Istoriko-ethnographicheskii atlas Sybiri*, Moscow-Leningrad: Nauka.

Smoliak, A. (1991) *Shaman: lichnost, funktsii, myrovozrnie (narody Niznego Amura)*, Moscow: Nauka.

Sunshugashev, Y. (1990) 'Petroglyphi Malogo Ozera v Khakasii', in M. Devlet (ed.) *Problemy izuchenia naskalnikh izobrajenii v SSSR*, Moscow: Institute of Archaeology, Russian Academy of Sciences.

Chapter Four

Shamans, heroes and ancestors in the bronze castings of western Siberia

Natalia Fedorova

INTRODUCTION

The northern part of western Siberia, the zone of *taiga* forest inhabited by the Ob'-Ugrian peoples (principally the Khanty and Mansi), is a unique area which affords the possibility for a continuous historical retrospective from the modern era back to prehistoric times. This is especially true with reference to the roots of the complicated phenomenon of shamanism.

The unique and (in both the physical and cultural senses) somewhat monotonous Siberian landscape, together with the specific environmental conditions which characterize it, have formed preconditions for a very slow rate of adaptation in the emergent systems of the region. This in turn has been reflected in a similarly slow pace of cultural change among the traditional west Siberian peoples. One result of this is a cultural continuity which can be traced back for at least five or six millenia, with the consequence that ethnographic data takes on a quite different relationship to archaeological investigations from what is common in many other parts of the world. In particular, this interplay of disciplines provides unusually direct and exact possibilities to access the cognitive dimension of past cultures, in this instance the shamanic world-view of the ancient Siberians.

Before proceeding to a more specific discussion, the Ob'-Ugrians themselves, whose ancestors form the focus of the present chapter, may require a few words of introduction. The name is a collective term for the modern peoples of the Khanty and Mansi, who following traditional language classifications are strictly speaking members of the Ugrian branch of the Finno-Ugric group within the Ural language family. Today they inhabit the *taiga* zone of the west Siberian plain, in the basin of the middle and lower Ob and Irtysh rivers. According to the state census of 1989, the Khanty numbered 22,283 persons and the Mansi 8,266. Several sub-groups can be distinguished within both the Khanty and Mansi peoples: the Khanty are divided into northern, eastern and western groups, while the Mansi contain distinctive northern, eastern, southern and western branches. To a greater or lesser degree, all these groups are distinguished from one another by their language and cultures (Golovnev 1995: 80).

The traditional economic base of hunting and fishing still holds for the modern Ob'-Ugrians. People live in small settlements, surrounded by areas used for the exploitation of these resources. Their religious beliefs focus upon a broad range of spirits, in relation to which people perform (or refrain from performing) certain rituals. In certain circumstances sacrifices are offered to these spirits.

The origins of the Ob'-Ugrians and the date of their appearence in western Siberia have not yet been fully established. Their ancient history, and the early stages of their ethnogenesis, have been explored through archaeological investigations augmented by retrospective analogy to more recent linguistic and folkloristic studies. It is important to understand that the entire material cultural heritage of these people derives from archaeological excavations. The majority of scientific researchers currently believe that the Ob'- Ugrians and their ancestors have constituted the aboriginal population of the region since at least the Bronze Age. However, it should be noted that the eighteenth-century descriptions of Ugrian society and culture do not tally with what is known of their much richer historical past (the primary published work on the culture of the Ob'-Ugrian peoples may be found in Gemuev 1990; Golovnev 1993, 1995; Kulemzin 1984; Kulemzin and Lukina 1992; Sokolova 1982; Haydu 1985; Chernetsov and Mozhinskaya 1974).

SHAMANISM AMONG THE OB'-UGRIANS

Research into shamanism among the Ob'-Ugrians has been characterised by a number of different interpretive standpoints, often mutually exclusive. In their more extreme polarised form, these can be summarised as follows:

- One understanding of shamanism sees it as a general conception of the spiritual, based around the central idea of the ability of some human beings to achieve direct contact with the world of the spirits. The researchers who share this point of view see the Ob'-Ugrian people's culture as being permeated by shamanism at every level, with, to some degree, every elderly man both maintaining the images of the household spirits and also being in contact with them in the role of shaman.
- An alternative understanding is exemplified by the work of K. Karjalainen, who wrote: 'If we would attempt to find the central idea underlying the whole structure of Ugrian religious perspectives, then this can only be characterised as a belief in spirits. And, in so doing, we should accept that this is a belief in the Ugrian spirits themselves, not a belief in shamanism' (Karjalainen 1927). This view is shared by one of the outstanding researchers of the modern spiritual life of the Ob'-Ugrian peoples, Vladislav Kulemzin, who similarly suggests that Ob'-Ugrian shamanism existed only in an underdeveloped form (Kulemzin 1976).

In relation to these two viewpoints, this chapter will address two main questions:

- What archeological sources can be used as evidence for ancient religious beliefs in this region, in particular from the period from the first century BC to the tenth century AD?
- Who was the primary actor in the rituals connected with this belief system: the shaman or the war chief, who later became transformed into the spirit-ancestor figure?

THE BRONZE CASTINGS OF WESTERN SIBERIA

The reconstruction of ancient religious beliefs from archaeological sources is naturally complicated by the fact that the latter represent only fragmentary remains of an originally highly diverse set of ritual practices. However, in this context we are nonetheless fortunate that the archaeological sites of the western Siberian *taiga* contain proportionately greater information than those of other Siberian regions. This is primarily because for most of the Iron

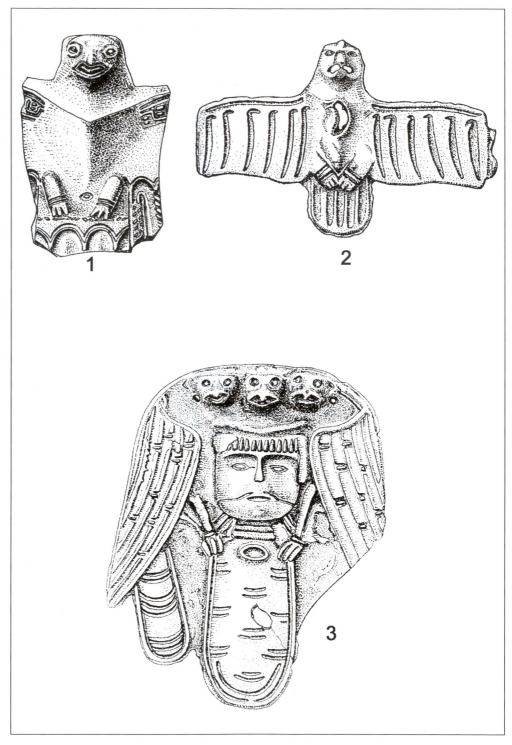

Figure 4.4 The bird images. The Cholmogorskaya collection, north-western Siberia (after Zykov and Fedorova 2001).

figure hostile to human beings. The key to deciphering this image may be twofold: first, the *combination* of the bird of prey and the warrior's face or figure was of indisputable importance; second, sometimes the image of the bear is substituted for that of the bird, with the bear being depicted with wings in such cases. It is extremely difficult to propose a comprehensive interpretation for the detail of these images, but we can suggest that they reflect major transformations in society, changes which it was necessary to set in an ideological context. For example, one plausible suggestion is that the combination (superimposition) of the two images, those of the bird of prey and a warrior, could perhaps symbolize certain individual qualities or abilities that were not conceptualized in the same way in earlier periods. These innovations chronologically coincide with the so-called 'heroic epoch' of the Ob'-Ugrians' ancient history, being the period of almost permanent military campaigns. The new social stratum of warriors needed to express and legitimate themselves, particularly in the spiritual sphere, and this may have been manifested in material culture.

BEARS IN BRONZE

The third type of bronze castings appearing around the first century BC is that of the bear figures representing the animal in a special posture, shown from the front with the head laid down between the paws, while the other parts of body are not seen at all (Figure 4.5; see Fedorova 1993 for a more detailed discussion of bear images in the Iron Age of western Siberia). This particular representation has been termed the 'bear in ritual posture', because it is exactly in this fashion that the bear, in the form of its skin with head and paws attached, is laid out in the Bear Festival of the modern Ob'-Ugrians. This Bear Festival forms the quintessence of Ob'-Ugrian spiritual life, encapsulating their view of the world, their folklore and drama cycles.

Within the scope of the present chapter it is not possible to present a detailed discussion of the historical roots of this highly complex phenomenon but, confining ourselves solely to the development of the bear's image we may note two points in particular. First, the Ob'-Ugrians consider(ed) the bear not only as an animal but mainly as a human being in reverted form, a so-called *bogatyr* or 'the son of god'; all examinations of the bear cult have noted these distinctive anthropomorphic traits of the bear figure, and the special links between bears and humans (Zen'ko 1997: 56). Secondly, the shaman was never established as a leader or primary orchestrator at this festival (Karjalainen 1927). The appearance of the bear figures in 'ritual posture' probably refers to the initial stage of the bear cult rituals, when the bear is a 'guest' at the festival: he is seen as an extremely strong man transformed into an animal, and in this form is 'invited' to the festivities. This symbolism

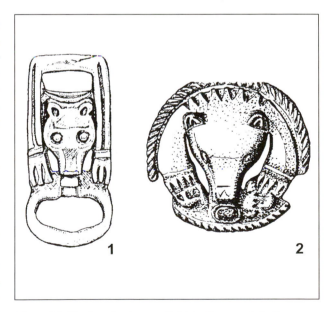

Figure 4.5 The bear in the so-called 'ritual posture'. 1. Barsova Gora; 2. The Saygatinsky 3 cemetery, Surgut region. All artefacts are previously unpublished, from the archaeological expedition archives of the Ural State University and Russian Academy of Sciences.

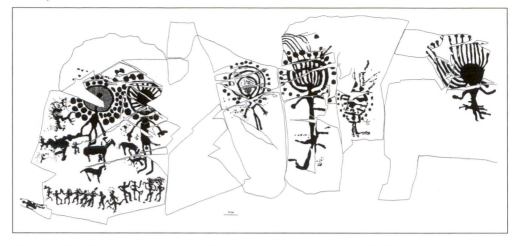

Figure 5.3 The big panel with 'sun-headed' petroglyphs newly traced by Muhiddin Huzanazarov and Andrzej Rozwadowski in 1997, Tamgaly Valley (Scale: 10cm).

in particular, display certain specific features which allow one to suggest that they may represent a symbolic context associated with shamanism.

The scenes which attract our attention specifically because of such associations in relation to features appearing in a 'sun god' context are located on the opposite side of the valley to the images described above. One of these scenes (Figure 5.4) presents five figures moving to the left, a horse fallen in the opposite direction, the image of a dog in the upper part, and several motifs

Figure 5.4 'Shamans' associated with the horse, Tamgaly Valley (Scale: 10cm).

which are difficult to unambiguously define. Each of the figures is holding in its hand a kind of staff in the form of a crosier, i.e. an object analogous to those indicated above. This scene is of particular interest due to several aspects which could suggest an association of these petroglyphs with shamanic practice and ideology.

The first, and clearest, kind of shamanic reference concerns the physical appearance of these figures. Short growths on the legs, torso and arms suggest a disguise. One should note that analogous elements are displayed by other figures, appearing as individual petroglyphs, holding the above-mentioned staffs (Figure 5.5). Furthermore, the context of this scene reveals a close similarity between these elements of appearance and the

Figure 5.5 Examples of dressed humans with crosier-like staffs (after Samashev 1999: fig. 5).

strongly defined horse's mane on the right-hand side of the composition. Ethnographical data concerning southern Siberian shamanism would support the assumption that we are dealing here with either a realistic representation of people disguised in a horse's hide or merely a symbolic identification of human with horse. In the light of these sources, the 'growths' visible on the bodies of the figures do not necessarily represent an actual dressing in a horse's hide, but may rather be *bakhroms*, i.e. dress accessories, usually of linen, attached to the outfit of the shaman at the arms, back and chest. Where these were long, they symbolised bird feathers, or the bird in general as a zoomorphological metaphor for shamanic journeying. Short *bakhroms*, on the other hand, were identified with the coat of a particular animal (Shvets 1998: 215), which, in this instance, corresponds well with their similarity to a horse's mane.

The next aspect to consider is the staff which the figures hold in their hands. This can be interpreted as being a shepherds' crook. However, the scene in question does not evoke associations with the daily life of shepherds, just as the length of these staffs barely lends itself to a purely functional interpretation. The five specifically attired human figures holding staffs are walking away from the horse, which is heading in the opposite direction. The scene therefore appears more likely to be of a symbolic rather than realistic nature. According to ethnographic data for the local territory, crosier-shaped shepherds' crooks were a common attribute of Central Asian shamans (Basilov 1976: 153; 1992: 288). In regional terms, this is also one of the key elements distinguishing the Central Asian shamanic complex from its northern Asian or Siberian equivalent. In the latter, the main attribute of the shamans was the drum, which in shamanic practices in southern Kazakhstan was used only sporadically. In this context, the classical drum of Siberian shamans could be related to the tambourine used by the shamans of Kazakhstan, which did not feature the drawings on its skin that are characteristic for Siberia. It should also be mentioned here that, for example in Altai, the use of the staff sometimes constituted an initial stage in the learning of the shamanic art by 'apprentices', who only later began to celebrate rituals with the drum (Sagalaev 1992: 108).

Determining how long the staff has been an attribute of local shamans is obviously a very complex process. Could it have fulfilled such a function in Bronze Age times? Theoretically, this cannot be excluded, at least when one considers that Bronze Age culture was associated with the pastoral life-style (Kuzmina 1994). Thus, it cannot be ruled out that the shepherd's crook may already have gained the symbolic value in question, all the more so since, at that time, the possession of livestock was most probably a sure index of status, both symbolically as well as economically.

The symbolical-ritual significance of this attribute is also confirmed by petroglyphs in the Karatau Mountains, where they appear in scenes with human figures, who, again, are distinguished by elements of their disguise (tails), and whose expressions suggest some form of ritual activity, perhaps dance.

Also worth mentioning in this context is the culture of the local dervishes, linked to the tradition of Sufism – a mystical version of Islam directed towards the direct knowledge of God through contact with the senses. This led to a strong development of specific trance techniques which enabled one to make momentary contact with God. To this end (especially in Central Asia where Islam overlapped with local shamanic traditions), the Sufis adapted certain shamanic techniques (the transmission of features between Sufism and shamanism was of a reciprocal nature), among which trance experiences were of key importance (Sukhareva 1960: 44–58; Gibb 1965: 108; Basilov 1992: 279–303). The stimuli for these trances were narcotics such as hashish, opium and wine, as well as song, music and dance (Składankowa 1996: 152). The definite closeness which appeared between Sufist and local shamanic practices, emphasising the importance of mystical experience, also led some shamans to enter, or to partially identify themselves with Sufist monasteries (Basilov 1992). Also not without significance here was the ideological pressure of Islam, propagated as the compulsory religion (Kośko 1999). The Sufis adapted not only ideological aspects of shamanic culture, but also a number of attributes relating to appearance or ritual guise. Of particular interest here is the use by Central Asian dervishes of crosier-shaped staffs (Figure 5.6), of precisely the same form as those recorded in petroglyphs of the Tamgaly Valley.

Any conclusions drawn on the basis of relatively recent ethnographical data relating to shamanic practices in Kazakhstan are obviously hypothetical. Further proof of the difficulty in transposing those data onto prehistoric times lies in the fact that in the analysis of the shamanism of this region there is no record of the custom of taking on specific disguises, a feature which is characteristic of Siberian shamans. Nevertheless, taking into account the strength of the shaman's link with the animal world throughout Central Asia, including Kazakhstan, one can suspect that this custom could have undergone a transformation, under the influence of the local cultural context – in early times, mainly the Iranian tradition, and later Islamic ideology – within which these regions of Asia were to be found as early as the seventh century, and which, albeit to a much lesser degree and significantly later, influenced the culture of the regions of southern Siberia.

The relation between the disguised crosier-wielding figures and the horse is suggestive for the following reasons. In the shamanism of Central Asia, the shamanic staff is often identified, on a symbolic level, with the horse. This is due to the swiftness of this animal. The shaman's staff was, therefore, his horse,

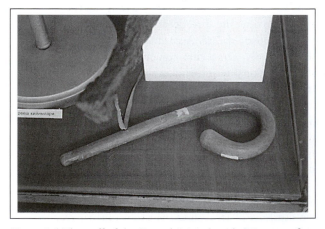

Figure 5.6 The staff of the Central Asian dervish (Museum of the Culture of Uzbekistan in Tashkent).

which just as speedily could transport him to another world in order to carry out a particular ritual. On the other hand, the horse was often not just a symbolic animal, but also an essential element in shamanic rituals, during which it was even put to death. Although these data are rather more connected with more northerly areas, the symbolic representation of the horse is also confirmed in Kazakh traditions of shamanism. Of particular interest here is the chthonic symbolism of this animal, which fulfilled the function of a go-between with the world of the dead (Toleubaev 1991: 137–48). Transporting the soul of the dead to the other world was one of the functions of the shaman, for whom the horse may therefore have been an essential symbolic element. The suggested symbolic context is all the more interesting due to the fact that right at the entrance to Tamgaly Valley, and in other locations nearby, can be found a Bronze Age cemetery (Mariyashev and Goryachev 1993; Rogozhinskij 1999). It is, therefore, certain that ceremonies connected with the burial of the dead took place here.

The symbolic representation of the transportation of souls to the afterworld may also be indicated by the way in which the two main compositional elements are directed: the people moving in the opposite direction to the horse. If the horse were a symbol of the departing soul, it must have made its way to the world of the dead, i.e. the opposite world to that of humans.

MEANING FOUND IN THE ROCK

Thus, the supposed symbolic representation of passing over may have been linked to burial ceremonies. The range of connotations could, however, be wider. On a symbolic level, the 'passing' motif is also a certain kind of transformation. Until now, our attention has been concentrated on that which was represented. However, besides the representation itself, of equally significant symbolic value could be *how* and *where* a given image was created. For example, the row of five figures (Figure 5.4) begins from the image which is not only smallest, but also the shallowest engraved, which is only noticeable on very close inspection of the rock face. Each of the following figures was made deeper, and each is bigger than its predecessor. Hence, one can observe a definite logic behind the presentation of these human images. They begin with the smallest and shallowest, ending with the largest and most deeply made. In addition, their principal 'transformation' occurs immediately after crossing the crack in the rock which divides the sequence into three smaller and two larger figures. Thus, both the method in which they were made and the selection of surface features of the rock appear to have been intentional, serving to express a particular symbolism connected with the whole composition. It is difficult to state for certain whether the crack concerned was of the same form at the time the petroglyphs were created, or whether it only developed much later. Today, the stone blocks are severely damaged, most probably as a result of earthquakes, which sporadically afflict this region of Asia. Nevertheless, some other Tamgaly Valley petroglyphs give credence to the hypothesis that stone cracks were deliberately selected for petroglyph compositions, in order to lend them a specific symbolic overtone.

A few dozen metres away there is an enigmatic petroglyph of an animal, centrally divided by two parallel cracks (Figure 5.7). Again, we can observe a certain transformation in the animal appearing at the place where the rock is split. It is clear from the visible mane that this is the image of a horse. To the right of the crack are shown its large head and neck; to the left we see only the extreme hindquarters and big tail. The proportions here are clearly uneven. At the point of the crack, where the large head and neck end, the small hindquarters and hind legs begin. It is also significant that it is not just the form of the animal that undergoes some transformation, but equally the technique with which it was made. The head and neck were made in a deep and strongly defined fashion, whereas the hindquarters are more vague and

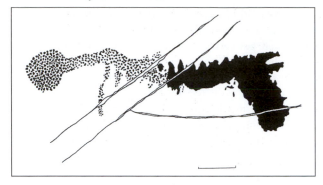

Figure 5.7 The horse divided by two parallel cracks, Tamgaly Valley (Scale: 10cm).

shallow pointed. It is worth noting that this transformation involves a horse: the same animal which was a crucial component of the scene analysed earlier which also displayed clear signs of a certain metamorphosis.

At a short distance from the scene displayed in Figure 5.4 is a further, barely distinguishable petroglyph, made using a loose and shallow point technique (Figure 5.8). It presents a human figure, or rather part of a figure, since the only parts clearly distinguished are the legs and part of the torso, which 'dissolves' on meeting two parallel cracks. Beyond that point, instead of the upper part of the torso and the head, is a relatively large, incomplete oval, surrounded by point-dots. It should be noted that the form of the 'head' of this figure belongs to the specific distinguishing traits of the enigmatic anthropomorphic figures which previous studies have identified with sun gods. In addition, the figure shown here is characterised by a tail ending in two balls. As we saw above, an analogous 'extremity' is displayed by the horse which undergoes a metamorphosis at the moment of contact with two analogous parallel cracks. This dispels the previous doubt that rock cracks, at least in the case of these few petroglyphs, played an integral role in the compositions in question, emphasising in a graphic way a certain transformation experienced by man and horse.

Figure 5.8 The transformed human figure associated with two parallel cracks, Tamgaly Valley (Scale: 10cm).

The possible shamanic context of these petroglyphs suggested above is thus provided with a further interesting argument, in the form of the possible use of cracks as a metaphor for the shamanic experience connected with the passage between two worlds: the earthly and the spiritual. This signification of cracks in shamanic ideology and practice has been convincingly suggested not just in Asian shamanism, but also in other shamanic traditions, and as such could appear to be a relatively universal phenomenon of the graphic expression of the shamanic state of trance.

In recent years, several lines of argument have been put forward in relation to the deliberate linking of rock images with those natural features of the rock surface which could fulfil an essential signifying function connected with shamanic experiences. This has been suggested in relation to a variety of contexts, such as southern Africa (Lewis-Williams and Dowson 1990; Dowson 1998a; Ouzman 1998: 36) and south-western regions of North America (Turpin 1994: 85; Whitley 1992, 1998). Equally, in Asian shamanic traditions narrow rock cracks have repeatedly been identified with places through which the shaman, with difficulty (metaphor for a perilous passage), enters the underworld (Kośko 1990: 77; Sagalaev 1992: 55–6; Vitebsky 1996: 70). An interesting context here is that of the practice of Siberian shamans connected with the consumption of toadstools, which led the shaman to enter an altered state of consciousness. One of the more common reactions of individuals under the influence of the hallucinogenic effect of this fungus was the impression of a making a great effort to squeeze their way into a small crack, which appeared to them to be a door. Other accounts more generally referred to an impression of passing through various kinds of narrow openings (Devlet 1998: 212–13).

The symbolic dimension of cracks in image-bearing rocks has also been noted in Siberia. There exists among the numerous peoples of Siberia the belief that petroglyphs were made in ancient times by local gods, with whom only the shaman could enter into direct contact. Another frequently shared view is that the stones or rocks on which these images appear are inhabited by the spirits considered to have created the petroglyphs, and that, in order to contact these spirits, the shaman had to find his way into the rock/mountain (Sagalaev 1992: 60–78). Ethnographic sources are rich in material related to the contemporary worship of such places. Various kinds of offerings are placed there, such as animals or other goods (objects, food). One intriguing feature of this worship is the squeezing of the offerings into the rock cracks, which it would be difficult to explain exclusively by the wish to prolong the life of these offerings by forcing them into the rock rather than simply laying them on the ground. Items placed into such cracks include arrows, wooden implements for starting a fire, and sticks which may have served in the past to suspend other ritual objects (Kochmar 1985; Tivanenko 1989: 93–7). An Altaic reflection of the belief in a posthumous journey into a mountain is probably provided by the frequent location of the graves of shamans at the foot of mountains, whilst their ritual attributes were buried in caves considered to be entrances to the other world. Also, according to Yakutsk legend, it was precisely through caves that a person could enter the underworld (Alekseyev 1984: 51). By contrast, in Sayano-Altai, there is evidence of the custom of 'burying' the bodies of those who died at an early age actually in the cracks (Sagalaev 1992: 78).

Also of interest in this context would appear to be the function of the hatchet, which some Altaic shamans used when performing rituals connected with the beginning of winter, in order to break the ice which separated them from the kingdom of Ulgen (the ruler of the upper world). They would then use the crack they had made in the ice to pass into that other world (Potapov 1991: 141). Could the shamanic staffs pictured in the hands of the figures associated with rock cracks in the Tamgaly Valley have had a similar function?

Hence, if the petroglyphs under analysis here were indeed connected with a shamanic context, then their relations with rock cracks not only do not run counter to such an interpretation, but actually strengthen its probability. Thus, there are two separate lines of argumentation supporting the linking of the enigmatic 'sun gods' with a shamanic context: (1) through ethnographic analogies (disguise in or imitation of animal hide, and shamanic staffs) and (2) universal sensations accompanying trance experiences expressed by the crack as a metaphor for a difficult passage.

This latter strand can be developed further. In recent years, of profound effect among researchers of rock art has been the neuropsychological model proposed by J.D. Lewis-Williams and T.A. Dowson (1988). This model met with extreme evaluations and, as Dowson (1999) himself asserts a decade later, led to a methodological impasse in the sphere of shamanistic interpretations of rock art. The greatest criticism was aroused by the application of this model to art of an unknown ethnographic context, and conclusions concerning its shamanistic overtones drawn simply on the basis of the identification of entoptic images, which, as Dronfield later showed (1996), can also be found in art which was not inspired by trance experience. However, if the possibility exists of complementing the neuropsychological model with other elements indicating a shamanic context for the art in question, the whole interpretation should gain a more convincing justification (cf. the prime example of linking different lines of evidence to suggest the shamanistic context of the Coso petroglyphs – Whitley *et al.* 1999), since there is no doubt that individuals entering an altered state of consciousness are receptive to the perception of certain defined geometrical images which, to a certain degree, appear to be universal (Siegel and Jarvik 1975). The only question which remains is whether to treat such an argument as fundamental, or as complementary to others.

Among the most widespread entoptic images recorded are a range of variants of the oval shape. These take the form of circles, concentric arrangements of point-dots, or lines radiating from a central point (Horowitz 1975: 178–9). A significant proportion of such images display crucial similarities to the head forms of the 'sun gods' under discussion here (Figure 5.9).[5] Hence, if the 'entoptic lead' is accepted as complementary to previous considerations, one may advance the thesis that the detailed analysis of these petroglyphs in their local context – the Tamgaly Valley – allows us to suggest an interpretation at variance with their identification with 'sun gods'. First, a shamanistic context would appear to be more credible; second, an acceptable contention is that they rather represent graphic metaphors, at least partially, of trance experiences – an essential distinguishing characteristic of shamanic practice:

Horse	Crack	'Sun heads'
↓	↓	↓
metaphor of shaman's journey	metaphor of 'trance-formation'	entoptic phenomena

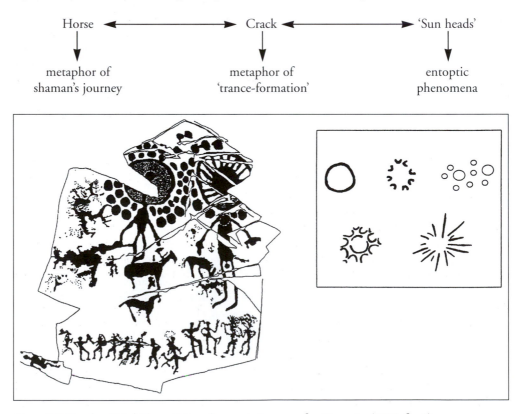

Figure 5.9 'Sun-heads' (cf. Figure 5.3) and entoptic imagery after Horowitz (1975: fig. 2).

SUN-HEADED IMAGES, SHAMANISM AND THE INDO-IRANIANS

The linking of these anthropomorphic figures with the horse motif does not exhaust their associations with other petroglyphs of the Tamgaly Valley. In several cases, they occur in the company of bulls. The intriguing aspect here is that in one of the scenes, the figure associated with the bull is distinguished by elements very reminiscent of a crosier-shaped staff (Figure 5.2), although these are not held in the hand, but rather appear to be attached to the shoulders. This example suggests a potential link between these figures and elements identified as shamanic staffs. From this, it would seem that 'sun gods' appear in association with both the horse and the bull. Of course, it is difficult to judge whether all anthropomorphic figures of this type belong to one cultural context, operating at an identical semantic level. Their symbolic representation could have been diverse, even within one single site. The form of their presentation could have been adapted by other societies, be it due to symbolic or to functional considerations. Such a stylistic form could have been perceived as more effective, with the aim of producing particular effects. Yet one cannot exclude the hypothesis that the majority are linked to a single cultural, and perhaps also ethnic, context. If we accept such a possibility, then these 'sun gods' could be regarded from a perspective which need not completely exclude the earlier interpretations, but may complement them constructively.

Researchers of these petroglyphs have, on more than one occasion, suggested a link between them and the tradition of Indo-Iranian peoples thought to have inhabited the territory of Central Asia in the second millennium BC, at the moment either just before their split into the Iranian and Indian branches or just after this separation, which occurred at least as early as the mid-second millennium BC. Datings of the rock art of Central Asia show that the petroglyphs in question are probably linked to this chronological context. Moreover, the comparative analysis of rock art and Indo-Iranian mythology suggest that the relations between the human form motif, the horse and the bull are clearly visible both among petroglyphs and in that mythology. Of particular interest is the fact that the arrangement of these elements plays a key role in the reconstruction of Indo-Iranian cosmogony (Lincoln 1975). Besides this, an analysis of the Tamgaly Valley petroglyphs enables one to confirm a crucial structural correspondence between the grammar of this rock art and Indo-Iranian mythology (Rozwadowski 1999d, In press).

Therefore, the linking of these petroglyphs with Indo-Iranian tradition is probably justified, especially in terms of their temporal-spatial context. In previous studies, there has been a conviction that these petroglyphs are of a purely mythological nature, perceived as representing gods of the pantheon of Indo-Iranian mythology. The interpretations outlined in this chapter could, therefore, be perceived as running contrary to previous hypotheses. A deeper analysis of this issue, however, shows that this is true only to a certain extent. The shamanic context of these petroglyphs which has been brought into relief here need not completely contradict their association with either Indo-Iranian tradition or the wider Indo-European tradition, since a thorough analysis of these brings to light many aspects which are strongly connected with shamanistic practices and ideology (Eliade 1964; Ogibenin 1968; Bongard-Levin and Grantovskiy 1974: 84–93; Rozwadowski 1999c), if, that is, we tend towards an understanding of shamanism as a complex of certain forms defining the practice which involves making contact with the other world by entering a state of trance.

A shamanistic context of Indo-Iranian tradition could be advanced both on a phenomenological level and in relation to Central Asian shamanic tradition. Since this subject lies beyond the framework of the present article (cf. Rozwadowski 1999c), only its main aspects will be indicated here.

Perhaps the most striking aspect is that of *soma/haoma* – the sacred ritual drink with hallucinogenic properties. The cult of *soma* has pride of place within Indo-Iranian culture, and although probably not every *soma/haoma* was a hallucinogenic drink (*Avesta* informs that the *haoma* plant was 'of many kinds' [Boyce 1975: 158]), in a large number of cases described in Vedic and Avestan texts it induces a state which could properly be referred to as distinctly trance-like (Flattery and Schwartz 1989; Jurewicz 1995). Also intriguing is the fact that the concept which Indo-Iranian tradition has presented of the threefold division of the cosmos into upper, intermediate and lower worlds is also one of the characteristic features of Central Asian shamanistic ideology. Although this is a relatively universal concept of cosmological construction, the fact that, according to mythological tradition, this division was established during a ritual act closely connected with the consumption of the mystical *soma* may suggest a close link between the *soma* ritual and the trichotomous perception of the world. Finally, an analysis of the ritual context of Indo-Iranian tradition allows one to suggest that the function of the priest, very strongly represented in Aryan culture, was developed from the more ancient shamanic practice.

The petroglyph analysis outlined here allows one to accept the hypothesis of the shamanic character of the so-called 'sun gods' of the Tamgaly Valley. In the light of previous considerations, one could also question the very hypothesis that these petroglyphs represent sun gods, since they could be interpreted as a graphical metaphor of shamanic rituals and of the personal experiences of the shamans performing particular rituals. Admittedly, one cannot exclude the thesis that these are images of gods with which the person identified during a trance (cf. Ripinsky-Naxon 1997: 71). It is, however, doubtful that they are simple representations of gods along the lines of illustrations of myths. Hence the second fundamental question to be discussed here, namely how to understand rock images in the context of their ontological status.

TAMGALY PETROGLYPHS VERSUS OTHER 'SUN-HEADED' IMAGES IN CENTRAL ASIA

As mentioned above, anthropomorphic images distinguished by the unnatural form of their heads are also known from other sites in Central Asia. On the basis of certain perceived formal analogies, researchers have tended to consider that they should be linked with an analogous semantic context. However, the relations between form and semantics can be extremely complex, and sometimes arbitrary. Admittedly, one cannot exclude the hypothesis of an analogous symbolic representation attributed to a particular stylistic convention, yet it is highly doubtful whether it is universally repeated in every instance. Thus by analysing the possible symbolic context of the petroglyphs at one particular site, we can inquire whether the interpretation of these motifs in the Tamgaly Valley could also be valid for the semantic context of similar motifs discovered at other sites.

The visual similarity between the head forms of these petroglyphs and entoptic images, as discussed above, could be accepted as a justified argument in favour of a shamanic interpretation, especially with the independent support from other rock art studies elsewhere. This being the case, the 'entoptic lead' becomes a potentially fruitful one, and as such should not be ignored. In presenting the potential value of such an interpretative indicator, I shall refer to several further examples of analogous petroglyphs, also distinguished by the specific head forms, found at other rock art sites in Central Asia.

One of the more spectacular examples is located in the Sarmishsay Valley in the Nuratau Mountains of central Uzbekistan (Figure 5.10 left). It shows the figure of a person standing with slightly bent knees and arms extended forwards, probably holding some form of attribute (rope?). The attribute is difficult to identify due to the exfoliation of the surface of the rock on which the image was engraved. Lines leading outwards from the level of the hips suggest that this person may have had a tail attached. The head of the figure was replaced by a proportionately very large oval shape, the inside of which was of a clear oval shape, while the outside was finished in a zigzag form. The right side of this 'head' is not visible, due to damage to the rock surface. However, one may suspect that originally it represented, or was intended to represent, a whole oval. Thus, again we are dealing with a human figure with an unnatural oval head form. Furthermore, as with the Tamgaly Valley petroglyphs, there is a striking similarity between the head form here and visional images recorded in laboratory studies (Figure 5.10 right).

As was mentioned above, after Tamgaly the second-largest concentration of so-called 'sun gods' in this part of Asia is the Saymaly-Tash site in the mountains of Kirghizstan. It is difficult to give a competent evaluation here of the petroglyphs of this site, since they are familiar to me only from publications, in which, once again, they are most frequently presented as single images, often isolated from the context which they forge with other petroglyphs (e.g. Martynov *et al.* 1992: Figs 49–54). This, in turn, is a consequence of the priorities of the overall explanatory scheme to which the documentation was subordinated. Starting from the *a priori* supposition that these images were representations of 'sun gods', care was taken to present only those petroglyphs which fitted this scheme. Hence the present impossibility of stating their relations to other petroglyphs or to features of the rock surface, which, in the case of the Tamgaly petroglyphs, proved to be of crucial

significance. Nevertheless, in the light of considerations hitherto available, it is possible to make certain suggestions relating to these petroglyphs. I would like to draw attention here to the numerous geometrical motifs noted in Saymaly-Tash, which again display crucial similarities to the frequently noted visional images. There we can find both a rather 'chaotic' zigzag pattern (Figure 5.11) and chain-like motifs. The latter have remarkably close analogies in art for which hypotheses have recently been put forward that it was inspired by states of trance (Figure 5.12). This concerns European megalithic tomb art (Bradley 1989: Figure 4; Hedges 1994: Figure 11a; Dronfield 1995: Figure 5) and the rock art of western North America (Hedges 1994: Figs 5, 7) and possibly of the Andes region of South America (Hedges 1994: 115; also Pia 1999a, 1999b). The analysis carried out by Hedges (1992, 1994) shows that the origins of 'crenellation design' may lie in visional experiences, the best record of which concern Tukano Indians (e.g. Reichel-Dolmatoff 1978). Therefore, it is probable that the presence of similar geometrical motifs among the petroglyphs of Saymaly-Tash is not entirely coinci-

Figure 5.10 The human figure with unnatural head (Sarmishsay Valley, Uzbekistan) versus visual imagery (right – 1, 2, 3) after Richards (1971: 90, 91). The dots indicate the centre of vision.

Figure 5.11 Zigzag motifs in Saymaly-Tash, the site in Kirghizstan with numerous 'sun-headed' petroglyphs (redrawn from the photo no. 13 in Martynov 1992 *et al.*).

dental, but may result from the common source of 'mental imagery' generated through trance experiences.

The suggestions put forward in relation to the Saymaly-Tash petroglyphs must, however, be qualified by the fact that an essential component of the art at this site is the image of a harnessed cart. Even if we accept that these are representations of a clearly symbolic character, their symbolism may be connected to certain forms of agriculture known to the artists of these petroglyphs. Such has also hitherto been the context in which the Saymaly-Tash petroglyphs have been interpreted (Golendukhin 1971). This represents one essential difference from the rock art in Tamgaly, where the few cart images that are present appear only occasionally, and not in scenes with the anthropomorphic figures under discussion here, in contrast to the case in Saymaly-Tash.

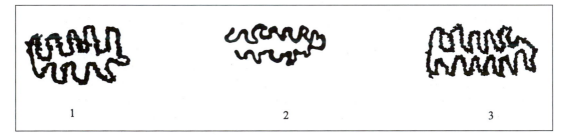

Figure 5.12 Comparison of double crenellation motifs in petroglyphs of: 1. Chile (after Hedges 1994: Fig. 8); 2. Arizona (after Hedges 1994: Fig. 5g); and 3. Saymaly-Tash (after Martynov *et al.* 1992: 11).

ESCHATOLOGY AND INTERACTION

The interpretations of the Saymaly-Tash images put forward here should, of course, be treated as suggestions rather than statements. Nonetheless, they arise from the analysis of similar petroglyphs in the Tamgaly Valley, the shamanic context of which appears to be likely. Of course, the meaning of these petroglyphs could have differed between various sites, yet it is possible that the origins of this form of expression of human figures in this part of Central Asia lie in shamanic experiences connected with entering an altered state of consciousness. Central Asian shamanism, as indicated at the beginning of this chapter, is an extremely ancient practice, evidence of which can be found in Bronze Age images discovered in tombs at Altai on the Karakol River (Figure 5.13), to which the Tamgaly Valley anthropomorphic figures are

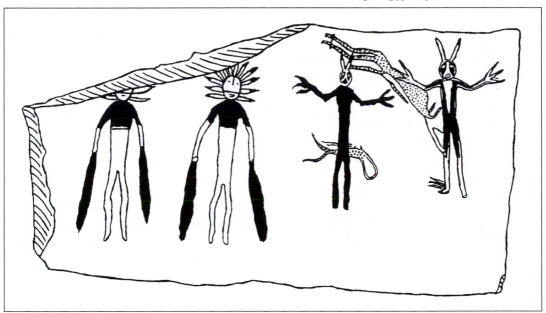

Figure 5.13 Painted images on the slabs of graves (third/second millennium BC) in Altai (after Kubarev 1988: fig. 18).

sometimes compared (e.g. Devlet 1997). These have been noted on the stone slabs used to construct *kurgan* graves, and on the basis of their archaeological context have been dated to the turn of the third- second or the mid-second millennium BC (Kubarev 1988). This complex is associated with the Okunievo culture. The similarities with the paintings and engravings from the tombs in Karakol concern the enlarged form of the heads of these figures and the guise in which they appear, which displays strong references to the ethnographically recorded ritual disguises of Altaic shamans. The aspect which appears to be of particular interest in this context is the fact that these figures appeared in art connected with a burial context, i.e. with the symbolic journey of the deceased to another world, probably the underworld. D.G. Savinov (1997) recently proffered the conclusion, based on an analysis of this kind of petroglyph in the wider context of southern Siberia, that most probably these figures should be symbolically linked to burial ceremonies. The interpretation of the Tamgaly petroglyphs advanced in the present chapter leads to similar conclusions. Therefore, we could be touching on a common symbolic context for such petroglyphs in Central Asia which are dated to a similar period (Bronze Age), where a key role was played by the shaman in the function of a psychopomp.

In conclusion, I would like once more to refer to the problem of the ethnic identification of the creators of these petroglyphs. As mentioned above, the majority of researchers have tended to work from the traditions of Iranian, Indo-Iranian or Indo-European peoples. This is justified insofar as the linguistic-archaeological context suggests that the expansion of the Indo-European tradition towards Central Asia most probably began at the turn of the third–second millennium BC (assuming, that is, that the homeland of the Indo-Europeans was the steppes of Eurasia – compare the opposite view of Gamkrelidze and Ivanov 1984; Renfrew 1989). Such is indicated by the historico-comparative linguistics thesis according to which the Indo-Iranian group of languages, already distinguishable from the original Indo-European family, began at this time to split into the Iranian and Indian branches (Allchin 1995: 56) – a split which must have taken place in a region of the Eurasian steppe difficult to define for certain (Mallory 1991). Taking into account the fact that the nomadic culture of the first millennium BC (Sakas) was linked to the Iranian tradition, it is highly likely that during the Bronze Age (second millenium BC) Central Asia was at least partly populated by Indo-Iranian peoples, or by the already distinct Iranian and Indian peoples. In questioning the interpretation of the petroglyphs under consideration here as representing gods of the Indo-Iranian mythological pantheon, the intention is not to state that Indo-Iranian mythology represents an unjustified interpretative context. It is undoubtedly a proven source for semantic-symbolic interpretation of rock art in Central Asia, as was also argued personally by the author of this chapter in other works (Rozwadowski 1997, 1999a, 1999d, in press). If, in addition, we take into consideration the presence in the Indo-Iranian tradition of certain ideas concerning a clear shamanic accent, it turns out that the shamanic context suggested in this chapter need not necessarily entirely exclude earlier interpretations. On the contrary, it would appear that it may significantly enrich our knowledge of Indo-Iranian tradition and of rock art in Central Asia.

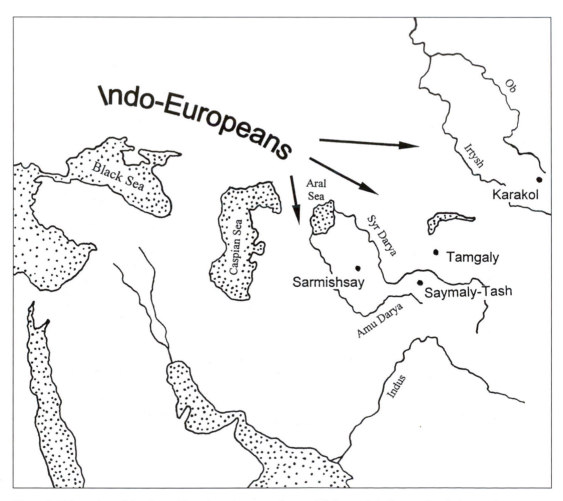

Figure 5.14 Location of the sites with rock art imagery of potential shamanistic features in relation to the hypothesis about expanding Indo-Europeans from the Eurasian steppes.

The assumed moment of appearance of this type of petroglyph in Central Asia steers us towards the question of the possible social context which may have stimulated the creation of these images. Their dating at the turn of the third-second millenium or the beginning of the second millenium BC clearly corresponds to the period of expansion of the new Indo-European cultural model (Figure 5.14), including the new model of life philosophy, which must have come into contact with various forms of autochthonous cultural traditions. Any attempt to define these traditions would, of course, be extremely hypothetical. What may well be supposed, however, is that this period could have witnessed pivotal confrontations between at least two distinct life philosophies – the newly arriving Indo-European model, and the local model, which is more difficult to define ('paleoasiatic', 'proto-turkic'). This could prove an important lead to a more complete understanding of rock art traditions in this part of Asia (cf. Jacobson 1993: 117–40), since shamanic activity is considered to have often become more vigorous at times of cultural and ethnic tensions (Dowson 1994, 1998b). Therefore, it is perhaps in the area of specific cultural confrontations that we could seek the origins of the petroglyphs analysed here. From this perspective, their shamanic context takes on a new dimension in relation to their linking with the tradition of Indo-Iranian peoples.

Notes

1 This chapter was written while I was in receipt of a scholarship from the Foundation for Polish Science.
2 Erdy (1999) identifies motifs connected with shamanic rituals found among that part of the rock art of southern Siberia which has been identified with the Xiong-nu culture of this period (probably the ancestors of the Huns).
3 In Altai and in southern Siberia, further locations are known of somewhat similar rock images of human figures with elaborate head forms, and others representing only human faces, which are often described under the analogous name 'sun-headed images' (cf. Devlet 1997).
4 The research undertaken in Tamgaly was part of a wider project, focussing on an analysis of the relation between rock art and Indo-Iranian mythology, carried out by the Adam Mickiewicz University in Poznan in co-operation with the Institute of Archaeology in Almaty and the Institute of Archaeology in Samarkand. I wish to express my indebtedness to Muhiddin Huzanazarov and Zaynulo Samashev for their fruitful collaboration.
5 With reference to the interpretation of these petroglyphs as sun gods, it is worth considering a certain variant of this explanation, according to which the two most spectacular anthropomorphic images in Tamgaly (Figure 5.3) represented a pair of heavenly bodies – Sun and Moon (Mariyashev 1994: 34). The figure characterised by rays projecting out from a circular head was supposed to represent Sun, whereas Moon was represented by the figure with a round head, but without the rays typical for the sun. This interpretation, albeit very close to earlier readings, does introduce an interesting lead, hitherto unnoticed, which again points to a possible shamanic context. Namely, that the sun and the moon belong to the most commonly found symbols of the upper world in the shamanism of numerous Siberian nations (Kośko 1990: 57–76). They can commonly be found represented on various ritual shamanic attributes, including the drum (Jankovics 1984). E. Devlet (1999) suggests that the graphic symbols of Sun and Moon may be present among other petroglyphs, particularly the so-called 'spectacle-signs' (two circular or oval shapes linked by one or more lines). The other intriguing aspect of this scene deals with its vertical arrangement, precisely the row of small humans 'dancing' below the two big figures. Such a theme is often observed in the Altaic shamans' drumhead paintings. Furthermore, the possible interpretation of the central figure in the row as having sexual relation with another inverted human can reflect the often reported idea of a sexual bond between the shaman and his tutelary spirit (cf. Ripinsky-Naxon 1997: 36–40).

References

Alekseyev, N.A. (1984) *Shamanizm tyurkoyazychnykh narodov Sibiri*. Novosibirsk: Nauka.
Allchin, F.R. (1995) 'Language, culture and the concept of ethnicity', in F.R. Allchin (ed.) *The Archaeology of Early Historic South Asia. The Emergence of Cities and States*, Cambridge: Cambridge University Press.

Basilov, V.N. (1976) 'Shamanism in Central Asia', in A. Bharati (ed.) *The Realm of the Extra-human*, Paris: Mouton.

—— (ed.) (1986) *Drevniye obryady, verovaniya i kulty narodov Sredney Azii*, Moskva: Nauka.

—— (1992) *Shamastvo u narodov Sredney Azii i Kazakhstana*, Moskva: Nauka.

Bayalieva, T.D. (1972) *Doislamskie verovaniya i ikh perezhitki u kirgizov*, Frunze: Ilim.

Bongard-Levin, G.M. and Grantovskiy, E.A. (1974) *Ot Skifii do Indii*, Moskva: Mysl.

Boyce, M. (1975) *A History of Zoroastrianism. Volume One: The Early Period*, Leiden/Köln: E.J. Brill.

Bradley, R. (1989) 'Deaths and entrances: a contextual analysis of megalithic art', *Current Anthropology* 30(1): 68–75.

Davis-Kimbal, J. and Martynov, A.I. (1993) 'Solar rock art and cultures of Central Asia', in M. Singh (ed.) *The Sun: Symbol of Power and Life*, New York: Abrams.

Devlet, E. (1999) 'Astronomical objects in rock art', *Astronomical and Astrophysical Transactions* 17: 475–82.

Devlet, M.A. (1997) 'Okunevskie antropomorfnye lichiny v ryadu naskalnykh izobrazheniy Severnoy i Centralnoy Azii', in D.G. Savinov and M.L. Podolskiy (eds) *Okunevskiy sbornik: Kultura. Istusstvo. Antropologiya*, Sankt-Peterburg: Petro-RIF.

—— (1998) *Petroglify na dne Sayanskogo Morya*. Moskva: Pamyatniki Istoricheskoy Mysli.

Dowson, T.A. (1994) 'Reading art, writing history: rock art and social change in southern Africa', *World Archaeology* 25(3): 332–45.

—— (1998a) 'Rain in Bushman belief, politics and history: the rock-art of rain-making in the south-eastern mountains, southern Africa', in C.C. Chippindale and P.S.C. Taçon (eds) *The Archaeology of Rock-art*, Cambridge: Cambridge University Press.

—— (1998b) 'Like people in prehistory', *World Archaeology* 29(3): 333–43.

—— (1999) 'Sztuka naskalna a szamanizm: impas metodologiczny', in A. Rozwadowski, M. Kośko and T.A. Dowson (eds) *Sztuka naskalna i szamanizm Azji Środkowej*, Warszawa: DIALOG.

Dronfield, J. (1995) 'Migraine, light and hallucinations: the neurocognitive basis of Irish megalithic art', *Oxford Journal of Archaeology* 14(3): 261–75.

—— (1996) 'The vision thing: diagnosis of endogenous derivation in abstract arts', *Current Anthropology* 37(2): 373–91.

Eliade, M. (1964) *Shamanism: Archaic Techniques of Ecstasy*, Princeton: Princeton University Press.

Erdy, M. (1999) 'The survival of shaman tradition in Siberian rock art: a Hunnic relic', in D. Seglie (ed.) *Siberian Rock Art – Archaeology, Interpretation and Conservation*, Pinerolo: CeSMAP.

Flattery, D.V. and Schwartz, M. (1989) *Haoma and Harmaline. The botanical identity of the Indo-Iranian sacred hallucinogen 'soma' and its Legacy in Religion, Language, and Middle Eastern Folklore*, Near Eastern Studies 21, Berkeley: University of California Press.

Francfort, H.-P. (1998) 'Central Asian petroglyphs: between Indo-Iranian and shamanistic interpretations', in C. Chippendale and P.S.C. Taçon (eds) *The Archaeology of Rock-art*, Cambridge: Cambridge University Press.

Gamkrelidze, T.V. and Ivanov, V.V. (1984) *Indoevropeyskiy yazyk i Indoevropeytsy*. Tibilisi: Izdatelstvo Tibiliskogo Universiteta.

Gibb, H.A.R. (1965) *Mahometanizm*. Warszawa: Państwowe Wydawnictwo Naukowe.

Golendukhin, Y.N. (1971) 'Voprosy klassifikatsii i dukhovnyy mir drevnego zemledeltsa po petroglifam Saymaly-Tasha', in R.S. Vasilevskiy (ed.) *Pervobytnoye iskusstvo*. Novosibirsk: Nauka

Goodman, N. (1968) *Languages of Art: An Approach to a Theory of Symbols*, Indianapolis: Bobbs-Merrill.

Hedges, K. (1992) 'Shamanistic aspects of California rock art', in L.J. Bean (ed.) *California Indian Shamanism*, Menlo Park: Ballena Press.

—— (1994) 'Pipette dreams and the primordial snake-canoe: analysis of a hallucinatory form constant', in S.A. Turpin (ed.) *Shamanism and Rock Art in North America*, San Antonio: Rock Art Foundation.

Hoppál, M. (1992) 'On the origins of shamanism and the Siberian rock art', in A.-L. Siikala and M. Hoppál (eds) *Studies on Shamanism*, Budapest: Akadémiai Kiadó.

Horowitz, M.J. (1975) 'Hallucinations: an information-processing approach', in R.K. Siegel and L.J. West (eds) *Hallucinations: Behaviour, Experience and Theory*, New York: John Wiley and Sons.

Jacobson, E. (1993) *The Deer Goddess of Ancient Siberia. A Study in the Ecology of Belief*, Leiden-New York-Köln: E.J. Brill.

Jankovics, M. (1984) 'Cosmic models and Siberian shaman drums', in M. Hoppál (ed.) *Shamanism in Eurasia*, Göttingen: Herodot.

Jasiewicz Z. and Rozwadowski, A. (1998) 'Malowidło naskalne z groty Zaraut-Kamar a malowid_o na ścianie domu z końca XIX wieku', *Lud* 82: 279–97.

Jettmar, K. (1986) *Religii Gindukusha*, Moskva: Nauka.

Jurewicz, J. (1995) 'Walka Indry z Wrytrą a Nāsadīya', *Studia Indologiczne* 2: 88–116.

Kadyrbaev, M.K. and Mariyashev, A.N. (1977) *Naskalnyye izobrazheniya khrebta Karatau*. Alma-Ata: Nauka.

Kochmar, N.N. (1985) 'Shenkeny pisanits yuzhnoy Yakutii', *Rerikhovskiye Chteniya* 1984 god: 180–92.

Konovalov, A.V. (1984) 'Perezhitki shamanstva u kazachov yuzhnogo Altaya', in I.N. Gemuyev and U.S. Khudyakov (eds) *Etnografiya narodov Sibiri*, Novosibirsk: Nauka.

Kośko, M.M. (1990) *Mitologia ludów Syberii*, Warszawa: Wydawnictwa Artystyczne i Filmowe.

—— 1999) 'Szamanizm: istotny komponent koncepcji światopoglądowej Kazachów', in A. Rozwadowski, M. Kośko and T.A. Dowson (eds) *Sztuka naskalna i szamanizm Azji Środkowej*, Warszawa: DIALOG.

Kubarev, V.D. (1988) *Drevnije rospisi Karakola*, Novosibirsk: Nauka.

Kuzmina, E.E. (1986) *Drevneyshiye skotovody ot Urala do Tyan-Shanya*, Frunze: Ilim.

—— 1994) *Otkuda prishli Indoarii*, Moskva: Kalina.

Lewis-Williams, J.D. (1997) 'Harnessing the brain: vision and shamanism in Upper Paleolithic Western Europe', in M. Conkey, O. Soffer, D. Stratmann and N.G. Jablonski (eds) *Beyond Art: Pleistocene Image and Symbol*, San Francisco: University of California Press.

Lewis-Williams, J.D. and Dowson, T.A. (1988) 'The signs of all times: entoptic phenomena in Upper Palaeolithic Art', *Current Anthropology* 29(2): 201–45.

—— (1990) 'Through the veil: San rock paintings and the rock face', *South African Archaeological Bulletin* 45: 5–16.

Lincoln, B. (1975) 'The Indo-European myth of creation', *History of Religions* 15(2): 121–45.

Maksimova, A.G. (1958) 'Naskalnye izobrazheniya ushchelya Tamgaly', *Vestnik Akademii Nauk Kazakhskoy SSR* 9: 108–42.

Maksimova A.G., Ermoleva, A.S. and Mariyashev, A.N. (1985) *Naskalnyye izobrazheniya urochishcha Tamgaly*, Alma-Ata: Onyer.

Mallory, J.P. (1991) *In Search of the Indo-Europeans*. London: Thames and Hudson.

Mariyashev, A.N. (1994) *Petroglyphs of South Kazakhstan and Semirechye*, Almaty: Institute of Archaeology of the National Academy of the Republic of Kazakhstan.

Mariyashev A.N. and Goryachev, A.A. (1993) 'K voprosu tipologii i khronologii pamyatnikov epokhi bronzy Semirechya', *Rossiyskaya Arkheologiya* 4: 5–20.

Martynov, A.I. (1988) 'The solar cult and the tree of life', *Arctic Anthropology* 25(2): 12–29.

Martynov A.I., Mariyashev, A.N. and Abetekov, A.K. (1992) *Naskalnyye izobrazheniya Saymaly-Tasha*, Alma-Ata: Kazniinki.

Ogibenin, B.A. (1968) *Struktura mifologicheskikh tekstov Rigvedy*, Moskva: Nauka.

Ouzman, S. (1998) 'Towards a mindscape of landscape: rock-art as expression of world-understanding', in C.C. Chippindale and P.S.C. Taçon (eds) *The Archaeology of Rock-art*, Cambridge: Cambridge University Press.

Pia, G.E. (1999a) 'Myths, shamans and drugs in the ancient rock art of South America', in D. Seglie *Proceedings of the International Rock Art Congress NEWS 95 Turin – Italy* (CD-rom edition), Pinerolo: Centro Studi e Museo d'Arte Preistorica di Pinerolo.

—— (1999b) 'East Bolivian ancient rock art related with present ayoreos', in D. Seglie *Proceedings of the International Rock Art Congress NEWS 95 Turin – Italy* (CD-rom edition). Pinerolo: Centro Studi e Museo d'Arte Preistorica di Pinerolo.

Pomaskina, G.A. (1976) *Kogda bogi byli na zemle . . . Naskalnaya galerya Saymaly-Tasha*. Frunze: Kyrgyzstan.

Potapov, L.P. (1978) 'K voprosu o drevetyurskoy osnove i datirovke altayskogo shamanstva', in (no editor) *Etnografiya narodov Altaya i Zapadnoy Sibiri*, Novosibirsk: Nauka.

—— (1991) *Altayskiy shamanizm*, Leningrad: Nauka.

Reichel-Dolmatoff, G. (1978) *Beyond the Milky Way. Hallucinatory Imagery of the Tukano Indians*, Los Angeles: UCLA Latin American Center.

Renfrew, C. (1989) *Archaeology and Language: The Puzzle of Indo-European Origins*, London: Penguin Books.

Richards, W. (1971) 'The fortification illusions of migraines', *Scientific American* 224(5): 88–96.

Ripinsky-Naxon, M. 1997) *Sexuality, Shamanism, and Transformation*, Berlin: VWB.

Rogozhinskij, A.E. (1999) 'Mogilniki epokhi bronzy urochishcha Tamgaly', in A.N. Maiyashev (ed.) *Istoriya i arkheologiya Semirechya*, Almaty: XXI vek.

Rozwadowski, A. (1997) 'Sztuka naskalna i Indoirańczycy: interpretacja etniczna petroglifów doliny Sarmišsaj' (with extended English summary – 'Rock art and the Indo-Iranians: Ethnic interpretation of the Sarmishsay Valley's petroglyphs'), in A. Kośko, T. Širinov and W. Rączkowski (eds) *Sztuka naskalna Uzbekistanu (Rock Art of Uzbekistan)*, Poznań: Instytut Historii UAM.

—— (1999a) 'Rock art and the ethnicity: semiotic system as an ethnic marker', in D. Seglie (ed.) *Proceedings of the International Rock Art Congress NEWS 95 Turin – Italy* (CD-rom edition), Pinerolo: Centro Studi e Museo d'Arte Preistorica di Pinerolo.

—— (1999b) 'Sztuka naskalna, szamanizm i Azja Środkowa: problemy relacji', in A. Rozwadowski, M.M. Kośko and T.A. Dowson (eds) *Sztuka naskalna i szamanizm Azji Środkowej*. Warszawa: DIALOG.

—— (1999c) 'Znikając w skale: szamanistyczne aspekty tradycji indoirańskiej jako kontekst dla interpretacji petroglifów Azji Środkowej', in A. Rozwadowski, M.M. Kośko and T.A. Dowson (eds) *Sztuka naskalna i szamanizm Azji Środkowej*. Warszawa: DIALOG.

—— (1999d) *'Kontekst interpretacyjny mitologii indoirańskiej w analizie sztuki naskalnej Azji Środkowej'*, unpublished Ph.D thesis, Poznań: Adam Mickiewicz University.

—— (In press) 'From semiotics to phenomenology or Central Asian petroglyphs and the Indo-Iranian mythology', in K. Helskog (ed.) *Theoretical Perspectives on Rock Art*.

Rozwadowski, A. and Huzanazarov, M. (1999) 'The earliest rock art of Uzbekistan in its Central Asian context: some dilemmas with chronological estimations in Central Asian rock art studies', in M. Strecker and P. Bahn, (eds) *Dating and the Earliest Known Rock Art*, Oxford: Oxbow Books.

Sagalaev, A.M. (1992) *Altay v zerkale mifa*, Novosibirsk: Nauka.

Samashev, Z. (1999) '"Szamańskie" motywy w petroglifach wschodniego Kazachstanu', in A. Rozwadowski, M.M. Kośko and T.A. Dowson (eds) *Sztuka naskalna i szamanizm Azji Środkowej*, Warszawa: DIALOG.

Samashev, Z. and Rogozhinskij, A. (1995) 'Tentative d'interprétation de pétroglyphes du ravin de Tamgaly', *Bulletin of the Asia Institute* 9: 198–207.

Savinov, D.G. (1997) 'K voprosu o formirovanii okunevskoy izobrazitelnoy traditsii', in D.G. Savinov and M.L. Podolskiy (eds) *Okunevskiy sbornik: Kultura. Istusstvo. Antropologiya*, Sankt-Peterburg: Petro-RIF.

Sher, Y.A. (1980) *Petroglify Sredney i Tsentralnoy Azii*, Moskva: Nauka.

Shvets I.V. (1998) 'Ryazhenyy personazh v naskalnom iskusstve Tsentralnoy Azii (problemy interpretatsii)', *Voprosy Arkheologii Kazakhstana* 2: 213–18.

Siegel R.K. and Jarvik, M.E. (1975) 'Drug-induced hallucinations in animals and man', in R.K. Siegel and L.J. West (eds) *Hallucinations: Behaviour, Experience and Theory*, New York: John Wiley and Sons.

Składankowa, M. (1996) *Zrozumieć Iran. Ze studiów nad literatura perską*. Warszawa: DIALOG.

Snesarev, G.P. 1973. *Pod nebom Khorezma*. Moskva: Mysl.

Snesarev G.P. and Basilov, V.N. (eds) (1975) *Domusulmanskie verovaniya i obriady v Sredney Azii*, Moskva: Nauka.

Sukhareva, O.A. (1960) *Islam v Uzbekistane*, Tashkent: Izdatelstvo Akademii Nauk Uzbekskoy SSR.

Tivanenko, A.V. (1989) *Drevnie svyatlishcha vostochnoy Sibirii v epokhu kamnya i bronzy*, Novosibirsk: Nauka.

Toleubaev, A.T. (1991) *Relikty doislamskikh verowaniy v semeynoy obriadnosti kazakhov*, Alma-Ata: Gylym.

Turpin, S.A. (1994) 'On a wing and a prayer: flight metaphors in Pecos river art", in S.A. Turpin (ed.) *Shamanism and Rock Art in North America*, San Antonio: Rock Art Foundation.

Whitley, D.S. (1992) 'Shamanism and rock art in far western North America*'*, *Cambridge Archaeological Journal* 2(1): 89–113.

—— (1998) 'Finding rain in the desert: landscape, gender and far western North American rock-art', in C.C. Chippindale and P.S.C. Taçon (eds) *The Archaeology of Rock-art*, Cambridge: Cambridge University Press.

Whitley, D.S., Simon, J.M. and Dorn, R.I. (1999) 'The vision quest in the Coso Range', *American Indian Rock Art* 25: 1–31.

Vitebsky, P. (1996) *Szaman*. Warszawa: Muza.

Chapter Six

The materiality of shamanism as a 'world-view': Praxis, artefacts and landscape

Peter Jordan

> Shamanism is not a 'religion' but rather a world-view system or a 'grammar of the mind' having many intercorrelations with ecology, economy, social structure for example. Shamanic folklore in shamanistic societies is partly collective knowledge shared by the clan, partly esoteric property known only by the shaman.
>
> (Pentikäinen 1998: 59)

INTRODUCTION

In this chapter I shall investigate the social and material contexts in which shamanism forms a means of communication. The Siberian Tungus word *šaman*, meaning approximately 'person with supranormal skills', was introduced into western languages in the seventeenth century by Protopop Avvakum. After being exiled to Siberia, this persecuted leader of the so-called Old Believers witnessed Tungusic Evenki rituals led by a 'shaman' ritual specialist (Pentikäinen 1998: 49, 81). Following the introduction of the word into the international literature, and the anthropological invention of the concept *shaman-ism*, contemporary usage of the word has spread far beyond its original meaning in particular cultural contexts (Pentikäinen 1998: 81). The distinction must therefore be made between specific Siberian groups who have a *šaman*, and cultures with similar concepts but different vocabulary. Khanty hunter-fisher-gatherers of western Siberia have the phenomenon (Pentikäinen 1998: 61) but not the word 'shaman' in their native lexicon, the term *elta-ku* being used instead to indicate a person who beats on the drum, summons helper spirits and cures illnesses (Kulemzin and Lukina 1992: 112).

In his classic analysis, 'Ecological and phenomenological aspects of shamanism', Åke Hultkrantz moves beyond the simplistic assumption that shamanism forms either the traditional religion of northern Eurasia, or indeed the religion of any 'primitive' society. Instead, he carefully disects the concept of *shaman-ism* to argue that it is a configuration of very specific values – a 'complex' (1996: 3). This shamanic complex displays several basic elements, turning around the idea that the shaman must experience an ecstatic level of consciousness and be assisted by helper spirits:

> The central idea of shamanism is to establish means of contact with the supernatural world by the ecstatic experiences of a professional and inspired intermediary, the shaman.
>
> (Hultkrantz 1996: 4)

These abilities enable the shaman to be an agent of change in the social group, a priest, spirit-healer or cultic official. Hultkrantz argues, however, that perhaps the most basic dimension to shamanism is what he terms the 'ideological premise'. In other words, the basic structures of historically constituted and socially sanctioned cosmologies enable the shaman figure to make communicative contact with the supernatural world, and to move between a number of different domains inhabited by spirits, deities and human persons either living or dead. As Pentikäinen argues, shamanism does not equate to a religion, with the associated Western assumptions that it forms 'just a sector of life among others', but rather it represents a more comprehensive *world-view* closely related to ecology, economy and social structures (1998: 61, 87).

Anthropologists have devoted great effort to the investigation of shamanism as a form of spiritual communication. Associated items of material culture including the shaman's costume and the heavily decorated drum, a central motif of northern Eurasian shamanism, have been singled out for special attention as cognitive maps of the multi-layered universe through which the shaman must fly (Pentikäinen 1998: 26–48; Pentikäinen *et al.* 1998). In this chapter, however, I would like to adopt a more holistic focus and expand the investigation of shamanism away from particular figures and their portable artefacts in order to explore its broader social and material contexts.

Thus, rather than presenting shamanistic cosmologies as timeless and overarching deterministic structures I will attempt to explore how specific understandings of the world are upheld by particular communities as forms of knowledge, which establish, through interactive social practices (praxis), relationships of power and authority between those who know. Moreover, these socially constructed world-views, reproduced and transformed through time and over inhabited spaces, are not 'free-floating' but grounded in the essential materiality of the human world. I will argue that the shaman be regarded as a member of a wider community, thereby giving acts of shamanising and the ideological premise that facilitates and legitimates them – a wider material and embodied social dimension (Figure 6.1). Drawing on a case-study of the Siberian Khanty[1] I will argue that the actions of the shaman form but one, albeit celebrated, dimension to a much wider dialogue between human and spiritual domains.[2] In this broader field of communicative contact the actions of creation, use and deposition of material culture form the essential media of communication (Figure 6.2). Moreover, investigating culturally constructed understandings of the inhabited landscape forms an important dimension to this study, for as Vitebsky notes 'there can be no landscape which is not already moulded by human consciousness and does not in turn form part of it' (1992: 223).

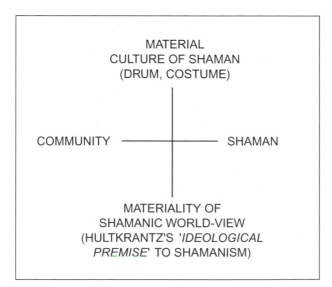

Figure 6.1 The social and material contexts to shamanism.

SOULS, SPIRITS AND KHANTY COSMOLOGY

There are several central themes running through Khanty understandings of the world, which can be argued to constitute major elements of what Hultkrantz (1996) describes as the ideological premise of shamanism:

- A three-tier construction of the world, existing on either a vertical or horizontal plane. The upper world, where everything is white, is inhabited by divine beings, including the *verkhnii khoziain* (upper master) *Torum*. The middle world, the domain of humans and animals, contains both black and white and good and evil. The mighty River Ob' runs through this world and drains off somewhere to the north where it empties downwards into the lower world and flows in the opposite direction. This black lower world is populated by the human dead who live their lives in reverse and by illness spirits whose master is *Kyn Lung*. From here illness spreads upwards into the middle world. In the horizontal construction of the universe the upper world equates with the warmer areas to the south, while the underworld is located in the cold northerly regions into which the main Siberian rivers drain, taking the souls of the dead with them (Balzer 1981; Chernetsov 1963: Golovnev 1984; Kulemzin 1984: 171–2; Kulemzin and Lukina 1992: 109).

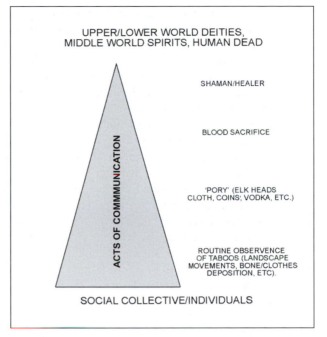

Figure 6.2 Acts of communication linking human and spirit domains.

- Human persons live out their lives in the taiga forests of the middle world. The Khanty believe that humans (and bears) have four or five souls depending on gender and while Chernetsov (1963) examines each of these in turn, others have argued that they amount to two essential life forces located within a material body (Kulemzin 1984; Kulemzin and Lukina 1977, 1992). The first of these is the free soul – an internal life force or *lil'* – which leaves the human body during dreaming, when it travels to the places seen in the dream. Involuntary departure is also caused by fainting but if the *lil'* soul does not or cannot return then illness and death result. This ability to depart from the body for short periods means that the free soul is particularly susceptible to being kidnapped or stolen. Evil illness-causing spirits (either *Kyn Lung* or the spirits he controls) may take the soul to the lower world, or it may be dragged away by souls of dead relatives who feel lonely on the 'other side' and cannot settle there. Thirdly the *lil'* soul may be displaced by the intrusion of illness-causing spirits in the middle world. In contrast to other human persons, the shaman's free soul may leave the body and wander into different realms although this remains an inherently risky practice. The second soul is the body soul, which remains with the body, yet can be destroyed when the physical integrity of the body is destroyed. This soul or 'life force' is closely linked not only to the physical form of the body but also to the shadow, reflection or impression that the body casts or makes. For this reason, sharp objects should never be stuck into shadows or into foot-prints in the snow for fear that they will cause the owner harm. Old clothes must be discarded with care for they maintain the body's impression, and are hence associated with its life forces. While the two life forces are to some extent independent they are both inextricably linked to the fate of an individual. Thus, illness and death can result from the loss of *lil'* but also from the destruction of the physical body, which in turn impacts upon or destroys the body soul. While the Khanty term *lilenky* describes living or animate beings (humans, animals) having the presence of a (*lil*) soul, the human dead are described as *suram*, that is not fully 'dead' but possessing some life forces. In contrast truly inanimate objects are described as being *entelilenky* (Kulemzin 1984; Kulemzin and Lukina 1977, 1992).

- Not only humans may be termed *lilenky*. The presence of *lil'* is revealed by the act of breathing, transformation and the ability to move so that trees, animals, flowing water and falling snow are also conceived to be animate or *lilenky*. Where these indicators are absent a tree stump or stone may also become animate if a supernatural being (*lung*) settles within it, for while human souls look like humans, and animal souls like animals, supernatural beings can assume any form. However, material objects may also come to be regarded as being animate if, through their physical form, they resemble other animate beings like humans or animals. Hence, sacred anthropomorphic spirit dolls and other items of material culture are thought animate as are natural feaures of the landscape, which may resemble human or animal features (Kulemzin 1984; Kulemzin and Lukina 1977: 154–5). For example, at a holy site on the Malyi Iugan there is a boulder singled out for special veneration due to its close resemblance to the form of a bear's head.

There is also an inherent fatalism in Khanty approaches to death (Balzer 1987: 1086), first because souls of the dead are reincarnated into the new-born living (see, for example, Chernetsov 1963). Kulemzin and Lukina (1992: 108) note that for elderly or middle-aged Khants the departure to the 'other side' was not regarded as a great tragedy, merely the departure from one group of close relatives to those of another who 'lived' on in the underworld of the dead. Here, time flowing backwards would ensure their eventual reincarnation, which, according to informants on the Malyi Iugan occurred 'within three years'. In the shorter term, however, it was widely believed that the length of a person's life has been decided in advance by *Torum*, the supreme being, or by *Pugos Anki* the 'Birth-Mother' (Balzer 1987: 1086). However, life could be cut short prematurely either by the intervention of illness spirits, as a result of the breach or violation of obligations towards normally benign deities, or by the failure to observe other taboos. In some areas *Kyn Lung* was seen as being equal in power to *Torum* (Kulemzin 1984: 117–29).

KHANTY SHAMANISM

Shamanism amongst the Khanty has common themes with that of other Siberian groups, although appears to have been quite idiosyncratic and to have developed to a less 'mature' degree (Sokolova 1989: 155, 162). A great range of Khanty spirtualists is documented, including singer-narrators, conjurers, the *niukul'ta-ku* foretellers of hunting luck, dream readers and sooth-sayers. The use of the hallucinogenic mushroom fly agaric – *mukhomor* (*amanita muscaria*) – was widespread, and unique *mukhomorshchiki* ate the mushroom in order to 'socialise' with spirits (Kulemzin and Lukina 1992: 117–20; Sokolova 1989).

I shall discuss two figures, the *isyl'ta-ku* healers and the *elta-ku*. It has been argued that only the latter are true shamanic figures (Kulemzin, cited in Sokolova 1989: 155; but see Balzer 1987), the term *elta-ku* meaning literally 'sorcery person' (*vorozhit' chelovek* in Russian; Kulemzin and Lukina 1992: 112). The shamanic calling was a tortured and painful one, with those 'chosen' unable to refuse (Balzer 1987; Kulemzin and Lukina 1992: 112; Pentikäinen 1998:

110–13). *Elta-ku* had true spirit initiations, which occurred in states of trance or ecstasy during which spirits of accreditation, usually directed by sky deities, tore apart the candidate's earth-bound soul and re-made it into a seeing and hearing shaman. In an agonising process of symbolic rebirth, spirits pierced the initiate with arrows and stripped away his or her flesh right down to the skeleton (Balzer 1987: 1087). After this process was complete the shaman was able to see and act as *posrednik*, 'intermediary', with the supernatural spirits invisible to ordinary people. While the shamanic call was made to both men and women, it was men who acquired the most helper spirits, enabling them to become the strongest shamans and to fly to the sky god. Balzer goes on to note that women became more powerful shamans only after the menopause. In the shifting cross-cultural contexts marking Soviet Siberian collective village life in the late 1970s, it was women who were more likely to maintain shamanic traditions while their overall prestige in the wider community waned (Balzer 1987).

Drums were often used in seances but tended to be devoid of any decoration (Kulemzin and Lukina 1992: 112; but see Balzer 1987: 1087). However, endurance drumming for a full night seance could not produce the desired results unless the particular helper spirits who could be summoned by drumming cooperated (Balzer 1987: 1086). Iugan River informants describe how the Khanty shaman's free soul (*iles*) could leave the body. Separating the free soul from the physical body was no easy task, even for the human dead, and only fully possible during shamanic activities (*kamlanie*) during which strong exhalations encouraged the departure (Kulemzin 1984: 25, 33).

In further contrast with other Siberian shamanic traditions, Khanty shamans did not generally possess elaborate or distinctive clothing (Sokolova 1989: 155), although Balzer (1987: 1087) mentions special costumes with dangling brass or iron ornaments. Moreover, shamans were non-professional and when not partaking in seances they hunted, fished and gathered like other human persons. Even in death they were not awarded special treatment, but were buried alongside their kinsfolk (Kulemzin and Lukina 1992: 112–13). Many other forms of ritual activity, including the bear festival, animal sacrifices and visits to a range of holy sites, were conducted without the participation of the shaman-figure (Kulemzin 1984: 118; Kulemzin and Lukina 1977: 149; Sokolova 1989: 162). Indeed, the adoption of a narrow analytical focus on shamanism alone would serve to obscure the rich diversity of Khanty ritual life.

The basic role of Khanty shamans was healing (Kulemzin and Lukina 1977: 149; 1992: 114) although the 'patient' could range in social scale, including:

- Individual clients, whose sickness was explicable through reference to either soul loss/theft or, more commonly, to the invasion of the body by invisible illness-bearing spirits (either *Kyn Lung* himself or his helpers) (Kulemzin 1984: 117; Kulemzin and Lukina 1977: 156–7; 1992: 106).
- Whole communities suffering from a more general malaise resulting, for example, from famine in the lean ice-bound months of the spring. At these times it was the duty of the shaman to restore a sense of harmony with the environment by cultivating favourable contacts with the spirits who controlled food supplies (Balzer 1987: 1087, 1091), perhaps suggesting the need for sacrifices (see Ingold 1986: 243–76 for a more general discussion).

Among some Khanty communities, for example those of the Agan River, shamans were thought quite weak, able only to appeal to *Torum* so that he, in turn, would make contact with *Kyn Lung* who would spare the kidnapped human soul. The use of the shamanic drum gave noise and power to the words of the request, for *Torum* lived so far away (Kulemzin 1984: 120). In other areas, such as Vakh, the shaman flew in person (i.e. their soul) to speak to *Torum*

(Kulemzin and Lukina 1992: 114). In general, the shaman (*elta-ku*) and other intermediaries (*isyl'ta-ku*) were able to be active on a number of world levels. 'Diagnosis of a given problem determined the arena of supernatural action' and 'helping spirits, usually in the form of spirit birds, horses, bears, hares or snakes, guided the shaman toward battle or mediation with spirits in multiple realms' (Balzer 1987: 1087):

- *Lower world* – the healers, *isyl'ta-ku*, were able to bargain for *lil'* (free soul), which had been stolen away to the underworld. After a person had apparently 'died' the room was emptied and a fire lit to keep the patient's body warm, allowing the *lil'* the potential to return. The healer lay down with the corpse for three days, travelling down into the *tsarstvo* (realm) of *Kyn Lung*, a journey taking more than a day. There he explains to *Kyn Lung* that the *lil'* of the dead person has arrived prematurely, perhaps bargaining with him and leaving gifts. There were two possible outcomes – *Kyn Lung* would release the soul and the 'dead' person would revive; conversely, he would refuse and the corpse would die forever, losing all final signs of life (Kulemzin and Lukina 1977: 159–60; 1992: 118).

- *Middle world* – the shaman was also able to remove sickness spirits who had invaded the patient's body by acting on the body itself (Balzer 1987: 1088–9). Again, these were the *isyl'ta-ku* healers who could cut open their own stomachs, remove innards and catch bullets and arrows in flight. This enabled them to cure many illnesses whereby they 'opened up' the stomachs of patients in order to extricate the carriers of illness, which usually took the form of a *cherviak* (worm) or similar creature (Kulemzin and Lukina 1992: 117). This illness-carrier was immediately eaten by the healer as all spirits were thought to be immortal and could only be destroyed by a shaman. Alternatively, the healer could open himself up and transfer the illness away from the patient to their own body (Balzer 1987: 1088). Kulemzin and Lukina (1992: 118) recount fieldwork observations made by Kulemzin, whereby an *isyl'ta-ku* from the Vakh River installed a *menkam* snake-like helper spirit in himself with the use of a metal file, enabling him to engage in this latter form of healing activity.

- *Upper world* – shamans were able to fly faster than a speeding arrow and pierced the sky on drums, flying to the golden residence of the sky god *Torum* in order to appeal for his assistance (Kulemzin and Lukina 1992: 111). Balzer appears to argue that seances of this form were more about the resolution of communal afflictions: the strongest shaman would, along with helper spirits, travel to the realms of the upper world, returning as a peddler of hope rather than a prophet of doom. Such seances also legitimated the authority of risky decisions, for example a move to new territories (Balzer 1987: 1089–91).

BROADER SOCIAL AND MATERIAL CONTEXTS TO KHANTY SHAMANISM

A number of issues arise from this discussion and relate to the conception of the shaman as an individual able to negotiate with spirits in order to secure community welfare:

- First, the actions of the shaman are situated within the practices of a wider community context. These uphold particular culturally constructed understandings of the world, which provide Hultkrantz's ideological premise to shamanism but which also have a material dimension ranging in scale from portable artefact to enculturated landscape. Thus, shamans were not so much the bearers of a society's ideology but the *otrazhatil'*, or reflector (Kulemzin and Lukina 1992: 114), of a wider sense of world-view expressed and reproduced through socially sanctioned praxis (see also Pentikäinen 1998).

- Second, this ideological premise or shamanistic 'philosophy of mind' (Pentikäinen 1998: 87), gives office to a particular gifted person. While the range of Khanty shamanistic seances defies typology, the 'unifying theme is the perceived need to deal with spiritual emergencies' (Balzer 1987: 1087) in order to benefit individual clients and the community as a whole. However, this focus on the shaman encourages the tendency to view the social collective, and the individuals comprising it, as being somewhat ambivalent, trapped between opposing upper and lower world forces of welfare (*Torum*) and illness (*Kyn Lung*). Within the narrow confines of these fatalistic structures the shamans constitute the only agents empowered with the ability to enact change, awarding them sole responsibility for ensuring the community's security within a dangerous and hostile world.

However, through an investigation of the individual's 'general life journey' Kulemzin illustrates how the shaman or healer may come to have only the most marginal influence on the fate on the individual. For example, Khanty informants took pains to stress to Kulemzin that shamans were only rarely asked to conduct 'sorcery' during the conduct of general procurement activity. Rather, it was up to the individual hunter to provide material offerings and ask *Wuhnt Lung*, the forest spirit, to give luck in hunting (Kulemzin 1984: 99). In other situations the influence exerted by a complex range of 'supernatural' beings, including dead relatives, was of much greater importance (Kulemzin 1984: 104–15). Thus, what appears to be the clearly defined role of the shaman as a supernatural communicator and agent of change may, in fact, shade off into a variety of other roles and practices, leaving the shaman at the narrow apex of a much larger 'cone' of communication (Figure 6.2). In order to explore these issues I would like to turn to a contemporary case-study of the material culture of Khanty communities living on the upper reaches of a river tributary to the Ob'.

THE KHANTY OF WESTERN SIBERIA

While the Khanty are, along with Mansi, Ket and Sel'kup groups, the oldest indigenous inhabitants in western Siberia, they have never lived in isolation but have traded extensively with groups to the south and west. For the Khanty communities who reside on the middle sections of the Ob' River, three historical developments have had particularly profound influences:

- First, the incorporation of northern Asia (i.e. Siberia) into the Russian Empire after the sixteenth century brought the imposition of colonial administrative policies whose primary focus was the extraction of *yasak* fur tax from the local taiga-forest hunting, fishing and gathering communities (Forsyth 1992; Konev 1998). At the same time, and despite a shift to a more dispersed settlement pattern, administrative territories appear to have been based to a large extent on pre-existing social groupings, with these in turn related closely to the drainage basins of the rivers tributary to the mighty Ob' (Martynova 1995). In order to pay the obligatory fur tax at annual *Jahrmarkt* trade fairs, indigenous communities were obliged to spend most of the yearly procurement round away from main Russian settlement centres, thereby sparing them massive face-to-face exposure to outside contacts. The basic structures of this extractive colonial relationship amounted to *de facto* apartheid, which in much of western Siberia continued largely unaltered right through the Communist period (Shimkin 1990).
- Secondly, indigenous belief systems were attacked by successive waves of missionaries leading to a partial blending of native and Russian Orthodox religion. Shamans were

singled out for special persecution in the Stalinist purges of the 1930s (Pentikäinen 1998) leading many to assume that shamanism had died out entirely by the middle of the twentieth century (Hoppál 1996). However, in the remoter areas seldom visited by state officials, traditional beliefs and religious practices were maintained in secret and continue to be respected and observed to the present day. The imposition of Russian-language boarding school education on indigenous communities after the 1930s had major cultural impacts, as did partially 'successful' collectivisation programmes conducted during the 1950s Krushchev era.

- Third, and most recently, the large-scale industrial exploitation of Siberia's mineral wealth has wrought massive ecological destruction in areas occupied by indigenous communities still practising traditional hunting and fishing lifestyles (Massey-Stewart 1995; Wiget and Balalaeva 1997a, 1997b). In addition, the urban centres tied to mineral extraction have boomed in recent years bringing into the remote taiga landscapes large influxes of migrant workers who have shown little respect for either the local ecology or the traditional lifeways of the Khanty.

MALYI IUGAN KHANTY MATERIAL CULTURE

Amongst the widespread environmental destruction around Surgut, where 'from the window of a helicopter one can see 300 flames shooting up from oil rigs' (Pentikäinen 1998: 103), pockets of traditional living continue to survive, albeit under the lengthening shadow cast by advancing mineral extraction industries (Massey-Stewart 1995; Wiget and Balalaeva 1997a, 1997b). This case-study explores the broader social, symbolic and material dimensions to practices of Khanty communities who maintain semi-nomadic lifestyles and reside on the upper stretches of the Malyi Iugan River, part of the larger Iugan River basin.[3]

The local taiga ecosystem is comprised of stands of woodland interspersed with lakes and extensive areas of bog. The climate is strongly continental, with warm summers and bitterly cold winters with deep snow cover. The summer thaw brings extensive flooding in this region of low-lying topography. The forests are home to numerous fur-bearing animal species including fox, wild deer, elk, sable, bear and squirrel. The rivers and lakes are rich in fish, especially in the summer and early autumn when migratory species return after the stagnant winter water has been flushed out during break-up. This strong seasonality leads to an uneven distribution of resources over the landscape at different times of the year. Traditional semi-nomadic Khanty lifestyles, based around hunting, fishing and gathering, alternate between the winter dispersal of household groups for forest hunting and their summer aggregation at riverside fishing sites.

The term *yurt* is used in the ethnohistorical literature to describe a small community of indigenous people who occupy different seasonal settlements in order to exploit general hunting, fishing and gathering territories (Martynova 1995). On the Malyi Iugan River, *yurt* communities comprise two to six households and are usually based around exogamous patrilocal lineages or *patronimia*. While successive generations of male hunters, bearing the same family name, tend to occupy the same territories, their wives are married into the *yurt* community from other *yurts* in the wider river basin (comprising the Bolshoi and Malyi Iugan branches of the Iugan River). At a broader level these lineages group to form non-localised clans or *sir*, comprising bear, elk and beaver clans (*pupi sir*, *nekh sir* and *makh sir*).

While 'Russians' (i.e. non-Khanty) are present in the local administrative centre located on the lower reaches of the main Iugan River, the population of the Malyi Iugan River remains exclusively Khanty in ethnic composition. This colonial settlement pattern developed after the imposition of the *yasak* fur tax system, part of which involved the establishment of forts and later church-administrative settlements at strategic points on arterial rivers. The pattern continued through the historical *longue durée,* with the Russian population of the taiga zone of western Siberia residing predominantly in urban settlements on the main Ob' River and having little, if any, contact with forest 'Ostiaks' (Khanty) (Lukina 1985: 16). Middle and upper reaches of tributaries like the Agan, Iugan and Vakh tended to remain indigenous 'hinterlands' providing fish and fur to the state economy, although more recently the inexorable advance of mineral extraction activities has radically transformed this ethnic mosaic much to the detriment of indigenous communities.

For Malyi Iugan households the seasonal round comprises movement between isolated huts located in winter hunting grounds (a period described as being *v urmane,* literally 'in the forest') and riverside base-settlement, also termed *yurt.* The hunting season is punctuated by a mid-winter break spent back at this base *yurt* when it becomes too dark and cold to hunt. Spring and autumn are also spent in the base *yurt* or at local fishing cabins. In the Communist era the whole community were obliged to take part in summer 'expeditionary fishing', which involved travelling, often en masse, to rich fishing sites on the lower Iugan and main Ob' Rivers. Thus a distinctive feature of this procurement activity is cyclical patterns of community aggregation and dispersal.

In order to secure success for the forthcoming hunting season, the house-hold must make *pory* gifts or fare (*ugoshenie* in Russian) for the forest spirit, *Wuhnt Lung* (*lesnoi shaitan* in Russian), who despatches game to the hunter. Although *Wuhnt Lung* is present in every part of the forest he is thought to reside in a series of *kot mykh* 'earth-houses', which, in the flat and boggy terrain, tend to be isolated island groves surrounded by open bog. At the sunny side of these islands white cloths are hung from trees, vodka is drunk and elk heads are cooked, consumed and the bones/bottles deposited (Figure 6.3). Each tract of the landscape has its own local earth-house and offerings must be left there when entering the area to hunt. Formerly, domestic reindeer were sacri-ficed at some of the more important earth-houses. As *yurt* communities tend to use the same hunting areas year after year, knowledge of particular sites, and the stories associated with them, tend to be passed down within the group (the following and subsequent quotations are taken from fieldwork interviews con-ducted in 1998 and 1999 on the Iugan River [see note 1]):

Figure 6.3 Lengths of white cloth (pory) hung from a tree at a sacred site on the Malyi Iugan River.

Petka A's parents were poor and hungry, but his father dreamt that they should do *pory* at *byrishkin kot mykh* (grandfather's grandmother's earth-house) so they went ahead and did that. Next morning, when they checked, they found a sable in every trap.

The members of the household are also protected throughout the course of the mobile seasonal round by the household idol who 'sees and hears all and does not let the illness spirits come close'. This anthropomorphic wooden idol is honoured monthly, often at times corresponding to the provisioning of the household with goods. The dolls themselves are fashioned from cedar wood and cut from trees growing on special earth-house island groves. Newly married couples travel to the girl's local grove where the male keeper (*khoziain*) of the site cuts the doll from a live tree. The couple make occasional return visits to leave offerings but after the death of the woman the doll is left '*bez khoziana*' (with no keeper) and is returned to foot of the same tree from which it was cut and left there to rot back into the ground (Figure 6.4).

In addition, each of the *yurt* communities strung out along the river has a local holy site spirit protector. These wooden images are housed in stilted *ambarchiks* or low open-fronted huts in dense areas of forest some distance away from the *yurt*. These places are known as settlements (*yurts*) but are described as being *bozhestvennyi* (i.e. sacred). Here live divine beings, the original residents of the land who were powerful warriors, heroes and elders and who lived in the distant past by hunting, fishing and gathering in the same way that the modern Khanty inhabitants do. Around these sites are areas of forest closed to all procurement activity, and while the game in these areas is thought to belong to the spirits, these zones of exclusion serve as unique sacred nature reserves (Novikov and Merkushina 1998). In order to request community health, welfare and hunting success, these sites are visited at times in the seasonal cycle when the community has aggregated again or is about to disperse (Figure 6.5). Lengths of white cloth and coins are left at the site along with remains of ritual meals consumed at the site, consisting of tea, vodka, elk heads and other fare. Reindeer and other domesticates are occasionally sacrificed and while the sacred sites remain fixed in place the wooden huts and dolls are replaced at intervals (Jordan In press a).

The chief of these local *yurt* protector spirits also resides in a stilted *ambarchik* and is the powerful patron protector of

Figure 6.4 Kot Mykh (earth-house) cedar tree from which a domestic idol has been cut.

Figure 6.5 Ritual meal at the *Daughters of Pugos Anki* holy site. The stilted ambarchik housing the idols is behind and to the left.

the wider river basin community. This hierarchical cultic tradition is found on other Khanty rivers (Martynova 1995: 90) with the main river deity being a son or daughter of *Torum* the sky god. For example, on the Bolshoi Iugan River this figure is *Iugan Iki*, the Iugan Elder, while on the Kazym River it is *Kazym Imi*, the Kazym Woman of that Kazym River. On the Malyi Iugan this deity is *Lon Lor Iki*. As one informant explained, '*Lon Lor Iki* is the general and the other local spirits are his officers' (Figure 6.6). Other important deities of this rank include the animal spirit master *Vojwort Iki*, who 'lives between the earth and the sky', the fish master *As Iki,* who despatches fish up the rivers, and *Kon Iki*. This latter figure rides on a horse and circles the world in an instant checking that all is well by acting as an intermediary between the high god and humans living on the middle earth (see also Kulemzin 1984). Another first generation descendant of *Torum* is *Pugos Anki,* the 'mother of all'. Her daughters were sent to live on the Malyi Iugan where they reside on the middle reaches of the river. They are tended by the local *yurt* community and are a focus of worship for Khanty from the local and adjacent river basins. Domestic animal sacrifices take place more frequently at the sacred sites inhabited by these more important deities (Figure 6.7).

In addition to these 'settlements of the sacred', Khanty believe that the souls of the dead live on after death in the cemetery – the settlement of the dead (Kulemzin 1984: 146). The cemeteries are visited at special times in order to hold special remembrance feasts, a time for communion with dead relatives. If the dead are made to feel comfortable in the cemetery there is less chance that their unsettled souls will wander back into the community at night. After communal visits the path is closed symbolically with felled saplings and at other times the

Figure 6.8 Carving of the bear on a cedar tree. The head and paws depict successful hunts with diagonal slashes recording the number of hunters who took part.

spirits are all able to exert influence and, for elk in particular, the animal spirit master *Vojwort Iki* is thought to have 'given' the animal to the successful hunter. After killing and consumption, the appropriate treatment and deposition of animal bones is important if this respectful relationship is to be nurtured (Jordan In press a). Feeding the 'clean' heart and head of elk to the dogs is thought particularly offensive and elk heads are often consumed at holy sites, forming one of the best sorts of *pory* or fare for the spirits. Relationships with the bear are more complex but also involve appropriate treatment of bones and their deposition in deep pools, whereas elk bones are returned to the forest to a 'clean place'. At the elk kill site a piece of fur is cut out from the animal's throat and hung from a tree so that '*Vojwort Iki* will know his elk has been killed'. For the bear, special carvings are made in cedar trees beside the path leading back into the *yurt*. These represent the head and paws of the bear, parts of the anatomy where the soul is thought to reside, and are cut so that *Torum*, the master of the bear, will not 'waste time looking for him' (Figure 6.8). The appropriate routine treatment of animals is also vital for the maintenance of the community's continued welfare.

DISCUSSION

I have gone some way in exploring the broader practices and social contexts which traditionally legitimated and gave authority to the abilities and actions of the shaman/healer. This more holistic analysis reveals that, far from being ambivalent pawns in a wider power struggle between opposing forces of illness (*Kyn Lung*) and benign assistance (*Torum*), individuals and the wider collective play an active but complex role in appealing for and securing their own health, welfare and hunting success. At this expanded landscape and community scale individuals have some, albeit constrained, ability to negotiate for their own fate, with the shaman playing only a very limited 'trouble-shooting' role in situations of crisis and uncertainty. In exploring the sets of relationships which link the human collective with various spiritual agencies, one has the sense of complex multiple webs of reciprocity stretching out over the landscape and flowing through time, so that at no point is any one person outside interlocking sets of obligations. The relationship is unbalanced: from the human side there is a general sense of tending relationships cautiously, by taking care to ensure that conduct is suitable in its both its timing, nature and spatial location. Yet there is also scope for interpretation, for the practical complexities of life bring forth the need for judgement, or even the taking of risk. From the powerful spirit side, there is an unfolding sense of uncertainty and unpredictability, for it is never clear whether human appeals will be successful, even if their timing and the manner in which they were made was thought appropriate.

Thus, rather than using Kulemzin's (1984) concept of a linear life journey, I feel a more appropriate metaphor would be the concept of an unfolding dialogue between humans and supernatural beings of the lower, middle and upper worlds. There are two dimensions to this dialogue: the media of communication and the locus of communication. To return to Hultkrantz (1996: 4), if a shaman-ism is about establishing some form of contact with the supernatural world then there are, following the Malyi Iugan Khanty case-study, additional conceptual levels at which this might proceed (Figs 6.2, 6.7):

- *Routine practice* – the observation of taboos relating to animal bones, prohibitions on hunting in, or walking or skiing in a full circle around sacred zones of exlusion (holy sites, cemeteries). Inappropriate treatment of old clothing may lead to (body) soul loss. For this reason clothes are hung from trees in the forest (see also Kulemzin and Lukina 1977: 151).

- *Preparation of* pory *at ritual sites* – the dedication to the spirit and consumption of 'clean' elk heads and vodka, and the deposition of bones and bottles; the offering of coins and cloths, which must be ritually smoked. In addition, remembrance feasts are held in cemeteries to prevent the souls of the dead from feeling lonely and trying to escape or send illness (Kulemzin 1984: 115).

- *Blood sacrifices* of domesticates (reindeer, sheep, goats) and the hanging of their skulls and skins from trees. In this way, not only is the animal's *lil'* or free soul released to the appropriate deity but also their body soul, relating to their physical form. In this sense the 'whole' animal is offered up, even though meat is consumed by humans at the meal (see e.g. Kulemzin and Lukina 1977: 153). In return, it is hoped that the deity will supply game, health or welfare to the hunter or community as part of a wider 'economy of souls' (see, for example, Ingold 1986 for an interesting wider discussion). Skulls and skins (and clothing and cloths) may only be hung from pine, birch or cedar, all of which are upper world tree species (Figure 6.9).

Figure 6.9 Skin of a sacrificed animal hung at a local holy site.

Kulemzin, V.M. and Lukina, N.V. (1977) *Vasiugansko-Vakhovskie Khanty v kontse XIX – nachale XX vv,* Tomsk: Izdatel'stvo Tomskogo Universiteta.

—— (1992) *Znakom'tec': Khanty.* Novosibirsk: Nauka.

Lukina, N.V. (1985. *Formirovanie material'noi kultury Khantov,* Tomsk: Izdatel'stvo Tomskogo Universiteta.

Martynova E.P. (1995) 'Obshchectvennoe ustroistvo v XVII–XIX vv', in N.V. Lukina (ed.) *Istoriia i kul'tura Khantov,* Tomsk: Izdatel'stvo TGU.

Massey-Stewart, J. (1995) 'The Khanty: oil, gas and the environment', *Siberica* 1(2): 25–34.

Novikov, V.P. and Merkushina, T.P. (1998) 'Ecological and economic significance of the 'Sacral Rivers' for Khanty and Mansi', in (no editor) *Proceedings of the International Conference 'Indigenous peoples. The oil. The law'. Khanty-Mansijsk, Russia, March 23–5, 1998.* Khanty-Mansiisk: No publisher listed.

Pentikäinen, J. (1998) *Shamanism and Culture,* Helsinki: Etnika Co.

Pentikäinen, J., Jaatinen, T., Lehtinen I. and Saloniemi, M. (eds) (1998) *Shamans,* Tampere: Tampere Museum.

Shimkin, D.B. (1990) 'Siberian ethnography: historical sketch and evaluation', *Arctic Anthropology* 27(1): 36–51.

Sokolova Z.P. (1989) 'A survey of the Ob-Ugrian shamanism', in M. Hoppál and O.J. von Sadovszky (eds) *Shamanism: Past and Present,* Budapest/Los Angeles: Fullerton.

Vitebsky, P. (1992) 'Landscape and self-determination among the Eveny. The political environment of Siberian reindeer herders today', in D. Croll and D. Parkin (eds) *Bush-Base: Forest-farm. Culture, Environment and Development,* London: Routledge.

Wiget, A. and Balalaeva, O. (1997a) 'Saving Siberia's Khanty from oil development', *Surviving Together* 46 (SPR): 22–5.

—— (1997b) 'Black snow, oil and the Khanty of West Siberia', *Cultural Survival Quarterly* 20: 13–15.

Chapter Seven

The medium of the message: Shamanism as localised practice in the Nepal Himalayas

Damian Walter

INTRODUCTION

In recent years, a significant shift in academic approaches to the study of shamanism has resulted in a move away from the essentialism of many earlier definitions, towards a more nuanced understanding of the localised specificity of shamanic practices. An important consequence of this approach is that it is no longer possible to consider the role of the shaman in isolation from other local ritual practitioners. In this chapter, I provide a description of lineage mediums (*kul-dhāmi*s) and shamans (*dhāmi-jhākri*s) in a predominantly Chetri (high-caste Hindu) village in the district of Solu Khumbu in Nepal. Unless otherwise noted, all the data presented below derive from my fieldwork undertaken there between 1995 and 1998, and is more fully described in my doctoral thesis (Walter 2001). In contrasting *kul-dhāmi*s and *dhāmi-jhākri*s belonging to a particular Chetri patrilineage (*kul*), I draw on an anthropological perspective that situates embodied practice in material culture, and attempts to account for differences between these ritual practitioners by drawing attention to the metaphorical properties of their respective practices.

Understood phenomenologically, space has no inherent meaning, but is itself a medium constituted through human praxis. Space is intrinsically relational, and in examining space as the locale of specific deities I argue that the *kul-dhāmi* can be satisfactorily studied in relation to the spatially designated deities and practices of the *dhāmi-jhākri*. Throughout this chapter, I draw attention to the ways in which these respective practices are framed by various orientational, spatial, percussive and transitional metaphors. In this context, metaphor is understood not just as a matter of language, but

> as a pervasive mode of understanding by which we project patterns from one domain of experience in order to structure another domain of a different kind. . . . Through metaphor, we make use of patterns that obtain in our physical experience to organize our more abstract understanding.
>
> (Johnson 1987: xiv–xv)

At an early stage in my fieldwork I became aware of significant differences in the ways in which *kul-dhāmi*s and *dhāmi-jhākri*s became possessed by their respective deities or spirits. The male *kul-dhāmi*'s possession by the lineage deities appeared to be almost instantaneous, while the ability of the *dhāmi-jhākri* to be possessed by his or her respective spirits was altogether a more elaborate affair, involving drumming and the gradual entry of spirits into his or her body. When I asked individuals to account for these differences in their respective practices, the general answer was that it was much easier for the *kul-dhāmi* to become possessed because the lineage deities were close by, while the spirits summoned by the *dhāmi-jhākri* had much further to travel, so not only did it take much longer for him or her to become possessed, but a drum was also required to summon the spirits in the first place.

In Nepal, the terms *dhāmi* and *jhākri* are often used interchangeably to refer to ritual practitioners believed to possess the ability to embody localised deities or spirits. Despite this apparent lack of distinction, ethnographic literature generally translates the terms into English as 'spirit medium' and 'shaman' respectively. My decision to retain the use of the combinative *dhāmi-jhākri* and *kul-dhāmi* is in keeping with local parlance, and has the added advantage of drawing attention to the terminological linkage between the two terms. In this sense, *dhāmi* refers to the actual individual who performs the function, while the hyphenated *kul-* and *-jhākri* refer to possession by the lineage deities (*kul-deutā*) in the former case, and utilisation of the *jhākri*'s equipment to gain access to spirits in the latter.

It is in this emphasis on technique that a meaningful distinction between these ritual practitioners suggests itself. More specifically, distinctions are often made according to the kind of equipment needed to utilise a particular kind of technique. A *dhāmi-jhākri*, for example, is most easily differentiated from other ritual practitioners by the typically shamanic equipment he utilises to access his possessing deities: typically a drum (*dhyāngro*), bells worn around the waist, long necklaces (*mālā*) of *rudrācche* and *ritho* seeds worn bandolier-style around the neck and shoulders, a particular kind of head-dress, and a white garment (*jāmā*) that typically resembles a long skirt that reaches to the ankles. This emphasis on the equipment of the *dhāmi-jhākri* becomes even clearer when it is noted that the term *jhākri* is used not only to refer to the human practitioner, but also describes some of the spirits he gains access to. The most common tutelary spirit of the *dhāmi-jhākri* is the *ban-jhākri*, a diminutive therianthropic spirit that inhabits the surrounding forest (*ban*). These forest spirits also make use of drums, *mālā* and bells, thus adding weight to the specific association between the word *jhākri* and the *dhāmi-jhākri*'s ritual accoutrements. The use of the drum in this context serves to metaphorically connect the *ban-jhākri* to its human counterpart, the *dhāmi-jhākri*.

THE SIGNIFICANCE OF SPACE

In contextualising the actual practices of the *kul-dhāmi* and *dhāmi-jhākri* it is necessary to describe some of the spatial properties that accrue to what Gaston Bachelard refers to as "the intimate values of inside space" (1994: 3). The Nepalese house (*ghar*) is suffused with symbolic significance. As Marc Gaborieau writes in his study of the Indo-Nepalese (Hindu) house in Central Nepal, "The house is both the family and residential unit in a patrilineal, patrilocal and virilocal society" (1991: 34). In terms of physical structure, a typical Chetri house in the area where I did my research tends to be rectangular in shape, and is built of rough stone coated with compacted earth, the exterior walls measuring on average 20 ft in length by 14 ft in width (Figs. 7.2, 7.3). The roof is thatched, and both the interior and exterior walls are plastered with lime. Each house consists of two storeys and a loft area. Houses are usually quite widely dispersed due to the nature of the steep slopes on which they are built, with the result that many houses are quite distant from their immediate neighbours.

The main entrance to the house is reached by crossing a veranda covered by thatched eaves supported on wooden pillars. Access to the interior of the house is denied to members of 'low'

Figure 7.1 A Chetri *dhāmi-jhākri* dances and drums on the veranda of the house during a familial healing ritual (*cintā*). A distinctive S-shaped drumstick (*gajo*) is used to beat the drum.

castes, such as members of tailor and blacksmith castes. To all intents and purposes, especially as far as visitors are concerned, the ground floor of the house *is* the interior of the house. Access to the upper levels is restricted to members of the immediate household. Both the veranda and the floor of the house are plastered with a smooth layer of clay and cow dung. Towards the rear of the house, the hearth (*aghyānu*) consists of a roughly shaped square depression set into the floor, delimited by stones, and containing a three-legged metal stand to hold pots and cooking implements placed over the fire.

Besides the hearth, the other main feature of the ground floor of the house is the specially constructed room that houses the lineage deities. This room is generally referred to as *kulko kothā* ('*kul*-room'), and consists of a small room built into the angle formed by the rear and side wall of the ground floor of the house. The *kul*-room's outer wall – some 5 ft long – is built parallel to the rear wall of the house, the interior of the *kul*-room measuring 3 ft in width. The entrance to the *kul*-room is barred either by a doorway or makeshift barrier that can be lifted out of the way when access to the room is required. The interior of the room is empty except for nine small clay braziers (*dhup-battī*) in which incense is burnt every month on the morning of the full moon. Each of the clay braziers corresponds to one of the deities associated with the lineage. All nine named deities are understood to be related, with the two most important ancestral deities of the lineage being conceptualised as 'brothers' (*dāju-bhāi*).

The area directly alongside the *kul*-room is also imbued with ritual significance, so that the ritual prohibitions that apply to the *kul*-room also extend, in large part, to an area of floor roughly coinciding with the general length and breadth of the *kul*-room, and extending from

Figure 7.2 A Chetri house in the Solu Khumbu district of Nepal.

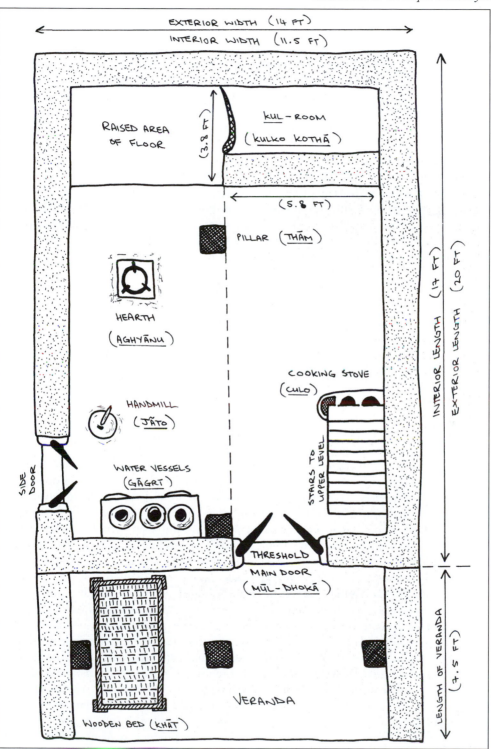

EXTERIOR WIDTH (14 FT)

INTERIOR WIDTH (11.5 FT)

RAISED AREA OF FLOOR

(3.8 FT)

KUL–ROOM

(KULKO KOTHÃ)

(5.8 FT)

PILLAR (THÃM)

HEARTH

(AGHYÃNU)

COOKING STOVE

(CULO)

HANDMILL

(JÃTO)

STAIRS TO UPPER LEVEL

INTERIOR LENGTH (17 FT)

EXTERIOR LENGTH (20 FT)

SIDE DOOR

WATER VESSELS

(GÃGRI)

THRESHOLD

MAIN DOOR

(MŨL–DHOKÃ)

WOODEN BED (KHÃT)

VERANDA

LENGTH OF VERANDA (7.5 FT)

Figure 7.3 Sketch plan of the ground floor of a Chetri house.

the entrance of the *kul*-room to the adjacent corner of the ground floor wall. This area is differentiated from the rest of the floor of the house by being slightly raised above ground level, but there is nothing else to indicate the particular restrictions that apply, and in terms of construction it is merely a raised continuation of the smooth clay and cow dung floor of the living area of the house itself. In most households, particular care is taken to keep this area swept clean, but even in households where no such care is taken, the same restrictions on access apply. Only certain members of the household, and appropriate members of the lineage, are permitted to set foot on this raised platform, and only when intending to gain access to the *kul*-room.

Worship of the lineage deities is restricted to senior male members of the lineage, and care is taken to ensure that anyone approaching the *kul*-room is in a state of ritual purity. Despite the unassuming appearance of both its exterior and interior, the *kul*-room remains the most important ritual space within the interior of the house. Any transgression of the various prohibitions that restrict access to its interior is considered inherently dangerous, and risks invoking the wrath of the lineage deities themselves. In such circumstances, threatened afflictions of the guilty party range from vomiting and bloody diarrhoea to losing the power of speech and paralysis.

Apart from the *kul*-room and the ritually proscribed area immediately alongside it, the actual living space of the ground level of the house consists of a single area without obvious partitions. In practice, however, this single area is subdivided into two different sections, despite the fact that there are no obvious physical indicators of differentiation. These subdivisions correspond to the immediate interior of the house to which most visitors are generally allowed access (an area extending roughly about halfway into the house), and the innermost half of the ground floor to which access is generally restricted to family members, relatives, and members of the same lineage or caste, including members of higher castes, such as Brāhmans.

The innermost part of the house is considered the most pure (*cokho*), and encompasses not only the previously described *kul*-room 'complex', but also the hearth on which most of the family's meals are cooked, and around which members of the family gather during meal-times both to eat and to talk amongst themselves. Depending on the particular household, this hearth is built either a short distance in front of the *kul*-room or in front of the raised area adjoining the *kul*-room. The majority of houses also possess a more elaborate cooking stove (*culo*), commonly situated beneath the stairs, but to all intents and purposes the rudimentary hearth (*aghyānu*) serves as the central cooking fire of the house, and takes precedence over the *culo* because of its closer physical proximity to the *kul*-room and its precinct. The roughly triangular area formed by the central hearth, the *kul*-room, and the raised area of floor next to the *kul*-room, together constitute the most significant ritual space inside the interior of the house.

The ground floor forms the collective heart of the household. The second floor, by contrast, is used as storage space for the household's food reserves. The upper level is loft space, and is located beneath the rafters of the roof itself. It is here that the *pūrbiyā* deities are located. These deities are associated with agricultural crops, and are propitiated with blood sacrifice before the new harvest can be consumed. These deities are more commonly associated with another major ethnic group in the area, the Kulung Rai, but are propitiated by Chetri householders because of this association with agricultural produce. These deities are kept spatially separate from the lineage deities that occupy the ground floor of the house, and great care is taken not to position the *pūrbiyā* deities directly above the *kul*-room two levels below. Insofar as the harvesting, storage, preparation, and consumption of agricultural produce remains integral to the household as a functioning entity, *pūrbiyā* are conceptualised as household deities, and it is in this capacity that their presence is tolerated by the lineage deities.

The lineage deities' acceptance of *pūrbiyā*, however, does not extend as far as the tutelary deity and attendant forest spirits associated with the *dhāmi-jhākri*. This is most clearly apparent in the explicit exclusion of the shamanic drum, the *dhyāngro*, from the interior of the house. On no account is the drum allowed to pass over the threshold. Because of this ban on the drum being allowed inside the house, the *dhāmi-jhākri* is necessarily restricted to the veranda of the house when performing his rituals. When not in use, the drum is kept in an annex building or hung from a wooden peg beneath the eaves on the outside of the house.

In a South Asian context, leather is widely regarded to be an impure or polluting substance. As such, it might seem reasonable to assume that the main reason why the drum is barred from the interior of the house is because of the use of animal skins in its manufacture. In contrast to the use of domestic animal skins to cover other kinds of musical instruments, however, what immediately distinguishes the *dhāmi-jhākri's* drum is that the leather used in its construction has to be taken from a particular species of mountain goat, the *ghoral*. Unlike the majority of domestic animals, Chetris consider wild animals – particularly those that inhabit the forests and mountains – to be *cokho* (pure). In itself, the leather used in the manufacture of the drum cannot explain the proscription on the drum's entry into the house. Distinguished by its permanent exclusion from the interior of the house, the drum quite explicitly embodies the antipathetic relationship between the household lineage deities and the *ban-jhākri*, the tutelary deity of the *dhāmi-jhākri*.

The spatial organisation of the house and the spatial positioning of the lineage deities inside the house – positioned, as they are, in a separate chamber in the innermost part of the house – tends to give rise to a general model that equates progressive restriction on access with increased movement into the depths of the house, what Gaborieau describes as "zones of intimacy and purity arranged in increasing order of importance" (1991: 53). Such a model, with its emphasis on linear progression and movement, only suggests itself when due attention is paid to the embodied experience of place. As Richard Lang has written, "Thinking of the house as embodied, as a kind of second body, means to see it in all its aspects not as a thing but as *access* to things" (1989: 204). The house embodies not only the principles and values of those who live within its walls, but is imbued with the same intricacies of identity that accrue to its human inhabitants.

The Nepali term *ghar* refers to both the physical structure of the house and its human inhabitants as a collective entity. Such a house does not exist in isolation, but forms part of a collective of similarly built and maintained houses. The network of paths and obligations that link these houses clearly demonstrate that the inside impinges on the outside, and vice versa. The distinctions I am drawing attention to can only ever be partial. The threshold of the house merely serves to delimit the effective spheres of inside and outside respectively. In the present context, however, my emphasis remains on these ritually designated differences between the interior and exterior. In what follows, I concentrate on the role of the shamanic drum – both as a physical and symbolic object – in providing a material basis for this distinction.

THE SHAMANIC DRUM

The drum (*dhyāngro*) is the main ritual implement of the *dhāmi-jhākri*. The drum used by *dhāmi-jhākri*s in the area of my research consists of a circular wooden frame covered on both sides with a leather membrane, and a carved tapered handle fixed into the underside of the frame. The drum is held in one hand, and a drumstick is used to beat out the rhythms. There is no simple corollary, however, between the beating of the drum and the ability of the *dhāmi-jhākri* to enter into a state of 'receptivity' in which contact with particular deities or spirits can be achieved.

Possession of a drum performs the symbolic function of representing physically the *dhāmi-jhākri*'s mastery of particular spirits. More specifically, it indicates the nature of the *dhāmi-jhākri*'s relationship with his tutelary deity, the *ban-jhākri*. During the formative period of his novitiate when the *ban-jhākri* first makes its presence felt – commonly characterised by an extended period of illness – the *dhāmi-jhākri* possesses none of the equipment which later forms an essential part of his repertoire. It seems clear that the *ban-jhākri* remains master of these early encounters until such time as he indicates to the *dhāmi-jhākri* (usually communicated through a dream) that he is now entitled to perform with a drum. Prior to this moment, the novice *dhāmi-jhākri* often performs with nothing more than a metal plate, which substitutes for a drum. From the moment he acquires a drum the relationship between the *dhāmi-jhākri* and his tutelary deity becomes characterised more by reciprocity than by mastery. This reciprocal relationship is metaphorically embodied in the drum itself. This idea of the drum as the physical embodiment of the *dhāmi-jhākri*'s relationship to his tutelary deity also accounts for why the drum is periodically 'fed' with blood on specific occasions (*guru-pūjā*). Other spirits do not share the same kind of relationship with the *dhāmi-jhākri*, and in these particular cases the drum – together with other elements of the *dhāmi-jhākri*'s equipment and repertoire – is used to summon, defend himself against, subdue, or generally gain mastery over these other kinds of spirits, ghosts, or deities.

Perhaps the most important point to emphasis is that the *ban-jhākri* is specifically associated with the forest. This association is necessarily both physical and symbolic. In this sense, the forest is represented as being spatially distant from the social domain of the house and village, and at the same time to be representative of all that is contrary to the principles that underlie this same social domain. That the *dhāmi-jhākri* shares many of these attributes with his tutelary deity is evident in the tales that are told by many *dhāmi-jhākri* describing their initial 'capture' by *ban-jhākri*, and the days or weeks they subsequently spend in the *ban-jhākri*'s lair deep in the heart of the forest. The forest is often described as the domain of wild animals, ghosts and bandits. It is a dangerous and threatening zone, free of the constraints that normally impose order on the social world. From the *dhāmi-jhākri*'s perspective it is also a domain rife with symbolic associations and transformative potential. It is the ultimate source of his own power (*śakti*), and binds him to a distinctly non-human *habitus*. The sound of the drum when played beats out a web of associations that stretch from the centre of the village community to the heart of the surrounding forest.

Seen from this perspective, the *dhāmi-jhākri*'s drum no longer becomes the *means* by which he achieves the desired result of being possessed by his tutelary deity – that is, it cannot be understood in purely Western terms as providing the physiological means by which entry into an 'altered state of consciousness' is achieved – but rather the means by which he marks out the differences between himself and the *kul-dhāmi*. This is expressed in terms of a locally meaningful idiom, in which the spaces that separate both types of ritual specialists from their respective possessing deities are understood as constituting both metaphorical and spatial degrees of differentiation.

'ALTERED STATES OF AWARENESS'

In preference to terms such as trance, ecstasy and altered or alternate states of consciousness, I suggest that the notion of an *altered state of awareness* merely supports the idea that in a culturally recognised 'trance' state – however defined – the subject learns to identify and give precedence to different visual, aural, somatic and mental criteria, without necessarily implying that he or she becomes disassociated from his or her immediate surroundings, and without prioritising etic categories concerned with the truth or falsity of what is believed to be taking place. To this extent, my discussion of the *dhāmi-jhākri's* drum and the notion of an 'altered state of awareness' can be seen as being fundamentally equivalent if both are understood for the purposes of the present argument as constituting *transitional* metaphors.

What characterises both *kul-dhāmi*s and *dhāmi-jhākri*s when embodying their possessing spirits is the fact that they 'shake' or 'tremble' (*kāmnu*). The 'shaking' is understood by both the ritual practitioner and his audience as indicating that particular spirits or deities are entering his body. The shaking starts as a barely perceptible tremor and slowly or more rapidly develops in intensity until his entire body seems to shudder uncontrollably. Despite the fact that the embodied expression of possession by their respective deities is described in very similar ways by both the *dhāmi-jhākri* and *kul-dhāmi*, these practices are also clearly differentiated from one another. Perhaps the most obvious distinction to draw attention to is that while the *dhāmi-jhākri* is generally regarded as being a solitary practitioner, the *kul-dhāmi* very rarely calls on the lineage deities (*deutī bolāunu*, literally 'to call or summon the deities') unless at least one other *kul-dhāmi* is present. The pronouncements uttered by the *kul-dhāmi*s while embodying the lineage deities are generally of a communal nature, and are often addressed to the lineage as a collective entity rather than to individual lineage members. It is not uncommon for three or four *kul-dhāmi*s to perform together.

MATERIAL CULTURE AND SOCIO-SPATIAL CONTEXT

Because the drum of the *dhāmi-jhākri* is barred from the interior of the house due to the presence of the lineage deities, the shamanic 'seance' (*cintā*) is invariably performed on the veranda of the house. A small 'altar' (*thān*) is built on the veranda of the house at the start of the *cintā* and serves as a focal point for the *dhāmi-jhākri* throughout the course of the evening's performance. The *thān* – consisting of a bed of husked rice, quartz crystals, black ammonite fossils, and horns and skull fragments of various deer and antelope – is generally positioned against the outside wall of the house. This orientation of the *thān* so that the *dhāmi-jhākri* sits facing the house reiterates the central focus of the majority of these healing rituals, the treatment or curing of an individual within a family within a household. The most important features of the *thān* are the small earthenware lamps (*diyo*) that are lit to mark the presence of the deities during the ritual.

Once the *thān* has been prepared, the *dhāmi-jhākri* takes up position in front of it in a cross-legged position. What most characterises the early stages of the *cintā* is the *dhāmi-jhākri's* extended chanting of his personal *mantra* and the gradual onset of the trembling that marks the arrival of the deities. During this initial period the drum is usually handled by one of his helpers rather than by the *dhāmi-jhākri* himself, and the drumbeat is slow and monotonous, a mere accompaniment to the *dhāmi-jhākri's* voice. The trembling that marks the onset of possession becomes only gradually apparent. It is often difficult to discern at first, often little more than a slight tremor in one of the *dhāmi-jhākri's* hands or his crossed legs. As he continues to chant his *mantra*, the trembling becomes more and more pronounced until his whole body starts shaking quite vigorously. It is at about the same time that one of the helpers – taking his cue from the *dhāmi-jhākri* – reaches forward and lights the wicks of the small lamps on the *thān*. It is only once all these preliminaries have been taken care of that the work of the *cintā* begins in earnest.

The most obvious difference between the *dhāmi-jhākri* and the *kul-dhāmi* is that the latter requires none of the outward trappings of the former. In marked contrast to the *dhāmi-jhākri* with his drum, plate, bells, *mālā*, and special clothing, the *kul-dhāmi's* practice is characterised by a paring down of equipment and clothing. Unlike the *dhāmi-jhākri*, the *kul-dhāmi* is required by the lineage deities to wear light-coloured clothing, and is not permitted to wear either a jacket or any kind of headgear. In the same way as the *thān* serves as the focal point for the *dhāmi-jhākri* during the course of the *cintā*, so the *kul*-room performs a similar function for the *kul-dhāmi*s when summoning the lineage deities. The *kul-dhāmi*s sit on the floor facing the outer wall of the *kul*-room. The area where they sit coincides with the roughly triangular area formed by the central hearth, the *kul*-room, and the raised platform next to the *kul*-room, which I have previously described as constituting the most significant ritual space inside the house. The *kul-dhāmi*s sit in front of the *kul*-room in the same cross-legged position as the *dhāmi-jhākri* adopts in front of the *thān*. Apart from incense, the only ritual equipment the *kul-dhāmi*s use consists of bundles of leaves and slender twigs (*syāulī*) bound with thread.

Sitting in a cross-legged position, each *kul-dhāmi* holds the spray of leaves in front of his chest with both hands and shakes them vigorously. Simultaneously, the *kul-dhāmi* starts to call on the lineage deities. As the rustling of the leaves fills the room, the *kul-dhāmi* is almost immediately possessed by the *kul-deutā*. He displays little of the gradual onset of possession characteristic of the *dhāmi-jhākri*. Instead, he jerks and 'shakes' with an intensity that is only matched by the *dhāmi-jhākri* when his *cintā* is well advanced. What also characterises the *kul-dhāmi* at this early stage is that his speech takes on a rapid, urgent tone, in which words and exhalations of breath coincide with increasing rapidity. This loud, aggressive tone is in marked contrast to the quiet, almost inaudible, way in which the *dhāmi-jhākri* marks the start of his own practice. At particular moments during the course of the evening, one or all of the *kul-dhāmi*s will get to their feet and dance to the entrance of the *kul*-room. The *kul-dhāmi* does not take the most obvious route to the *kul*-room, but instead traces a short circuitous route which leads from where he is sitting, around the outer edge of the hearth so that the hearth is between himself and the *kul*-room, before stepping up onto the raised platform and entering the *kul*-room. Once inside, the *kul-dhāmi* bows (*dhognu*) to the clay braziers representing the lineage deities before retracing the same route back to where he was originally seated.

FRAMEWORKS OF DISTANCE, PROPERTIES AND POLARITY

I initially envisaged the relationship between the *kul-dhāmi* and the lineage deities as being one of verticality – both in terms of the inherent hierarchical nature of their relationship, and because, in a more abstract sense, there seemed to be no clear distinction between the places occupied by both the *kul-dhāmi* and his possessing deities within the interior spaces of the house. By contrast, the *dhāmi-jhākri*'s relationship with his or her possessing spirits seemed to be one of horizontality – the hierarchical nature of this relationship was not present to the same degree, and, more importantly, the spirits were situated outside, at some distance from the *dhāmi-jhākri*. When summoned, the shamanic spirits had to move *between* places, which I tended to equate with horizontal distance.

I realise, however, that such a framework for thinking about the differences in practice between the *kul-dhāmi* and the *dhāmi-jhākri* is not all that helpful, not least because the landscape of Nepal is anything *but* horizontal, characterised as it is by deep-sided valleys, steep hillsides, and imposing mountain-ridges, and to continue to describe it as such – even if only as a theoretical construct – is to downplay the very characteristics of *place* which form an important part of these ritual practices. A further problem is that any discussion of vertical and horizontal distinctions remains inherently abstract, and constitutes what the philosopher Edward Casey has described as "Anesthetized conceptions of space" (1993: 49). In such a model, there is no space for the lived characteristics of place, or for the particularities of agency and praxis.

In Casey's discussion of the inherent properties of place, he draws attention to the 'lived aspects' of various binary pairs of attributes which are crucial to the relationship between body and place. In particular, he highlights two sets of related polarities – here–there, and near–far – which he describes as general traits of the body's experience of place. This aspect of his argument provides a useful framework for discussing some of the means by which the *kul-dhāmi*'s practice can be differentiated from that of the *dhāmi-jhākri*. In particular, it demonstrates the immutability of the relationship between corporeality and the lived experience of place, with the result that the 'structural' similarities and differences I have drawn attention to between these different ritual practitioners become much less rigid in practice. In other words, the distinction between inside and outside, for example, becomes maintained *in practice*, rather than being an inherent quality of abstract space itself.

In relation to the initial framework I proposed above, the vertical–horizontal distinction is more usefully replaced by the here–there, near–far distinction outlined by Casey. In such a model, the lived body itself serves as the basis of orientation. The body is always *here* in place, but is necessarily also implicated in the plurality of *theres* that surround it (Casey 1993: 66). Despite the tension that exists between these two terms – the imminent potentiality of here becoming (t)here, and vice versa – Casey maintains that this particular dichotomy fails by itself to fully reflect the lived experience of place. In order to add 'depth' to this initial binary pair, Casey introduces a second set of terms, near and far. Unlike here and there, near and far are "matters of degree" (1993: 57). As Casey states, "We can engage more or less fully in nearness or farness" (1993: 57). *Here* and *there* are absolute terms; *near* and *far*, by contrast, are expressions of gradual difference and "continuous transition" (Casey 1993: 57). The broad field of experience is characterised as being either 'here' or 'there'. By contrast, objects, places and people *within* that same field of experience are characterised as being 'nearer' or 'farther away' from other people, places and objects.

All of this is in accordance with Casey's notion of 'non-simple location', the idea that none of these categories is solely reducible to "geographic actuality" (1993: 57). The here–there, near–far binary pairs are never just straightforward categories designating relative distance. To describe something as *just* here or *just* there is to ignore the role of the lived body (the body-in-place) in providing meaning to these particular categories. The near–far dyad, in particular, possesses a dynamic quality, which indicates that near or far refers not only to relative closeness or distance, but possesses a metaphorical quality as well. 'Nearness', for example, refers as often to traits of shared commonality as it does to shared physical proximity.

What I am mainly concerned with arguing is that the apparent 'immediacy' of the *kul-dhāmi*'s possession by the lineage deities – compared, that is, to the *dhāmi-jhākri*'s more gradual possession by different deities – can be explained by reference to this same set of principles. Here, however, it is precisely the *twofold* 'nearness' of the *kul-dhāmi*'s relationship with his possessing deities – the sense of shared commonality exemplified by the existence of the lineage, and the close physical proximity of the *kul-dhāmi* to the 'housed' lineage deities themselves – that helps to account for this difference. The *kul-dhāmi*'s possession requires none of the trappings of the *dhāmi-jhākri* precisely *because* he shares these traits of 'nearness' with his possessing deities. The sense of movement engendered during the *kul-dhāmi*'s possession – his physical circumambulation of the hearth and entry into the *kul* room, and the vigour of his shaking – demonstrates the immediate parameters within which this sense of 'nearness' is realised. This association between the *kul-dhāmi*'s ritual practice, and the hearth and *kul*-room of the house is reiterated on a broader communal level during *devālī*, an important celebration in honour of the lineage deities, during which the spatial component of the *kul-dhāmi*s'

Figure 7.4 A Chetri *kul-dhāmi* uses bundles of leaves (*syāulī*) to indicate his possession by the lineage deities. The onlookers listen attentively to the possessing deities' pronouncements.

performance expands from a concern with the immediate parameters of the house to the communal parameters of the patrilineage itself.

This argument can equally be extended to the fact that the shamanic spirits, by contrast, are 'far away', both in terms of distance because of their association with the forest, and also in the more immediate sense that they share none of the inherent commonalities of identity which are intrinsic to the relationship between the *kul-dhāmi* and the lineage deities. The situation is made more complicated, by the fact that this simple dichotomy between the 'nearness' of the lineage deities and the 'farness' of the shamanic spirits becomes more problematic in practice. Despite being both literally and metaphorically more 'distant' than the lineage deities, it is precisely in the *dhāmi-jhākrī's* ability to summon these spirits that his skill as an intercessor lies. The spirits travel between places, but it is a movement necessarily dictated by the *dhāmi-jhākrī's* summons: from (t)here to here, from far to near, from the places which they inhabit to a place where their presence is temporarily required or requested. It is the occasion and performance of the *cintā* itself that creates the ritual space in which practitioner and spirits alike come to occupy the same place. Once the spirits have been summoned the *dhāmi-jhākri* displays all the immediacy of the *kul-dhāmi's* possession. What continues to differentiate the *dhāmi-jhākrī's* practice from that of the *kul-dhāmi*, however, is the presence of those ritual accoutrements – the drum, plate and bells, in particular – that are used to summon the spirits in the first place.

Returning briefly to Edward Casey's 'dyadic structures' outlined above, it is useful to consider one further point he makes in highlighting the differences between *here–there* and *near–far*. As he writes, "the near–far is thoroughly *spatio-temporal* in its experience and presentation. Where the here–there is primarily spatial, the near–far can be temporal or spatial, and is often both at once" (1993: 58). Just as the possessing spirits of the *dhāmi-jhākri* are spatially distant from the veranda of the house where he performs his ritual, so the gradual onset of his possession reflects the fact that the spirits are temporally distant as well. By contrast, the 'spatio-temporal' nature of the relationship between the lineage deities and the *kul-dhāmi* is very different. Sharing as they do spatial, symbolic and metaphorical 'nearness', the temporal nature of this relationship is negligible. The *kul-dhāmi* invokes the deities inside his own or another lineage member's house, and shares a sense of 'nearness' with the lineage deities as a consequence of both physical proximity and a shared commonality of identity.

Spatial distance also constitutes symbolic and metaphorical distance. Unlike the *kul-dhāmi* who operates in a context *integral* to his own sense of identity as a member of a particular lineage, the *dhāmi-jhākri* operates outside of any particular context that derives its significance from pre-existing categories of identity. In order to operate outside the normal constraints imposed by his situatedness within a caste-based society, the *dhāmi-jhākri* necessarily needs to 'distance' himself from his normal social persona. In such a context, distance becomes synonymous with difference, and the *dhāmi-jhākri's* ritual accoutrements serve to physically accentuate this difference. The donning of the headgear and costume, the setting up of the *thān*, and the cacophony of sound that accompanies the performance of shamanic ritual – the thumping of the drum, the whistles and shouts, and the accompanying clatter of the metal plate – all draw attention to the symbolic and metaphorical distance that separates the *cintā* and, more importantly, the *dhāmi-jhākri* from the everyday.

RESONANCE AND MEANING

The drum, in more than one sense of the term, *resonates* with meaning. As a concept, this is not dissimilar to Victor Turner's emphasis on the "polysemy or multi-vocality" of important ritual symbols (1967: 50). By this, he means that a significant symbol often has many associated meanings. As such, it serves as the focal point for a "fan" or "spectrum" of referents (Turner 1967: 50). Importantly, this notion of resonance refocuses attention on the drum as a percussive instrument. It is first and foremost an instrument that *sounds*. The drum rhythms that are beaten out on its surface support and structure much of the ritual activity that takes place during the *cintā*. The percussive rhythm captures the attention of deities and spirits from elsewhere, and summons them to attend. Control of rhythm indicates mastery of the ritual space and, by implication, mastery of encounters with gods and ghosts alike.

In considering why percussion is intrinsic to the *dhāmi-jhākri's* practice, while being of only minor significance to the *kul-dhāmi*, I argue that the former's greater reliance on percussion serves as a metaphorical expression of spatial organisation to the extent that the 'spatio-temporal' nature of the *dhāmi-jhākri's* relationship with his possessing spirits is fundamental to his need for a percussive instrument capable of transmitting sound over specific distances and attracting their attention. Percussion can also be usefully understood as an important indicator of 'transition', particularly in a ritual context where it serves to indicate the process or period of change from one state or condition to another.

According to Rodney Needham, the reason why percussive sound occurs so frequently in ritual contexts is that it marks, better than any other medium, the different phases inherent in transitional rituals that indicate the "formal passage from one status or condition to another" (1967: 611). According to Bruce Knauft, "percussion is a primary metaphor which uses the sensory effects of marked auditory stimulation to enhance and enrich the structure of ritual transitions" (1979: 189). To the extent that both the rustle of leaves and the beating of the drum perform a similar function in creating the appropriate environment in which particular rituals unfold, and in attracting the attention of the respective deities, percussion serves as an important signifier of both the *kul-dhāmi* and the *dhāmi-jhākri*'s ritual practice. Significantly, though, the most important difference between the shaking leaves of the *kul-dhāmi* and the sonorous pounding of the *dhāmi-jhākri*'s drum is the essentially *muted* nature of the former in relation to the latter. Unlike the *dhāmi-jhākri*, the 'transitional phase' required by the *kul-dhāmi* to change from one state to another is altogether less significant precisely because the change from one state to another is less rife with significance itself. Possessed by the lineage deities, the *kul-dhāmi*'s social role is enhanced, rather than altered, and the concomitant distance between these two aspects of his persona remains one of degree rather than difference. As such, the *kul-dhāmi*'s bundle of leaves carry little of the metaphorical and symbolic weight of the percussive equipment in the *dhāmi-jhākri*'s repertoire.

CONCLUSION

In providing a framework for considering the different practices of both the *dhāmi-jhākri* and *kul-dhāmi*, I have attempted to explore the multiple ways by which the complementarity of these oppositions is reflected in actual practice. What has been suggested is a distinction between interior and exterior spaces, which encompasses within these admittedly broad parameters a number of interrelated themes. I have argued that the drum embodies complex metaphorical associations that reflect these differences between the *dhāmi-jhākri* and the *kul-dhāmi*, suggesting alternative avenues for exploring the significance of percussion in shamanistic ritual. I have also drawn attention to the house as the locus of ritual and spatial differentiation, and demonstrated the complex interplay between ritual and domestic spaces.

The interior, exemplified by the house, is associated with caste and lineage exclusivity. The possessing deities of the *kul-dhāmi* are household lineage deities and necessarily occupy the same spaces as the *kul-dhāmi*. The *kul-dhāmi*'s, membership of the lineage, and the performance of collective rituals associated with the lineage are connective links in an exclusive social order. The specific nature of this relationship is represented in terms that make sense both spatially and in practice by the apparent ease with which the *kul-dhāmi* becomes possessed by these deities, exemplified by the almost instantaneous entry of the deities into his body. Intimately associated with his possessing deities, the *kul-dhāmi* requires nothing more than the susurrating rustle of leaves and twigs (*syāulī*) to indicate his embodied incorporation of the lineage deities.

The exterior, by contrast, is differentiated in a number of important respects. The spaces beyond the house necessarily reflect a loosening of familial, lineage and caste imperatives. The pull is towards the forest, and towards the undifferentiated spaces the forest represents. While the *kul-dhāmi* necessarily belongs to a particular lineage, the *dhāmi-jhākri* shares many affinities with *dhāmi-jhākri*s from other castes and ethnic groups. The ritual practices of the *dhāmi-jhākri* and the propitiation of local deities can be seen as connective links in the wider social field. This association necessarily relates back to the cultural anxieties shared by the members of individual households for whom the *dhāmi-jhākri* serves as an intercessor with the gods, ghosts and spirits of the local environment. Here the emphasis is on the related themes of contact with spirits that exist outside the immediate social order, and the concomitant greater social and spatial distances that have to be traversed if meaningful engagement with these spirits is to take place. In closing, it remains to emphasise that these different spatial 'zones' are necessarily contiguous, and reflect some of the variety of ways in which individuals attempt to negotiate the ritualised and permeable boundaries of their collective social worlds.

REFERENCES

Bachelard, G. (1994) [1964] *The poetics of space*, Boston: Beacon Press.

Casey, E. (1993) *Getting back into place: toward a renewed understanding of the place-world*, Bloomington: Indiana University Press.

Gaborieau, M. (1991) 'The Indo-Nepalese house in central Nepal: building patterns, social and religious symbolism', in G. Toffin (ed.) *Man and his House in the Himalayas: Ecology of Nepal*, New Delhi: Sterling Publishers.

Johnson, M. (1987) *The Body in the Mind: The Bodily Basis of Meaning, Imagination, and Reason*, Chicago: University of Chicago Press.

Knauft, B. (1979) 'On percussion and metaphor', *Current anthropology* 20: 189–91.

Lang, R. (1989) 'The dwelling door: towards a phenomenology of transition', in D. Seamon and R. Mugerauer (eds) *Dwelling, Place and Environment: Towards a Phenomenology of Person and World*, New York: Columbia University Press.

Needham, R. (1967) 'Percussion and transition', *Man*, 2: 606–14.

Turner, V. (1967) *The Forest of Symbols: Aspects of Ndembu Ritual*, Ithaca: Cornell University Press.

Walter, D. (2001) 'Blood and stones: ritual, shamanic practice, and the presence of place in the Nepal Himalayas', Unpublished Ph.D thesis, Department of Anthropology and Sociology, School of Oriental and African Studies, University of London.

Part Three

North America and the North Atlantic

Chapter Eight

The gendered peopling of North America: Addressing the antiquity of systems of multiple genders

Sandra E. Hollimon

INTRODUCTION

The purpose of this chapter is to discuss the antiquity of systems of multiple gender in native North American societies, with particular reference to the social role of the shaman. Central to this discussion is the much-debated notion of a broad cultural continuity across much of the circumpolar region, coupled with the contention that it was from eastern Asia and Siberia that the population of North America ultimately derived. One aspect of this discussion has been typified by Kroeber (1952: 314), considering linkages between northern Asian and North American gender and belief systems, who stated 'that the institution is a single historic growth'. Perhaps La Barre (1970: 161) put it best, when noting that, 'The worldwide distribution of functionaries recognizable as shamans ... testifies to their antiquity' and that,

> . . . the aboriginal New World, seen in its common essence, is a kind of ethnographic museum of the late Palaeolithic – Mesolithic of Eurasia, whence came the American Indian in very ancient times. Indian religious culture is of the same date and origin as their material culture, and it is as copiously documented.

This sentiment is echoed by Furst (1977: 20), who notes that:

> . . . we must assume that at least the fundamentals of the system were well established *before* the earliest peopling of North America in the Late Pleistocene, so that these may well have been part and parcel of the intellectual *baggage* of the first Paleo-Americans as they drifted across the Bering Land bridge that once linked Siberia to Alaska. (emphasis in original)

The recognition of similarities in the material culture, physical characteristics, and socio-cultural adaptations of Asian and North American natives has a long history in anthropology (e.g. Jochelson 1930), and the study of these similarities has produced a large corpus of data. Indeed, our most complete information about 'transformed' (alternative gender) shamans in Siberian cultures comes from Jochelson and Bogoras, two exiled ethnographers hired by the Jesup North Pacific Expedition, whose explicit purpose was to investigate the origins of American Indians by examining cultural similarities on both sides of the Bering Strait (Freed *et al.* 1997: 9).

The geographic distribution of societies that share fundamental similarities in belief suggests a great time depth for these cosmologies. Therefore, in this chapter I reiterate Kroeber's argument that the first people to migrate to North America were members of societies that recognised gender 'difference' (cf. Roscoe 1999: 8), the ability of an individual to change gender, and that these qualities were frequently associated with supernatural power. Following this argument, it is suggested that systems of multiple gender in native North American cultures have considerable time depth, and should be considered by archaeologists who interpret the material record of these societies. As Kirkpatrick (1999: 397) notes:

> Widely divergent cultures across the Americas have a broadly similar although by no means unitary way of incorporating transgender homosexual behavior (Williams 1992; Lang 1998), and this suggests that the original human migrants into the Americas 12,000 years ago had similar cultures.

Nevertheless, some archaeologists and other students of prehistory have argued that societies which lack an ethnographic or ethnohistoric record, or for whom these records have no mention of alternative genders, apparently lacked such genders, and they need not be considered in the reconstruction or examination of prehistoric gender systems (see Williams 1992: xiii–xiv). I argue, in contrast, that the distribution and antiquity of these belief/gender systems suggests the ubiquity of alternative genders in native North American societies, and that the deductive assumption should be that they were present, until effectively demonstrated otherwise (see Callender and Kochems 1983: 444–6; Roscoe 1999: 202–3).

SHAMANISM AND GENDER IN ANTHROPOLOGICAL RESEARCH

For the purposes of this chapter, the term 'shaman' is taken to include religious, ritual, or supernatural specialists found in northern Eurasia (especially Siberia) and North America, north of the present-day border of the USA and Mexico (see Schmidt 2000). Following Eliade's (1964: 4) definition, it is the ecstatic experience – the trance state or direct contact with the supernatural – that is the salient characteristic, and technique, of the shaman. While there are certainly significant variations within and among these traditions, it is the experience of manipulating supernatural power, especially that perceived to be housed in sexual energy, that is of concern here.

Recent studies of shamanism have approached the topic from a sex/gender theoretical perspective, highlighting the importance of gender 'difference', and sexuality-as-spirituality, as unifying principles in these far-flung belief systems. As Basilov (in Hoppál 1993: 276) notes, 'The ritual (including the shamanistic) "gender change" must be studied in a broad perspective, as interconnected with facts associated with an archaic, dualistic world view'. Examples of these analyses include those of Balzer (1981, 1996a and b), Basilov (1978), Bogoras (1930), Grambo (1989), Hamayon (1984, 1996), Jochelson (1930), Ripinsky-Naxon (1997), Saladin D'Anglure (1986, 1988, 1989, 1992a and b, 1993), Schmidt (2000), Siikala (1978), Taylor (1989), and Van Deusen (1999). Indeed, the work of Saladin D'Anglure specifically suggests that among the Inuit of arctic Canada, the category of 'shaman' is conceptualised in such a way as to constitute a third gender, along with the genders 'woman' and 'man'. In this formulation, his work echoes that of Marie Czaplicka on Siberian shamans: 'Socially, the shaman does not belong to either the class of males or to that of females, but to a third class, that of shamans' (Czaplicka 1914: 253). These shamans 'have special taboos comprising both male and female characters. The same may be said of their costume, which combines features peculiar to the dress of both sexes' (Czaplicka 1914: 253).

While it is not my intention to suggest that every instance of gender 'crossing', 'mixing', or 'ambiguity' is evidence of an individual's status as a shaman, I do draw attention to the association of gender 'difference' with supernatural power. This feature is so common in Siberian and North American belief systems as to qualify it as a ubiquitous aspect of these religions. In other words, not all shamans were of 'alternative' gender, nor were all alternative gender persons shamans; nevertheless, spiritual sanction was required to be a shaman, an alternative gender person, or both, in nearly all these societies (see Roscoe 1987: 85, 1999: 203, 276–7, notes 10 and 12).

The geographic distribution of societies with shamanistic religions has long suggested to anthropologists that these belief systems are of great antiquity, beginning with E.B. Tylor (Eliade 1964: 333). Examples are numerous, and include the early examinations of Bogoras (1930) and Czaplicka (1914; see Eliade 1964: 333–4, note 146 for a summary of sources prior to 1950). Building on this foundation, Kroeber (1952) considered the linkages between Asian and North American systems. The major synthetic works followed, epitomised by Eliade (1964), and then considered by Bäckman and Hultkrantz (1978: 29), Furst (1994), Grim (1983), Grambo (1989), and Hultkrantz (1981).

These theoretical issues have led some researchers to attempt to reconstruct ancient beliefs and the systems of social relations in which they were embedded. The studies of concern here are those which incorporate rather broad generalizations across large geographical areas, comparing material culture, mythology and linguistics, but which nevertheless point to the similarities that are most likely indicative of great time depth. Examples include the 'Proto-Uralic' cosmology posited by Napolskikh (1992), which draws upon comparative evidence from Siberia, Eastern Europe, Central Asia and North America; von Sadovszky's (1989, 1993, 1996) comparison of the Siberian Ob-Ugrian and California Penutian systems of shamanism; Zvelebil's (1993, 1998) work that suggests continuity from the Mesolithic to recent hunter-gatherers of the circumboreal zone; and an evolutionary framework focusing on Upper Paleolithic and circumpolar studies (Irimoto 1994: 430–1). These analyses join synthetic works whose examples include those of Anisimov (1963), Bäckman and Hultkrantz (1978), Bogoras (1930), de Laguna (1994), Grambo (1989), Hallowell (1926), Hultkrantz (1981, 1994), Ingold (1986), Lowie (1934), and Vasilivic (1963).

A significant conclusion of many of these studies is that the element of ritual transvestism, or even the change of sex/gender of the shaman, is a very ancient feature of these disparate belief systems. While there is certainly controversy concerning the possible Palaeolithic origins of shamanistic religions in northern Eurasia, there does appear to be substantial agreement that these belief systems have very ancient roots, and that the widespread distribution of several elements argues for ancient and perhaps ongoing contacts and diffusion (see Balzer 1996a: 174–5; Eliade 1964: 333–6; Grambo 1989: 110). Specifically, Grambo (1989) considers the northern geographic distribution of gender-transformed shamans to be an indication of an archaic belief system. Features shared by Eurasian and North American religions include the 'world tree' or 'cosmic pillar' that unites a tri-partite cosmos of universe, earth, and underworld; the ritual significance of animals that mediate between or among these realms, such as ravens and bears; the presence of 'shamanic flight'; and the shaman's ability to pierce his/her flesh without injury, among others (see Eliade 1964: 333–5; Hultkrantz 1994).

SHAMANISTIC POWER AND SEXUALITY

The recognition of gender 'difference' associated with shamanism in Eurasia and North America has been discussed by several authors (see Basilov 1978; Balzer 1996a and b; Basilov 1984;

Bogoras 1930; Grambo 1989; Jochelson 1908; Saladin D'Anglure 1986, 1988, 1989, 1992a and b; Siikala 1978). One notable observation among many of these studies is that shamanistic power and reproductive capability (human fertility) are considered incompatible (Balzer 1996a: 177, note 2; Czaplicka 1914: 252; Hollimon 2000). For example, Bogoras (1904: 455–6) reported the case of a Chukchi woman who was transformed into a man after receiving spiritual instruction to do so, and she undertook this transformation after menopause. She had children of her own when young, and then entered a mutual marriage with a young woman whose children were fathered by a genitor, and the transformed person was recognised as the pater (Bogoras 1904: 455–6).

In another example from the Koryak, a woman's fertility is a threat to her shamanistic power. Childbirth might result in a complete or temporary loss of this power, and a menstruating woman is not allowed to touch the shamanistic drum (Jochelson 1908: 54; see also Czaplicka 1914: 252).

Alternatively, the gender ambiguity of male shamans may be interpreted as their appropriation of birth symbolism and power from women. As an example, Fienup-Riordan (1994: 307) describes Yup'ik shamans as 'male mothers' whose mediating activity 'dramatically transcended these [gender] boundaries so scrupulously maintained during daily life'. The ambiguous gender of the shaman was sometimes reflected in ceremonial masks that depicted their helping spirits as hermaphrodites (Kaplan 1984: 2; see also Black 1977: 99).

The association between shamanic power and gender ambiguity has been documented among societies that cover a wide geographic area. These include the Sámi of Fenno-Scandia (Lundmark 1987); the Hungarians of Central Europe (Dömötör 1984; Hoppál 1993; Klaniczay 1984; Kürti 1996); and the Central Asian Uzbek (Basilov 1978). Numerous Siberian groups have also been described with regard to these phenomena, including the Khanty-Vakht (Balzer 1981), Nivkh-Gilyak (Black 1973; Chard 1961; Shternberg 1925, 1999), 'Samoyed' (Hajdú 1968), Koryak (Czaplicka 1914; Jochelson 1908), Kamchadal-Itelmen (Czaplicka 1914; Krasheninnikov 1972), Chukchi (Bogoras 1904; Siikala 1978; Van Deusen 1999), Evenk-Tungus (Vasilevic 1968), and Ob-Ugrian (Sokolova 1989).

Among the Sakha (Yakut), the sexual symbolism of the shaman is manifested when the shaman gives birth to animals in an altered state of consciousness (Popov, cited in Balzer 1996a: 177, note 2). Also among the Sakha, Jochelson (1908: 53, note 3) reported that on the third day after giving birth, a woman is believed to be attended by the deity of fecundity. At this time, the house is off-limits to men, but not to shamans. Sakha shamans also perform ceremonies in order to instill women with sexual desire (*dzalin*) and promote the forces of reproduction (Diachenko 1994: 270).

Perhaps the most profound example of this principle is the notion of a sexual union between the shaman and the helping spirit (Ripinsky-Naxon 1993: 75, 77; 1997: 36). In many Siberian cultures, the transformed shaman is believed to have a supernatural or spirit 'husband', hence the shaman's sex must change in order to receive this guidance (see Bogoras 1904: 452). Similar beliefs of shaman/spirit intercourse are found among the Goldi of the Amur River area (Shternberg 1925), the Sakha (Yakut) of Siberia (Shirokogoroff in Ripinsky-Naxon 1997: 36), Nivkh (Gilyak) of Sakhalin (Shternberg 1925; see also Chard 1961; Grant 1999), the Yup'ik (Fienup-Riordan 1994: 307), and the Inuit of St Lawrence Island, Alaska (Murphy 1964; see also Foulks 1972) and Baker Lake (Butler 1974).

These beliefs are reflected in the oral traditions of cultures that recognise gender flexibility (see Hollimon 1998). A common motif is the gender transformation of the shaman, whether the change is permanent or temporary. Examples include the Inuit (Boas 1901–1907: 325; Fleming 1956: 189; Rasmussen 1929: 302, 1931: 303–4, 500–1), the Koryak (Jochelson 1908:

52–3, 304–5, 323), in Chukotka (Van Deusen 1999) and throughout the North Pacific (see Meletinsky 1980; Novik 1990; Shternberg 1925; Utley 1974).

MEDIATION

Miller (1982: 275) describes the cultural importance of mediating figures in native North American belief systems. Mediators display attributes of each member of a pair, such as female and male, as well as qualities from a third dimension that are unique to mediators (Miller 1982: 275). In this way, Miller finds analogies between third gender males ('*berdaches*') and bears. The human-like qualities of bears, their large size, and association with supernatural power led many native North American groups to espouse a fictive kinship with these creatures, echoing beliefs held widely throughout Siberia (Hallowell 1926; Miller 1982: 275–6). For example, on both sides of the North Pacific, beliefs that the bear is merely a kind of human clad in a bearskin are remarkably similar (e.g. Alekseenko 1968: 176–7; Balzer 1999; Miller 1982: 276; Unsgaard 1985).

Bears

The importance of bears, especially as a mediating symbol, has been described throughout Eurasia and North America (Balzer 1996a; Czaplicka 1914; Irimoto 1994; Kroeber 1952: 315–16; Miller 1982: 275–6). In western Siberia, the bear is seen as a mediating category between the living and the dead (Gemuev 1989: 181), and in Eurasia and North America bears are considered to be masters or guardians of other animals (Zvelebil 1993: 58). This symbolism is reflected in the widespread occurrence of 'bear doctors' and the role of bears as spirit guides in shamanic practice (Delaby 1984; Hallowell 1926; Kroeber 1952).

Those groups that recognise a supernatural significance of bears, and/or those who practise bear ceremonialism, include the Ainu (Akino 1999; Kono and Fitzhugh 1999), Ket (Alekseenko 1968), Khanty (Balzer 1996a and 1999), Nanai (Diószegi 1968), Turkic-speaking Siberians (Dyrenkova 1930), Ob-Ugrians (Kálmán 1968; Schmidt 1989; Sokolova 1989), Nivkh (Shternberg 1999: 160–1), Sámi (Unsgaard 1985, 1987; Zachrisson 1985). While bear ceremonialism is also widespread throughout North America (see Hallowell 1926 and Miller 1982), it appears to be particularly strong in the Northwest Coast culture area, fostering ties of cultural and ethnic renewal between contemporary North American native groups and the Ainu of northern Japan (Kono and Fitzhugh 1999: 118–19).

Ravens

Similar to the symbolism of the bear in these religions is the mediating figures of the raven. While many birds are considered important spirit guides throughout Eurasia and North America due to the association with magical flight, the raven has a particularly pronounced role in the beliefs of many Siberian and Northwest Coast groups (Balzer 1996b; Jochelson 1908; Meletinsky 1980; Novik 1990; Van Deusen 1999: 168, note 11). The obvious intelligence of the species accounts in some part for its role as a trickster in many mythological traditions, but other behaviors also contribute to its mediating qualities (see Balzer 1996b; Goodchild 1991; Driver 1999: 291, Table 1 for a summary). For example, the raven was symbolically equated with a gender-changing shaman in an oral tradition motif from Siberia (Meletinsky 1980: 126).

The great time depth of ravens' symbolic importance is demonstrated by the apparently intentional burial of two complete ravens at a Paleoindian site in British Columbia, *c.*10,500 BP

(Driver 1999). While it cannot be determined whether humans deliberately buried these birds in a ritual or ceremonial context, it seems likely that some aspect of ideology or symbolism is reflected in this remarkable archaeological find, joining other sites in North America that contain raven remains (see Driver 1999: 291–2 for a summary of this evidence).

Shamans

Referring specifically to the Inuit of arctic Canada and Alaska, Saladin D'Anglure (1994: 208) provides a useful definition of the remarkable qualities of the shaman found in many cultures:

> The shaman is the individual who, in addition to living in the visible world like everyone else, is also able to function in the reality of myth. He is the one who can readjust the pillars holding up the worlds, who can find babies pushed up from the ground and give them to sterile women, who can bring back game animals to areas where none are to be found. He is the one who through levitation frees himself from the pull of gravity, who through metamorphosis, crosses the gender boundary, who through glossolalia speaks through the language of others, and who through clairvoyance sees through the obscurity and across all obstacles into the past or into the future. Like the great spirits, he also benefits from telescopic vision together with a tenfold increase in strength and speed. Like them, he is insensitive to pain. . . . He seeks aid from helping spirits of the opposite sex to transcend the sexual boundary more easily.

This observation is echoed by the Sakha (Yakut) ethnographer Alexander A. Popov (cited in Balzer 1996a:177, note 2), who noted that the most revered of shamans could mediate three worlds: celestial, earthly, and underground (see also Irimoto 1994: 428–9; Miller 1982). The principle of mediation, or unification of opposing qualities, is epitomised by the shaman in many Eurasian and North American cultures. Ripinsky-Naxon (1997: 49) notes,

> . . . shamans appear to combine in their persons the feminine (earth) and the masculine (heaven) principles. . . . Consequently, such individuals are viewed as intermediaries, the intercepting axis, between the heavenly and the worldly realms, a nexus for the divine and the human.

THIRD AND FOURTH GENDERS

Among native North American societies, there is a strong underlying principle that individuals who occupy an intermediate or ambivalent position are spiritually powerful (see Fulton and Anderson 1992: 609; Roscoe 1999: 8, 26). Those who are more-or-less permanently in a liminal position, or are what Turner (1969) calls 'threshold figures', are those who can mediate between earthly and supernatural realms. Certainly this describes shamans, but it can also apply to those who express differences in gender identity, sexuality, or other aspects of self. Thayer (1980: 292), referring to gender diversity in Northern Plains societies, clearly states this notion:

> It was from this interstitial character that the berdache's [sic] mediating powers spring: as half-man/half-woman he had powers to mediate or cross sexual boundaries and roles, and, since he was a creation of a vision like other shamans, he mediated as well between the divine and human worlds.

Similarly, folklorists and scholars of comparative religion in Eurasia recognise that boundary transcendence is an important aspect of defining the sacred (Balzer 1996a : 174–5, emphasis added):

. . . we can see varied gender transformations as one aspect of repeated and *ancient* attempts to harness, define, and redefine the power of sex by explorations of gender ambiguity and reversal in Siberian concepts of the sacred.

An individual who can straddle gender boundaries should be able to span all boundaries (Saladin D'Anglure 1992a: 18). Balzer (1996a: 176) continues, 'Instead of seeing gender reversals as deviant, we may see the mirror image: anomaly turned into sacred power.' Ripinsky-Naxon (1997: 49), describing Siberian shamans, notes, '. . . such individuals are viewed as the intermediaries, the intercepting axis, between the heavenly and the worldly realms, a nexus for the divine and the human'. Furthermore, shamans are capable of:

. . . the harnessing of both male and female sexual potential. For many this means having male shamans accept female spirit helpers as guides, and vice versa, incorporating their power and even their gendered essence in trance and during seances. It can involve tapping the gendered spiritual force of a tree, for instance the female birch, to cure a male patient. And in a particularly dramatic form, the greatest shamans, even if they are males, are able to themselves give birth to spirit animals.

(Balzer 1996a: 164)

The way in which 'different' persons are regarded by their societies can include many aspects, such as admiration, awe, and fear, and these feelings may be held simultaneously. Speaking to his Nivkh (Gilyak) consultant, Grant (1999: 209–10) asked about turn-of-the-century ethnographer Shternberg's notes concerning hermaphrodites, and what native attitudes were/are about such people. Ms Liutova replied:

It may also be a case of just being afraid of anyone born differently. Any time anyone was born with an extra finger, or with any physical differences, people went out of their way to treat them specially, to treat them well, in case they might have some special powers. People felt that if someone was born differently there must be a reason.

(Grant 1999: 210)

This echoes a sentiment expressed by a Lakota *winkte* (third gender male) with whom spiritualist John Fire Lame Deer conversed. The *winkte* said that 'if nature puts a burden on a man by making him different, it also gives him a power' (Fire/Lame Deer and Erdoes 1972: 149).

This recognition of persons with 'extra' supernatural power may explain the belief in some societies that shamans with gender difference were the most powerful of all. For example, among the Chukchi, 'transformed' shamans were the most greatly feared, even by untransformed shamans, for they were considered to be the most supernaturally powerful of all (Bogoras 1904: 453). Throughout North America, there are examples of religious/ritual specialists who are gender variant (Callender and Kochems 1983; Fulton and Anderson 1992; Thayer 1980). In some societies, third or fourth gender persons were shamans, according to Eliade's definition. These include the Ingalik (Osgood 1940), Inuit (Saladin D'Anglure 1986), Maidu, Achumawi, and Shasta (Voegelin 1942), Mattole, Chilula, and Hupa (Driver 1939), Modoc (Ray 1963), Mohave (Devereux 1937), Tolowa (Driver 1937), Wappo (Willoughby 1963) and Yurok (Kroeber 1925).

ARCHAEOLOGICAL IMPLICATIONS

These principles are important to the interpretation of native North American archaeological remains for several reasons. It is my contention that the first people to migrate to North America from North Asia were members of societies that recognised more than two genders. Therefore, archaeologists and prehistorians should operate from the deductive position that multiple genders were present in these societies, until substantial evidence to the contrary emerges. The lack of ethnographic or ethnohistoric information about 'alternative' genders is not sufficient 'proof' that such genders did not exist; many sources may have omitted information about these genders, primarily due to ethnocentrism and an intolerance of native religious and sexual practices (see Callender and Kochems 1983; Roscoe 1999; Williams 1992). Therefore, we should assume that absence of evidence is not evidence of absence.

In addition, the accuracy of archaeological interpretations of prehistoric lifeways is predicated on an understanding of the gender system, and its interconnections with ritual, cosmological, economic, and symbolic systems. Gender is an underpinning for the division of labor, for marriage and kinship practices, and for many other aspects of culture. As such, archaeologists must consider gender, in the general sense, and multiple genders, specifically, if we are to more fully understand the material record of past lives.

REFERENCES

Akino, S. (1999) 'Spirit-sending ceremonies', in W.W. Fitzhugh and C.O. Dubreuil (eds) *Ainu: spirit of a Northern people*, Washington, DC: Smithsonian Institution.

Alekseenko, E.A. (1968) 'The cult of the bear among the Ket (Yenisei Ostyak).', in V. Diószegi (ed.) *Popular Beliefs and Folklore Tradition in Siberia*, Bloomington: Indiana University Press.

Anisimov, A.F. (1963) 'Cosmological concepts of the peoples of the North', in H.N. Michael (ed.) *Studies in Siberian Shamanism,* Toronto: University of Toronto Press for the Arctic Institute of America.

Bäckman, L. and Hultkrantz, Å. (1978) *Studies in Lapp shamanism*, Stockholm Studies in Comparative Religion 16, Stockholm: University of Stockholm.

Balzer, M.M. (1981) 'Rituals of gender identity: markers of Siberian Khanty ethnicity, status, and belief', *American Anthropologist* 83: 850–67.

—— (1996a) 'Sacred genders in Siberia: shamans, bear festivals and androgyny', in S.P. Ramet (ed.) *Gender Reversals and Gender Cultures: Anthropological and Historical Perspectives*, London: Routledge.

—— (1996b) 'Flights of the sacred: symbolism and theory in Siberian shamanism', *American Anthropologist* 98(2): 305–8.

—— (1999) *The Tenacity of Ethnicity: a Siberian Saga in Global Perspective*, Princeton: Princeton University Press.

Basilov, V.N. (1978) 'Vestiges of transvestism in Central-Asian shamanism.', in V. Diószegi and M. Hoppál (eds) *Shamanism in Siberia*. Budapest: Akadémiai Kiadó.

—— (1984) 'The study of shamanism in Soviet ethnography', in M. Hoppál (ed.) *Shamanism in Eurasia, part 1*, Göttingen: Edition Herodot.

Black, L. (1973) 'The Nivkh (Gilyak) of the Sakhalin and the Lower Amur', *Arctic Anthropology* 10(1): 1–110.

—— (1977) 'The Konyag (the inhabitants of the island of Kodiak) by Iosaf [Bolotov] (1794–1799) and by Gideon (1804–1807)', *Arctic Anthropology* 14(2): 79–108.

Boas, F. (1901–7) *The Eskimo of Baffin Land and Hudson Bay*. New York: American Museum of Natural History.

Bogoras, W.G. (1904) *The Chukchee*, New York: American Museum of Natural History.

—— (1930) 'The shamanistic call and the period of initiation in Northern Asia and Northern America', in (no editor) *23rd International Congress of Americanists*, New York: International Congress of Americanists.

Butler, K.J. (1974) 'My uncle went to the Moon', *Artscanada* 184/187: 154–8.

Callender, C. and L.M. Kochems. (1983) 'The North American Berdache', *Current Anthropology* 24: 433–56.

Chard, C. (1961) 'Sternberg's [sic] materials on the sexual life of the Gilyak', *Anthropological Papers of the University of Alaska* 10(1): 13–23.

Czaplicka, M.A. (1914) *Aboriginal Siberia*. London: Oxford University Press.

Delaby, L. (1984) 'Shamans and mothers of twins', in M. Hoppál (ed.) *Shamanism in Eurasia, part 1*, Göttingen: Edition Herodot.

van Deusen, K. (1999) *Raven and the Rock: Storytelling in Chukotka*, Seattle: University of Washington Press.

Devereux, G. (1937) 'Institutionalised homosexuality of the Mohave Indians', *Human Biology* 9: 498–527.

Diachenko, V. (1994) 'The horse in Yakut shamanism', in G. Seaman and J.S. Day (eds) *Ancient Traditions: Shamanism in Central Asia and the Americas*, Denver: University of Colorado Press/ Denver Museum of Natural History.

Diószegi, V. (1968) 'The three-grade amulets among the Nanai (Golds)', in V. Diószegi (ed.) *Popular Beliefs and Folklore Tradition in Siberia*. Bloomington: Indiana University Press.

Dömötör, T. (1984) 'The problem of the Hungarian female *táltos*', in M. Hoppál (ed.) *Shamanism in Eurasia, part 1*, Göttingen: Edition Herodot.

Driver, H. E. (1937) *Culture Element Distributions 6: Southern Sierra Nevada*, University of California Anthropological Records 1(2). Los Angeles: UCLA.

—— (1939) *Culture Element Distributions 10: Northwest California*. University of California Anthropological Records 1(6). Los Angeles: UCLA.

Driver, J.C. (1999) 'Raven skeletons from Paleoindian contexts, Charlie Lake Cave, British Columbia'. *American Antiquity* 64(2): 289–98.

Dyrenkova, N.P. (1930) 'Bear worship among Turkish tribes of Siberia', in (no editor) *23rd International Congress of Americanists*, New York: International Congress of Americanists.

Eliade, M. (1964) *Shamanism: Archaic Techniques of Ecstasy*, Princeton: Princeton University Press.

Fienup-Rirodan, A. (1994) *Boundaries and Passages: Rule and Ritual in Yup'ik Eskimo Oral Tradition*. Norman: University of Oklahoma Press.

Fire/Lame Deer, J. and Erdoes, R. (1972) *Lame Deer: Seeker of Visions*. New York: Simon and Schuster.

Fleming, A.L. (1956) *Archibald the Arctic*, New York: Appleton-Century-Crofts, Inc.

Foulks, E.F. (1972) *The Arctic Hysterias of the North Alaskan Eskimo*, Anthropological Studies 10, Washington, D.C.: American Anthropological Association.

Freed, S.A., Freed, R.S. and Williamson, L. (1997) 'Tough fieldworkers: history and personalities of the Jesup Expedition', in L. Kendall, B. Mathé and T.R. Miller (eds) *Drawing shadows to stone: the photography of the Jesup North Pacific Expedition, 1897–1902*, New York: American Museum of Natural History.

Fulton, R. and Anderson, S.W. (1992) 'The Amerindian 'man-woman': gender, liminality and cultural continuity', *Current Anthropology* 33(5): 603–10.

Furst, P.T. (1977) 'The roots and continuities of shamanism', in A.T. Brodsky, R. Danesewich and N. Johnson (eds) *Stones, Bones and Skin: Ritual and Shamanic Art*, Toronto: Society for Arts Publications.

—— (1994) 'Introduction: an overview of shamanism', in G. Seaman and J.S. Day (eds) *Ancient Traditions: Shamanism in Central Asia and the Americas*, Denver: University of Colorado Press/ Denver Museum of Natural History.

Gemuev, I.N. (1989) 'Bear cult in Western Siberia', in M. Hoppál and J. Pentikäinen (eds) *Uralic mythology and folklore*. Budapest: Ethnographic Institute of the Hungarian Academy of Sciences.

Goodchild, P. (1991) *Raven Tales*, Chicago: Chicago Review Press.

Grambo, R. (1989) 'Unmanliness and *seiðr*: problems concerning the change of sex', in M. Hoppál and O.J. von Sadovszky (eds) *Shamanism: Past and Present*, Budapest: Istor Books.

Grant, B. (ed.) (1999) 'Editorial commentary', in L. Shternberg. *The social organization of the Gilyak*, Seattle: University of Washington Press.

Grim, J.A. (1983) *The Shaman: Patterns of Siberian and Ojibway Healing*. Norman: University of Oklahoma Press.

Hajdú, P. (1968) 'The classification of Samoyed Shamans', in V. Diószegi (ed.) *Popular Beliefs and Folklore Tradition in Siberia*, Bloomington: Indiana University Press.

Hallowell, A.I. (1926) 'Bear ceremonialism in the northern hemisphere', *American Anthropologist* 28(1): 1–175.

Hamayon, R. (1984) 'Is there a typically female exercise of shamanism in patrilinear societies such as the Buryat?', in M. Hoppál (ed.) *Shamanism in Eurasia, part 2*, Göttingen: Edition Herodot.

—— (1996) 'Game and games, fortune and dualism in Siberian shamanism', in M. Hoppál and J. Pentikäinen (eds) *Northern Religions and Shamanism*. Budapest: Akadémiai Kiadó.

Hollimon, S.E. (1998) '"Berdaches", giants, and cannibals: depictions of gender and humanness in native North American myths', paper presented at the 14th International Congress of Anthropological and Ethnological Sciences, College of William and Mary.

—— (2000) 'Archaeology of the *'Aqi*: gender and sexuality in prehistoric Chumash society', in R.A. Schmidt and B.L. Voss (eds) *Archaeologies of Sexuality*, London: Routledge.

Hoppál, M. (1993) 'Studies on Eurasian shamanism', in M. Hoppál and K.D. Howard (eds) *Shamans and Cultures*, Budapest: Akadémiai Kiadó.

Hultkrantz, Å. (1981) 'North American Indian religions in a circumpolar perspective', in P. Hovens (ed.) *North American Indian Studies: European Contributions*, Göttingen: Edition Herodot.

—— (1994) 'Religion and environment among the Saami: an ecological study', in T. Irimoto and T. Yamada (eds) *Circumpolar Religion and Ecology: An Anthropology of the North*, Tokyo: University of Tokyo Press.

Ingold, T. (1986) *The Appropriation of Nature: Essays on Human Ecology and Social Relations*, Manchester: Manchester University Press.

Irimoto, T. (1994) 'Concluding remarks', in T. Irimoto and T. Yamada (eds) *Circumpolar Religion and Ecology: An Anthropology of the North*, Tokyo: University of Tokyo Press.

Jochelson, W. (1908) *The Koryak*, New York: American Museum of Natural History.

—— (1930) 'The ancient and present Kamchadal and the similarity of their culture to that of the Northwestern American Indians', in (no editor) *23rd International Congress of Americanists*, New York: International Congress of Americanists.

Kálmán, B. (1968) 'Two purification rites in the bear cult of the Ob-Ugrians.', in V. Diószegi (ed.) *Popular Beliefs and Folklore Tradition in Siberia*, Bloomington: Indiana University Press.

Kaplan, S.A. (1984) 'Note', in E.S. Burch (ed.) *The Central Yup'ik Eskimos*. Supplementary issue of *Études/Inuit/Studies* 8:2.

Kirkpatrick, R.C. (1999) 'The evolution of human homosexual behavior", *Current Anthropology* 41(3): 385–98.

Klaniczay, G. (1984) 'Shamanistic elements in Central European witchcraft', in M. Hoppál (ed.) *Shamanism in Eurasia, part 2*, Göttingen: Edition Herodot.

Kono, M. and Fitzhugh, W.W. (1999) 'Ainu and Northwest Coast peoples: a comparison', in W.W. Fitzhugh and C.O. Dubreuil (eds) *Ainu: Spirit of a Northern People*. Washington, DC: Smithsonian Institution.

Krasheninnikov, S.P. (1972) [1755] *Explorations of Kamchatka 1735–1741*, Portland: Oregon Historical Society.

Kroeber, A.L. (1925) *Handbook of the Indians of California*. Washington, DC: Smithsonian Institution.

—— (1952 [1940] 'Psychosis or social sanction', in A.L. Kroeber (ed.) *The Nature of Culture*, Chicago: University of Chicago Press.

Kürti, L. (1996) 'Eroticism, sexuality, and gender reversal in Hungarian culture', in S.P. Ramet (ed.) *Gender Reversals and Gender Cultures: Anthropological and Historical Perspectives*. London: Routledge.

de Laguna, F. (1994) 'Some early circumpolar studies', in T. Irimoto and T. Yamada (eds) *Circumpolar religion and ecology*, Tokyo: University of Tokyo Press.

La Barre, W. (1970) *The Ghost Dance: Origins of Religion*. London: Dell.

Lang, S. (1998) *Men as Women, Women as Men: Changing Gender in Native American Cultures*, Austin: University of Texas Press.

Lowie, R.H. (1934) 'Religious ideas and practices of the Eurasiatic and North American areas', in E.E. Evans-Pritchard, R. Firth, B. Malinowski and I. Schapera (eds) *Essays Presented to C.G. Seligman*, London: Kegan Paul, Trench, Trubner & Co. Ltd.

Lundmark, B. (1987) 'Rijkuo-Maja and Silboe-Gåmmoe – towards the question of female shamanism in the Saami Area', in T. Ahlbäck (ed.) *Saami Religion*, Åbo: Donner Institute.

Meletinksy, E..M. (1980) 'The epic of Raven among the Paleoasiatics: relations between Northern Asia and Northwest America in folklore', *Diogenes* 110: 98–133.

Miller, J. (1982) 'People, Berdaches, and left-handed bears: human variation in Native America', *Journal of Anthropological Research* 38: 274–87.

Murphy, J.M. (1964) 'Psychotherapeutic aspects of shamanism on St. Lawrence Island, Alaska', in Kiev, A. (ed.) *Magic, Faith, and Healing*. New York: The Free Press.

Napolskikh, V.V. (1992) 'Proto-Uralic world picture: a reconstruction', in M. Hoppál and J. Pentikäinen (eds) *Northern Religions and Shamanism*. Budapest: Akadémiai Kiadó.

Novik, E.S. (1990) 'Ritual and folklore in Siberian shamanism: experiment in a comparison of structures', in M.M. Balzer (ed.) *Shamanism: Soviet Studies of Traditional Religion in Siberia and Central Asia*, Armonk, NY: M.E. Sharpe.

Osgood, C. (1940) *Ingalik Material Culture*, Publications in Anthropology 22, New Haven: Yale University.

Rasmussen, K. (1929) *Intellectual Culture of the Iglulik Eskimos*. Report of the Fifth Thule Expedition 1921–24, vol. 7(1), Copenhagen: Gyldendalske Boghandel, Nordisk Forlag.

—— (1931) *The Netsilik Eskimos: Social Life and Spiritual Culture*, Report of the Fifth Thule Expedition 1921–24, vol. 8(1–2). Copenhagen: Gyldendalske Boghandel, Nordisk Forlag.

Ray, V.F. (1963) *Primitive Pragmatists: The Modoc Indians of northern California*, Seattle: University of Washington Press.

Ripinsky-Naxon, M. (1993) *The Nature of Shamanism: Substance and Function of a Religious Metaphor*, Albany: State University of New York Press.

—— (1997) *Sexuality, Shamanism, and Transformation*, Berlin: Verlag für Wissenschaft und Bildung.

Roscoe, W. (1987) 'Bibliography of Berdache and alternative gender roles among North American Indians', *Journal of Homosexuality* 14(3/4): 81–171.

—— (1999) *Changing Ones: Third and Fourth Genders in Native North America*, New York: St Martin's Press.

von Sadovszky, O.J. (1989) 'Linguistic evidence for the Siberian origin of the Central California Indian Shamanism', in M. Hoppál and O.J. von Sadovszky (eds) *Shamanism: Past and Present*. Budapest: Istor Books.

—— (1993) 'The Wintu shaman', in M. Hoppál and K.D. Howard (eds) *Shamans and Cultures*, Budapest: Akadémiai Kiadó.

—— (1996) *The Discovery of California: a Cal-Ugrian Comparative Study*, Budapest: Akadémiai Kiadó.

Saladin D'Anglure, B. (1986) 'Du foetus au chamane: la construction d'un "Troisième Sexe" Inuit', *Études/Inuit/Studies* 10(1–2): 25–113.

—— (1988) 'Penser le 'féminin' chamanique, ou le 'tiers-sexe' des chamanes Inuit', *Recherches Amérindiennes au Québec* XVIII (2–3): 19–50.

—— (1989) 'La part du chamane ou le communisme sexuel Inuit dans L'Arctique central Canadien', *Journal de la Société des Américanistes* 75: 133–71.

—— (1992a) 'Shamanism and transvestism among the Inuit of Canada', in A.I. Gogolev (ed.) *Shamanizm kak religiia*. Yakutsk: Yakutsk University.

—— (1992b) 'Rethinking Inuit shamanism through the concept of "Third Gender",' in M. Hoppál and J. Pentikäinen (eds) *Northern Religions and Shamanism*. Budapest: Akadémiai Kiadó.

—— (1993) '*Sila*, the ordering principle of the Inuit cosmology', in M. Hoppál and K.D. Howard (eds) *Shamans and Cultures*, Budapest: Akadémiai Kiadó.

—— (1994) 'Brother Moon (*Taqqiq*), Sister Sun (*Siqiniq*), and the Direction of the World (*Sila*): from arctic cosmography to Inuit cosmology', in T. Irimoto and T. Yamada (eds) *Circumpolar Religion and Ecology: An Anthropology of the North*. Tokyo: University of Tokyo Press.

Schmidt, É. (1989) 'Bear cult and mythology of the northern Ob-Ugrians', in M. Hoppál and J. Pentikäinen (eds) *Uralic mythology and folklore*, Budapest: Ethnographic Institute of the Hungarian Academy of Sciences.

Schmidt, R.A. (2000) 'Shamans and Northern cosmology: the direct historical approach to Mesolithic sexuality', in R. Schmidt and B. Voss (eds) *Archaeologies of Sexuality*, London: Routledge.

Shternberg, L. (1925) 'Divine election in primitive religion', in (no editor) *21st International Congress of Americanists*, The Hague: International Congress of Americanists.

—— (1999) *The Social Organization of the Gilyak*, Seattle: University of Washington Press.

Siikala, A.-L. (1978) *The Rite Technique of the Siberian Shaman*, Helsinki: Suomalainen Tiedeakatemia.

Sokolova, Z.P. (1989) 'A survey of the Ob-Ugrian shamanism', in M. Hoppál and O.J. von Sadovszky (eds) *Shamanism: Past and Present*, Budapest: Istor Books.

Taylor, J.G. (1989) 'Shamanic sex roles in traditional Labrador Inuit society', in M. Hoppál and O.J. von Sadovszky (eds) *Shamanism: Past and Present*, Budapest: Istor Books.

Thayer, J.S. (1980) 'The Berdache of the Northern Plains: a socioreligious perspective', *Journal of Anthropological Research* 36: 287–93.

Turner, V.W. (1969) *The Ritual Process: Structure and Anti-structure*, Chicago: Aldine Publishing Co.

Unsgaard, S. (1985) 'Gesture and posture in Saami bear ceremonialism', in T. Ahlback (ed.) *Saami Religion*, Stockholm: Almqvist and Wiksell.

—— (1987) 'On time reckoning in old Saami culture', in L. Bäckman and Å. Hultkrantz (eds) *Saami Pre-Christian Religion: Studies of the Oldest Traces of Religion among the Saamis*, Stockholm: Almqvist and Wiksell.

Utley, F.L. (1974) 'Four channels to the Americas', *Current Anthropology* 15(1): 5–27.

Vasilevic, G.M. (1963) 'Early concepts about the universe among the Evenks (Materials)', in H.N. Michael (ed.) *Studies in Siberian Shamanism.* Toronto: University of Toronto Press for the Arctic Institute of America.

—— (1968) 'The acquisition of shamanistic ability among the Evenki (Tungus)', in V. Diószegi (ed.) *Popular Beliefs and Folklore Tradition in Siberia,* Bloomington: Indiana University Press.

Voegelin, E.W. (1942) *Culture Element Distributions 20: Northwest California,* Anthropological Records 7(2). Los Angeles: UCLA.

Williams, W.L. (1992) *The Spirit and the Flesh: Sexual Diversity in American Indian Culture,* Boston: Beacon Press.

Willoughby, N.C. (1963) *Division of Labor among the Indians of California,* Reports of the University of California Archaeological Survey 60. Los Angeles: UCLA.

Zachrisson, I. (1985) 'Archaeological finds from Saami territory', in L. Bäckman and Å. Hultkrantz (eds) *Saami Pre-Christian Religion: Studies of the Oldest Traces of Religion among the Saamis*, Stockholm: Almqvist and Wiskell.

Zvelebil, M. (1993) 'Concepts of time and 'presencing' the Mesolithic', *Archaeological Review from Cambridge* 12: 51–70.

—— (1998) 'Hunter-gatherer ritual landscapes: questions of time, space and representation', paper presented at the European Association of Archaeologists' 4th Annual Meeting, Gothenburg, Sweden.

Chapter Nine

Shamanism and the iconography of Palaeo-Eskimo art

Patricia D. Sutherland

INTRODUCTION

The Palaeo-Eskimos were the first widespread occupants of Arctic North America. They are associated with archaeological complexes related to the Arctic Small Tool tradition, among them the Denbigh Flint Complex, Independence, Saqqaq, Pre-Dorset and Dorset cultures. The archaeological evidence of their occupation extends from southwestern Alaska to northeastern Greenland. The Palaeo-Eskimos first appeared between 4000 and 5000 years ago, and continued in some regions of the Central and Eastern Arctic until well into the past millenium when they disappeared from the archaeological record (Figure 9.1). Their demise is often related to the eastward movement of ancestral Inuit people from their original homelands in Alaska (McGhee 1996).

An association between Palaeo-Eskimo art and shamanic thought has long been recognised, and was explicitly stated in an important pair of articles published in 1967 by archaeologist W.E. Taylor Jr. and art historian George Swinton. Taylor and Swinton, in company with other scholars who have examined the art of the Palaeo-Eskimos, usually dealt with 'shamanism' or 'shamanic thought' as a distinctive and uniform entity characterizing the world-view and religious beliefs of peoples occupying the circumpolar regions of the globe. If specific relationships have been proposed between the shamanic art of the Palaeo-Eskimos and the religious thought of a particular northern people, the suggested link has almost invariably been with Inuit culture, as it is known from Arctic Canada and Greenland.

Such an association between Palaeo-Eskimo and Inuit cultures seemed natural when Taylor and Swinton were writing their articles in the late 1960s. At that stage in our knowledge of Arctic prehistory, most archaeologists assumed some form of ancestor-descendant relationship between the two widespread prehistoric cultures known from Arctic North America. Such a relationship was implied in the name Palaeo-Eskimo which was derived from the speculative historical ethnology of the early twentieth century, and was readily attached to Arctic Small Tool tradition materials.

Although similarities had been noted between Arctic Small Tool tradition artifact styles and those of the Siberian Neolithic, the tradition was viewed as having developed primarily in Alaska, perhaps from early cultures of the Alaskan interior or the Aleutian Islands. The Arctic Small Tool tradition was thought to have given rise to a series of more recent Alaskan cultures, and to have made a major contribution to the cultural ancestry of the Eskimo peoples, if not

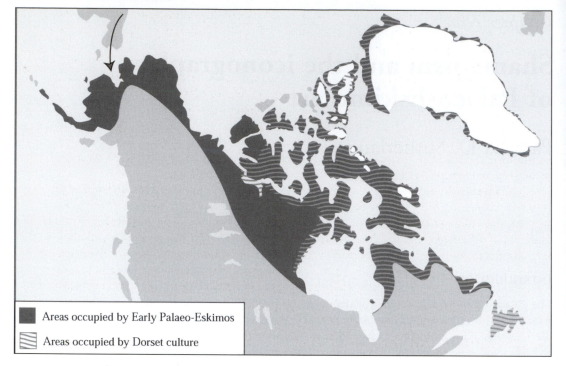

Figure 9.1 Map showing areas occupied by Early Palaeo-Eskimos and the Dorset culture.

providing its entire foundation. This relatively simple picture of Arctic prehistory has not stood the test of time and more adequate archaeological knowledge. On the one hand, archaeological work in northern North America has failed to discover a possible ancestor for the Arctic Small Tool tradition/Palaeo-Eskimo materials which appear suddenly in Alaska at some time shortly after 5000 years ago. The archaeology of northeastern Siberia, on the other hand, has extended our knowledge of the existence of Palaeo-Eskimo-like Neolithic cultures at the same time period (Mochanov 1969). As a result, the Siberian Neolithic origin of the Palaeo-Eskimos has become a widely accepted view among prehistorians working in Arctic North America. Further, it is increasingly likely that Eskimo origins are grounded in the ancient cultures of southern Alaska, adjacent to the homelands of the linguistically related Aleuts (Dumond 1998). If the Palaeo-Eskimo peoples of central and northern Alaska played a significant role in the development of Inuit culture, this role is not clearly apparent in the archaeological record.

In view of the current reconstruction of Arctic prehistory, it no longer seems appropriate to look exclusively to Inuit shamanic thought as a means of interpreting the imagery of Palaeo-Eskimo art. Rather, the postulated Siberian origin of the Palaeo-Eskimos suggests that more fruitful interpretations may be derived from comparisons with the shamanic thought and practices of Siberian peoples.

Before attempting to investigate such comparisons, one must acknowledge that archaeological evidence is clearly inadequate as a means of reconstructing the totality of a past belief system. Although religious practices can to some extent be reconstructed from the physical artifacts associated with these practices, the systems of mythological beliefs which give rise to or validate religious rites and practices remain largely hidden. As well, even a superficial examination of the ethnographic literature indicates that circumpolar shamanism is not the broad and uniform entity which is implied in much of the work attempting to interpret the art of the Palaeo-Eskimos. Rather, the traditional world-views and religious beliefs of northern peoples as described over the past one or two centuries show significant diversity across cultural boundaries. It is also apparent that our knowledge of the shamanic beliefs of any individual culture is limited both by the inherent complexity of belief systems and the inadequacy of ethnographic interpretation and reporting of those systems. Saladin D'Anglure (1997) has recently pointed out that the study of shamanism has been largely neglected among the Canadian Inuit since the time of Rasmussen, as a result of the linguistic deficiencies of ethnologists, and their frequent dependence on missionary hosts in Inuit communities. Similar problems have probably constrained the study of shamanism among other northern peoples, or have resulted in an incomplete or confused understanding of an extremely complex subject.

Given these constraints in the archaeological evidence and in ethnographic knowledge of northern shamanic practice, is it possible to make useful observations on the relationship between shamanic thought and the iconography of Palaeo-Eskimo art? It is the position of this author that a limited range of observations can be made, and that the importance of these inferences is augmented by the preservation of the Palaeo-Eskimo artistic system over a broad geographical range and a time period of several millennia. This preservation allows a unique opportunity to observe the dynamics of artistic change, and less directly the dynamics of change in the belief system in which the art is based.

DESCRIPTION OF PALAEO-ESKIMO ART

The portion of Palaeo-Eskimo artistic activity which is archaeologically preserved consists primarily of small sculptures carved in ivory, driftwood, antler, bone and occasionally soapstone. The only exception to this statement comprises a number of localities along the southern shore of Hudson Strait where petroglyphs representing human-like faces have been etched into soapstone outcrops (Saladin D'Anglure 1962; Arsenault *et al.* 1998). These petroglyphs, as well as the overwhelming majority of carvings, are associated with the last 2,000 years of Palaeo-Eskimo occupation, the period ascribed to the Dorset culture; the art of the Palaeo-Eskimo peoples of Canada and Greenland is therefore commonly referred to as 'Dorset art'. Close to one thousand such carvings have been recovered from archaeological excavations. The majority of the objects which we call 'art' in Palaeo-Eskimo assemblages can be interpreted as personal amulets used for hunting and other types of magic, and objects that appear to have been used in shamanic ritual. Most of the sculptures portray humans or animals in a wide variety of realistic and abstract representations. Almost all animals of the Arctic world are depicted, from bears to swans to sculpins. However, the frequency of depiction of a species varies greatly, with humans and bears being portrayed most often.

The relative frequencies with which species are portrayed are far from constant through time and space. There is, for example, a significant increase in the frequency of portrayal of humans, seals, and bears during the 'Late Dorset' period, in the centuries between approximately AD 700 and 1300. This is the period which saw a major florescence in artistic activity, and which produced the majority of Palaeo-Eskimo carvings in museum collections. Not all species representations increased however; for example, the relative frequency of walrus depictions declined during Late Dorset times. This may be related to the wide geographic distribution of Late Dorset collections, for this period saw the expansion of Palaeo-Eskimos into many areas where walrus were not a significant economic resource. Economic, environmental, and historical factors, as well as those relating directly to religious thought, appear to have had some influence on regional and temporal variants of Dorset art (Sutherland 1997a).

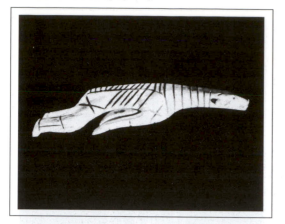

Figure 9.5 Ivory flying bear with skeletal markings, *c.*AD 0–500 (Photo: Canadian Museum of Civilization; NhHd-1:2655).

either the spirit-helper of a shaman, or the shaman himself in bear form and in the act of flying to another realm. Such an interpretation is supported by the presence of a skeletal pattern that is often incised on the surface of the bear carvings, suggesting that a spirit creature rather than an ordinary animal is being portrayed. A wood carving representing a human which seems to take the same posture as the bear, with arms held close to the body and feet tilted so that the toes point backwards, may also represent a figure in flight. This theme is also suggested in the bear-human transformation figure noted earlier, as well as in a number of other representations of human figures.

The concept of flight appears to have a widespread distribution among northern peoples (Balzer 1996). Its prominence in Inuit belief encouraged scholars to interpret Dorset carvings of bears in this posture as flying bears, or even specifically as the *Tornarssuk* spirit-helper figure of Greenlandic and eastern Inuit belief (Swinton 1967; Taylor 1967). However, an alternative explanation, first proposed by Larsen (1970) but not widely accepted, might be reconsidered: that these carvings represent a hanging bear skin, such as those featured in the bear-cult rituals of Siberian peoples and American Indians of the northern forests. Supporting this interpretation is the fact that some of the Dorset bear figures have a ventral slit or groove, occasionally showing traces of red ochre, which suggest that the animal represented has been eviscerated and that perhaps the skin alone, or skin and symbolic skeleton are portrayed. While the ritual treatment of killed bears was practised among Inuit groups, it does not appear to be a prominent feature of Inuit culture (Hallowell 1926; Larsen 1970), but may have been more important to their Palaeo-Eskimo predecessors in Arctic North America. Evidence in support of such a suggestion comes from Late Dorset sites on Dundas Island in the High Arctic, where the skulls and fore-leg bones of several bears were found in the vicinity of the dwellings, and at least one bear skull had been painted with dots of red ochre, suggesting that these bones had been retained for a ritual purpose (McGhee 1975; personal communication 1996). This evidence, and perhaps the interpretation of 'flying bear' carvings as depictions of bear skins undergoing ritual treatment, hint at similar practices in the cultures of Siberia and subarctic North America (Hallowell 1926). It may be that both interpretations of the bear figures apply, in that the shaman and his helping spirits are often linked to hunting magic and intercession, and that several distinct layers of meaning may be attributed to specimens such as these.

A third interrelated theme, the spiritual importance of the skeleton in Palaeo-Eskimo belief, has been proposed on the basis of its representation on depictions of 'flying bear' figures, as well as on portrayals of humans, seals and other animals (Figure 9.6). Among northern hunting peoples, the view of the skeleton as not simply a remnant of a dead animal, but as a container or representative of the soul or spirit of the creature is a widely held belief (Pavlinskaya 1994). It has been of particular importance to shamanic practice, with both Siberian and Inuit shamans symbolically reducing themselves to skeletal form in order to attain the abilities of flight and intercession (cf. Rasmussen 1929: 114). The incised X-ray motifs of Palaeo-Eskimo art are consistent with such a view of the skeleton, but the specific reasons which led to the carvings of these motifs are more difficult to discern. It is apparent that the artistic representation of the skeleton is extremely stylised, with bones represented as a standardised series of lines and joints by '+' or 'x' marks. Such stylization must be the result of a long process of abstraction, during which particular meanings of the markings must have undergone considerable mutation. It is interesting to note that the recently discovered frozen body of the 'Ice-Man' from the glaciers on the Austrian–Italian

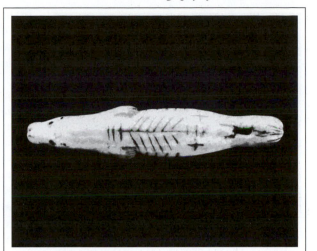

Figure 9.6 Ivory seal with skeletal markings, *c.*AD 1000 (Photo: Canadian Museum of Civilization; QiLd-1:2215).

border, bore tattooed '+' marks on the knee and ankle, remarkably similar to those which appear on the joints of Dorset 'flying bears' and other carvings (Spindler 1995: 168). This 5,000–year-old find suggests that joint-markings must have had a widespread distribution in Eurasia at the time that ancestral Palaeo-Eskimos reached North America, and that the interpretation of such markings may be quite different than the explanations of beliefs concerning the skeleton given by nineteenth- or twentieth-century informants on northern shamanic traditions.

In addition to sculptures that carry the 'X-ray' motif, carvings representing isolated limbs, sections of the vertebral column, and skulls of animals point to the importance of the skeleton in the Palaeo-Eskimo belief system.

OTHER IMAGERY IN PALAEO-ESKIMO ART

Potential insight into Palaeo-Eskimo belief systems is also provided by a class of artifacts which are found in limited numbers in Dorset culture assemblages. These are small, flat disks cut from bone, usually from the thin portion of a scapula. They are perforated with a central hole, and marked with radiating lines which often number eight or sixteen. Similar disk-shaped objects are widely distributed among Siberian peoples, where they are commonly associated with the clothing of shamans (Prokofyeva 1963: 137). They have been interpreted as representations of a cosmological plane with the central opening or the ice-hole leading to a submarine or subterranean world, and as representations of the sun and moon (Jochelson 1934; Lommel 1967; Martynov 1991). Many of the disks are also divided into multiples of four and may have additional meaning, perhaps associated with the cardinal directions. As with so many other elements of shamanic symbolism, a variety of interpretations suggests either a diversity of beliefs or a multi-layered symbolic system which alluded to several levels of understanding. The recurrence of such a specific form in Palaeo-Eskimo culture strongly suggests that the idea derives from a Siberian connection and that Dorset people may have maintained similar views of the world.

Comparable imagery is known from the ancient cultural traditions of Alaska, occurring in the Old Bering Sea and Ipiutak cultures which existed contemporaneously with Dorset culture

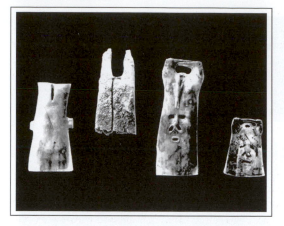

Figure 9.7 Four bell-shaped tubes, carved in ivory. From left to right: (a) 500–1BC; (b) *c*.AD 0; (c) *c*.AD 1000; (d) *c*.AD 1000 (photo: Canadian Museum of Civilization; QiLd–1: 12; K kHh–3: 914; NiHf–4:115; SiHw–1: 453).

in the Eastern Arctic (Chaussonnet 1995: 65; Larsen and Rainey 1948: 138). However, such images occur very rarely in the later Inuit cultures of Alaska, Canada and Greenland. The most striking example, an ivory disk with sixteen divisions, was excavated from an early Inuit archaeological site in High Arctic Canada, a region where Dorset people may have survived and directly contacted their Inuit successors (Sutherland, 1993: 329). The recurring appearance of quartered or eight-sectioned circles in contemporary Inuit art may be fortuitous, or further evidence of the tenuous survival of an ancient Palaeo-Eskimo symbol into a later culture (e.g. Blodgett and Bouchard 1986: 118, 119).

Imagery on other Palaeo-Eskimo artifacts appears to represent complex symbolism, but a symbolism which is not clearly related to that known from any other northern peoples. An example of this occurs on bell-shaped ivory tubes carved from the root ends of walrus tusks. These objects first appear about 2500 years ago as unadorned tubes, but an example from about 2000 years ago has had the edges extended in the form of two bear-heads facing one another across the top of the tube. A few centuries later the bears were replaced by walrus with their bodies extending up the outer edges of the artifacts and their tusks interlocking across the top. A pair of human faces have now been added to the opposite sides of the tube, and on one Late Dorset example a bear and a seal are portrayed on opposite sides above the faces (Figure 9.7). In another Late Dorset example, a seal–human transformation figure is added. Lemoine *et al.* (1995) have suggested that the depiction on these tubes of humans, walrus, and occasionally bear and seal may relate to a specific complex mythological narrative. If that is the case, then this narrative may have been unique to the Palaeo-Eskimo tradition and may have changed considerably over two millennia before disappearing with the last of the Palaeo-Eskimos. It should not be surprising that a people as isolated as the Palaeo-Eskimos would have developed a distinctive mythological tradition, portions of which may not relate to the myths and beliefs of other northern peoples.

CONCLUSIONS

When William Taylor and George Swinton examined the shamanic associations of Palaeo-Eskimo art, they dealt with the art as a unitary phenomenon which was interpreted as sharing in a widespread and uniform shamanic belief system common to northern peoples, and which shared specific attributes with the belief system of the Inuit people. Since the time of their study, the corpus of known Palaeo-Eskimo art has grown significantly and now comprises material from a broader geographical and temporal range. In examining the material currently available in museum collections, the most immediate impression is of diversity (Lyons 1982; Sutherland 1997b). The art of the Palaeo-Eskimos was obviously not static, but very dynamic, changing over time in many different directions and probably in reaction to many different stimuli. Changes are apparent in the overall rate of artistic production, in the relative frequency with which specific subjects or symbols are portrayed, in the degree of abstraction or complexity of symbolic combinations, and in the forms of symbols themselves. The best example is in the portrayal of bears, but changes of various kinds are also very apparent in the portrayal of humans. For example in the enduring tradition of carving small ivory maskettes, the form changes from the earliest known example, a serene tattooed face from 3,900 to 3,600 years ago (Helmer 1986), to a vaguely animal-like face of 2,000 years ago, to the grotesque faces found on maskettes carved about 1,000 years ago.

It is tempting to suggest that changes in the art of the Palaeo-Eskimos reflect a similar set of changes which occurred in the symbolic system and the belief system with which the art was clearly associated. Rather than seeing a 'shamanic belief system' as the product of an ancient and continuous cultural pattern, possibly rooted in the beliefs of Palaeolithic hunters, we should perhaps interpret the evidence for diversity and change in Palaeo-Eskimo art as evidence that shamanic beliefs have also been mutable in the cultural traditions of the past several thousand years.

An acceptance of this view implies that interpretations of Palaeo-Eskimo art based on direct comparisons with the belief systems of nineteenth- and twentieth-century peoples have been somewhat naive. Rather than viewing evidence for similarities between Palaeo-Eskimo and Inuit cosmological or religious beliefs as indicative of a 'common symbolic reservoir', as has been suggested by Lemoine *et al.* (1995), we might more aptly visualise parallel symbolic streams flowing from an ancient past and contributing in unique ways to the reservoir of beliefs among the northern peoples of recent centuries. From this viewpoint, Dorset art is a uniquely preserved cultural stream which can provide information on the reservoir's formation.

Also viewed from this perspective, we should not be surprised at apparent disjunctions between the symbolic system of the Palaeo-Eskimos and those of recent Inuit culture. If the Palaeo-Eskimos originally derived from Siberia about 5,000 years ago, at a time when ancestral Inuit were occupying southern Alaska, then one might expect the Palaeo-Eskimo religious and symbolic systems to hold more in common with the descendants of similar 5000 year old Siberian cultures. This may in fact be seen in evidence from Dorset art, which hints at the importance of human/bird transformation, complex ritual associated with bears, and the perforated disk as a symbol of cosmological order.

But Palaeo-Eskimo art cannot be seen as a simple transfer of Siberian beliefs and symbols to North America. Rather, it should be interpreted as a palimpsest of layered beliefs: some originating in the Siberian shamanism of 5,000 years ago, which must have been considerably different than the shamanism of the past century; some perhaps adopted through contact with American Indian peoples living in adjacent forested areas; some modified through contacts with the evolving Eskimo cultural traditions of Alaska. Just as scholars have suggested that Christian missionary influence has modified aspects of the mythology and belief systems of northern peoples in recent times (Sonne 1986), contact and influences in the past must have also produced significant changes.

The most interesting aspect of Palaeo-Eskimo art may not be in specific interpretations of the iconography, but in the insight which it provides into the malleable and dynamic nature of the symbolic and belief systems of a hunting society.

ACKNOWLEDGEMENTS

I would like to acknowledge Jean Blodgett and Robert McGhee with whom I have had many useful discussions on the subject of Palaeo-Eskimo art. All photographs were taken by Harry Foster from the Canadian Museum of Civilization.

REFERENCES

Arsenault, D., Gagnon, L. and Gendron, D. (1998) 'Investigations archéologiques récentes au sud de Kangirsujuaq et sur le site à pétroglyphes de Qajartalik, détroit d'Hudson, Nunavik', *Études/Inuit/Studies* 22 (2): 77–115.

Balzer, M.M. (1996) 'Flights of the sacred: symbolism and theory in Siberian shamanism', *American Anthropologist* 98 (2): 305–18.

Blodgett, J. and Bouchard, M. (1986) *Jessie Oonark, a retrospective,* Winnipeg: the Winnipeg Art Gallery.

Chaussonnet, V. (1995) *Crossroads Alaska, Native Cultures of Alaska and Siberia,* Washington, DC: Arctic Studies Center, National Museum of Natural History, Smithsonian Institution.

Dumond, D. (1998) *The Hillside Site, St Lawrence Island, Alaska,* University of Oregon Anthropological Papers 55, Eugene: University of Oregon.

Fitzhugh, W.W. and Kaplan, S.A. (1982) *Inua, Spirit World of the Bering Sea Eskimo,* Washington, DC: Smithsonian Institution Press.

Hallowell, A.I. (1926) 'Bear ceremonialism in the northern hemisphere', *American Anthropologist* 28 (1): 1–175.

Helmer, J. (1986) 'A face from the past: an Early Pre-Dorset ivory maskette from Devon Island, N.W.T.', *Études/Inuit/Studies* 10(1–2): 179–202.

Issenman, B.K. (1997) *Sinews of Survival, the Living Legacy of Inuit Clothing.* Vancouver: UBC Press.

Jochelson, W. (1934) *The Yakut,* Anthropological Papers of the American Museum of Natural History, 33. New York: American Museum Press.

Larsen, H. (1970) 'Some examples of bear cult among the Eskimo and other northern peoples', *Folk,* 11–12: 27–42.

Larsen, H. and Rainey, F. (1948) *Ipiutak and the Arctic Whale Hunting Culture,* Anthropological Papers of the American Museum of Natural History, 42, New York: American Museum Press.

Lemoine, G., Helmer, J.W. and Hanna, D. (1995) 'Altered states: human–animal transformational images in Dorset art', in K. Ryan and P.J. Crabtree (eds) *The Symbolic Role of Animals in Archaeology,* MASCA Research Papers in Science and Archaeology 12, Philadelphia: University of Pennsylvania Museum.

Lommel, A. (1967) *Shamanism, the Beginnings of Art,* New York: McGraw-Hill.

Lyons, D. (1982) 'Regionalism of Dorset art styles: a comparative analysis of stylistic variability in five Dorset art samples', unpublished Master's thesis, Department of Archaeology, University of Calgary.

Martynov, A. (1991) *The Ancient Art of Northern Asia,* Urbana and Chicago: University of Illinois Press.

McGhee, R. (1975) 'Late Dorset art from Dundas Island, Arctic Canada', *Folk,* 16–17: 133–45.

—— (1996) *Ancient People of the Arctic.* Vancouver: UBC Press.

Mochanov, I.A. (1969) 'The Bel'kachinck Neolithic culture on the Aldan', *Arctic Anthropology* 6(1): 104–14.

Pasztory, E. (1982) 'Shamanism and North American Indian art', in Z.P. Mathews and A. Jonaitis (eds) *Native North American Art History: Selected Readings,* Palo Alto: Peek Publications.

Pavlinskaya, L.R. (1994) 'The shaman costume: image and myth', in G. Seaman and J.S. Day (eds) *Ancient Traditions, Shamanism in Central Asia and the Americas,* Niwot, Colorado: University of Colorado Press.

Prokofyeva, Y.D. (1963) 'The costume of an Enets shaman', in H.N. Michael (ed.) *Studies in Siberian shamanism,* Arctic Institute of North America, Anthropology of the North, Translations from Russian Sources 4, Toronto: University of Toronto Press.

Rasmussen, K. (1929) *Intellectual Life of the Iglulik Eskimos,* Report of the Fifth Thule Expedition 1921–24, VII(1), Copenhagen: Gyldendalske Boghandel, Nordisk Forlag.

Saladin D'Anglure, B. (1962) 'Découverte de pétroglyphes à Qajartalik sur l'ile de Qikertaaluk', *North* IX(6): 34–9.

—— (1997) 'Pour un nouveau regard ethnographique sur le chamanisme, la possession et la christianisation'/'A new look on shamanism, possession and christianization', *Études/Inuit/Studies,* 21(1–2): 5–36.

Serov, S.I. (1988) 'Guardians and spirit-masters of Siberia', in W.W. Fitzhugh and A. Crowell (eds) *Crossroads of Continents, Cultures of Siberia and Alaska.* Washington, DC: Smithsonian Institution Press.

Sonne, B. (1986) 'Toornaarsuk, an historical proteus', *Arctic Anthroplogy* 23 (1):199–219.

Spindler, K. (1995) *The Man in the Ice,* London: Phoenix.

Sutherland, P.D. (1993) 'The history of Inuit culture', in (no editor) *In the shadow of the sun, perspectives on contemporary native art,* Canadian Ethnology Service, Mercury Paper 124. Hull, Québec: Canadian Museum of Civilization.

—— (1997a) 'Real and imagined: the representation of animals in Palaeo-Eskimo art', unpublished paper presented at the 1997 North Atlantic Biocultural Organization Conference, St John's, Newfoundland.

—— (1997b) 'The variety of artistic expression in Dorset culture', in R. Gilberg and H.C. Gulløv (eds) *Fifty Years of Arctic Research, Anthropological Studies from Greenland to Siberia,* Copenhagen: National Museum of Denmark.

Swinton, G. (1967) 'Prehistoric Dorset art: the magico-religious basis', *The Beaver* 298: 32–47.

Taylor, W.E. Jr. (1967) 'Prehistoric Dorset art: the silent echoes of culture', *The Beaver* 298: 32–47.

—— (1968) *The Arnapik and Tyara Sites, An Archaeological Study of Dorset Culture Origins.* Memoirs of the Society for American Archaeology, 22, Salt Lake City: Society for American Archaeology.

Chapter Ten

Social bonding and shamanism among Late Dorset groups in High Arctic Greenland

Hans Christian Gulløv and Martin Appelt

INTRODUCTION

The 'Dorset culture' is the term used by archaeologists to describe a homogenous artefactual complex extending from Greenland to the eastern Canadian Arctic, the latter comprising the northern Canadian archipelago and mainland coastal regions from east of Coronation Gulf to subarctic Newfoundland. During the approximately 2,000 years of its existence – terminating around 1300 AD in the High Arctic Smith Sound region and some hundred years later along the southern shores of Hudson Strait – the Dorset culture complex was continuously represented in the region around the Foxe Basin. However, no evidence of the culture has been found in the northernmost Canadian arctic and in Greenland during the Middle Dorset, i.e. the centuries around the beginning of the common era. Despite extensive investigations, no remains of dog sledges (or dog bones), seagoing vessels and other means of transport have ever been found, and the problem as to the arrival of the Dorset people in these areas remains unresolved.

Artefacts and faunal material from excavated sites indicate that the hunting of caribou, walrus and seal formed the basis of subsistence for the Dorset people. Beautiful carved representations of regional fauna and zoomorphic creatures, together with incised decorations on tools and weapons, were all common in the Dorset culture and have long been thought to indicate a developed complex of shamanistic thought, the coherence of which has been documented through similarities in workmanship and subjects chosen (Sutherland, this volume).

At the beginning of the second millennium AD, people of the Neo-Eskimo Thule culture and ancestors of the modern Inuit spread eastwards from Alaska. They were whale-hunters, well equipped with effective and fully developed means of transportation. Reaching the eastern Arctic they seem to have met the Palaeo-Eskimo Dorset people in the terminal phase of the latter's culture. From around 1300 AD onwards in the High Arctic the Dorset disappear from the archaeological record, but their use of soapstone for seal-oil lamps and snow-knives of the type used for building igloos subsequently became incorporated into the technological repertoire of the Thule culture.

WHO WERE THE 'STRONG TUNIT'?

In Inuit oral tradition stories were told about the 'Tunit' people (sing. *Tuneq*, etymologically suggested as referring to the concept of strength or firmness), and examples have been recorded from all regions of Greenland and Arctic Canada east of Coronation Gulf. The stories derive from the remote past when the Inuit were not the only inhabitants of the country in which they live at the present time. Another tribe similar to them shared their hunting grounds, but they were on good terms, both tribes living in harmony in their villages. According to the stories, the Tunit were much taller than the Inuit and were extremely strong, being able to lift large boulders which were far too heavy for the Inuit. It is said that they were able to hold on to a harpooned walrus as the Inuit hold a seal. The Tunit did not build any *kayaks*, but as they were aware of the advantages afforded by their use in hunting they stole the boats from the Inuit, who did not dare to defend their property as the Tunit were by far their superiors in strength. One story relates how a young Tuneq had taken the *kayak* of a young Inuk without asking him, and had damaged it by knocking in the bottom. The Inuk got very angry and ran a knife into the nape of the Tuneq's neck while he was sleeping. The Tunit then became afraid that the Inuit would kill them all and preferred to leave the country for good. They assembled at a certain place, and in order to deceive any pursuers they cut off the tails of their jumpers and the women tied their hair into a bunch protruding from the crown of the head (this seems to have been of importance in relation to the supernatural world as a means of 'cheating' evil spirits, and it seems also to have functioned as an ethnic marker). Many old songs either mention the Tunit or are reported to have been sung by them.

The story is a typical one told by the Inuit about the Tunit. This version was noted down by Franz Boas, who in the 1880s spent a year among the Baffin Islanders (Boas 1964: 226–8). The core of the story – the fact of friendly co-existence, the strong Tunit, and the conflict – is common to many of the versions known. But who were these Tunit and where did they disappear to? The question has engaged archaeologists since 1925, when the Dorset culture was for the first time interpreted as a prehistoric society older than that of the Thule (Jenness 1925). A further advance was made in the 1950s when joint Danish-Canadian investigations were carried out in the Foxe Basin region of the central Canadian Arctic, and local Inuit could add a number of additional illuminating stories which included descriptions of the Tunit's dwellings and tools. After having excavated a number of Palaeo-Eskimo structures in the area, the excavator Jørgen Meldgaard concluded that, 'it became obvious that the Tunit had nothing to do with the Thule culture – they were the Dorset people!' (1955: 176).

In subsequent decades, archaeologists were unable to find any *in situ* evidence for the contemporaneity of the Dorset and Thule cultures. The oral traditions about the Tunit were therefore seen as a rationalization created by the neo-Eskimos when entering the eastern Arctic with its abandoned Dorset sites. But in spite of generally poor archaeological results in specific relation to this problem, the time gap between the two cultures was reduced after excavations in High Arctic Canada seemed to indicate that some of the Thule winter houses must have been built 'very shortly after the Dorset settlement had been abandoned, perhaps even in the same season' (McGhee 1996: 218).

IN SEARCH OF THE DORSET PEOPLE AT THE 'GATEWAY TO GREENLAND'

Over decades of investigations the enigmatic Dorset culture has revealed parts of its character, but much remains to be done before the people themselves appear in flesh and blood as described in the oral traditions about the Tunit.

The stories emphasize how Tunit women were seen as very desirable by Inuit men, who then married them and brought them to live in Inuit villages. If we are to believe these tales, this would provide an explanation for a continuation of Tunit cultural traditions among the Inuit, an example being the use of snow-knives. When the Tunit decided to leave their homelands for good, a decision which must have been made somewhere in central Arctic Canada, then two routes would have been possible: one to the south, crossing the Hudson Strait where terminal Dorset culture remains from northern Québec province have been radiocarbon dated to the fifteenth century AD; and an alternative route northwards, to the Smith Sound area.

Here, at the so-called 'Gateway to Greenland', joint Danish-Greenlandic-Canadian archaeological investigations were carried out over three field campaigns in the late 1990s. The project focused upon the Late Dorset remains that had been surveyed in the early 90s by the local museum in Qaanaaq, in the Thule district. The project was part of a larger programme entitled *Man, Culture and Environment in Ancient Greenland,* which has identified three sets of cultural categories which can together describe this relationship: resource utilization and management; migration and diffusion; and cultural contacts and exchanges (Arneborg and Gulløv 1998).

The Gateway to Greenland project has produced a large number of new finds from the Late Dorset, excavated and recorded for the first time in Greenland within a well-defined cultural context. Supplemented by some fifteen radiocarbon datings made on terrestrial materials, the investigations suggest that a substantial settling of Late Dorset took place within a period that lasted about 500 years, from approximately 800 AD to about 1300 AD (Appelt and Gulløv 1999).

The initial settling of the study area around 800 AD corresponds to the general settling of the eastern High Arctic archipelago (Schledermann 1990), probably an expansion from the southern core areas (Maxwell 1985). The Terminal Dorset lasted at least one century after the emergence of the Thule culture in the region, and surveys in other parts of the district clearly demonstrate that the settlement pattern identified by the project is but one aspect of a larger settlement system. The chronological overlap with the early Thule culture, as well as supposed face-to-face contact with Norse hunters in the study area, no doubt led to changes in the political landscape of the Late Dorset, but the results of these cultural meetings are almost invisible (Gulløv 2000).

With our present knowledge of the distribution of Late Dorset sites, the Greenland Late Dorset group seems to have been isolated from other Late Dorset groups when the pioneers of the Thule culture arrived – an isolation that may have meant that the group had reached the limit of its social flexibility and was unable to respond to further changes caused by the newcomers. Unfortunately, we are still unable to make any sort of firmly founded assumptions on the subsequent fate of the Late Dorset groups: did they end in acculturation, through migration further north and east, and/or did they die of new viruses brought in by the newcomers? However, their influences are still to be seen in the material remains of the Thule culture, and also survive in the oral tradition of contemporary Greenlanders (Gulløv 1997). In the following we will accept the Tunit in the oral tradition of Inuit as a reality within our archaeological concept of the Late Dorset.

EXCAVATION OF A MEGALITHIC STRUCTURE

The Late Dorset sites within the study area were situated on small promontories, minimizing the distance to open water or the ice edge. One site consists of four to six house structures. The architecture of the excavated houses showed a squared ground-plan divided by the well-known

Palaeo-Eskimo mid-axial feature for cooking and storing purposes. On the mainland, close to each site, a megalithic structure was also situated.

Such megalithic structures, normally termed 'longhouses' in the archaeological literature, were recorded from 33 sites containing at least 43 structures, all thought to be Late Dorset in age (Damkjar 2000). They are distributed between four regions: the Ungava Bay/Hudson Strait area with thirteen structures; Victoria Island with eleven structures; the Arctic islands south of Ellesmere Island (Somerset, Bathurst, Devon, Little Cornwallis and Bylot) with nine structures; and the Smith Sound region with 10 structures (Damkjar 2000; figure 10.1). Interior length ranges from 8 to 45m, the average width being 4.5 m. Average datings of the structures mainly fall into the period from the eighth to the thirteenth centuries (Damkjar 2000).

Other Late Dorset structures have been recorded from the megalith sites, especially the so-called hearth rows. Several of the megalithic structures have been archaeologically tested, and a few have been excavated, but one very well-preserved example has recently been the subject of a total internal documentation (Appelt and Gulløv 1999). No Late Dorset dwellings were found at the site in question.

The site is situated on the Greenland side of the 40 km wide Smith Sound on the mainland in Hatherton Bay, 1 km south of the adjacent Late Dorset site at the small promontory Qeqertaaraq. Its most striking feature is a so-called 'longhouse'. Associated with this are no

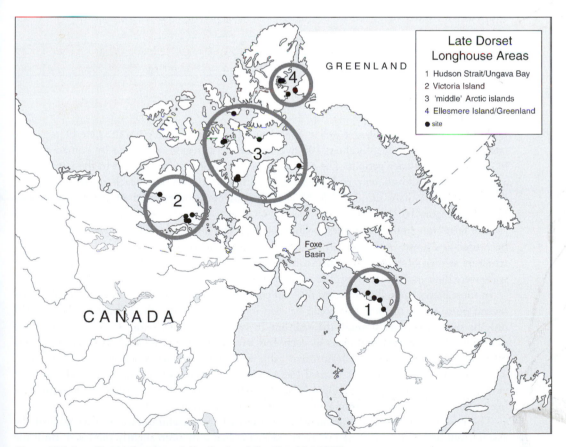

Figure 10.1 Late Dorset 'longhouse' distribution (after Damkjar 2000).

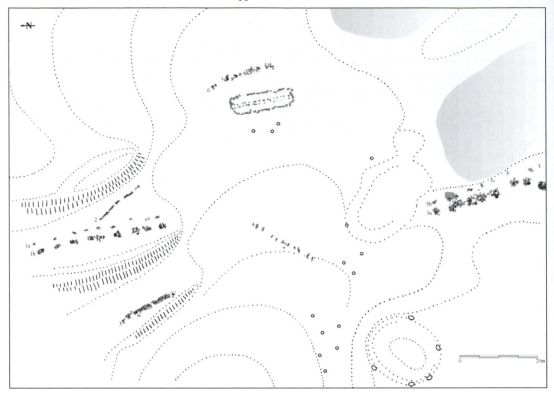

Figure 10.2 General plan of the Greenland megalithic site, Hatherton Bay, Smith Sound.

fewer than eight hearth rows, as well as a large number of caches, all from the Late Dorset. The core area of the site, which is about 100 m from the coast, seems untouched by human activity in either earlier or later periods. The only features which cannot be assigned to the Late Dorset are a few Neo-Eskimo tent rings and meat caches found on the beach northwest of the 'longhouse'. The main site can thus be described as undisturbed, and all structures are well preserved (Figure 10.2).

The term 'longhouse' is of questionable value, as this kind of structure never seems to have been used as a house in the normal sense of the word. The long-walls appear in the rectangular structure as rows of raised stones, half-ton boulders and stacked slabs. The slightly convex gable walls were built in the same way. The walls enclose an area of 4.5 by 15.5 m (Figure 10.3).

In most places the walls still stand 60–100 cm high on their original positions, and although several openings in the wall-line could be seen in both long-walls, the occupation layer could only be seen expanding through the wall-line in two places. It therefore seems likely that the structure only had two entrances in each end of the western long-wall. An approximately 50 cm-wide break in the central, northern gable wall may also have functioned as an entrance. This possible third entrance is formed like a door-step, some 30 cm high. A similar type of entrance is found in another Hatherton Bay 'longhouse'. Some of the stones in the walls have been tilted systematically at some point after the structure went out of use.

The two long-walls were constructed using two different techniques, the main part of the eastern wall being raised in a natural frost crack that had only been slightly modified. Both the internal and external faces of the wall were retained by the use of wedge-stones placed at the

Figure 10.3 The megalithic structure prior to excavation.

base. In six places, larger wedge-stones served as platforms for fireplaces containing small amounts of burnt material, the latter consisting primarily of blubber-soaked moss. If the same regularity that we generally see in constructions of this kind is applied to all the structural elements, we may suggest that there were originally nine of these fireplaces spaced at approximately 1.5 m intervals. Several of the wedge-stones had been removed and lay up to 2 m from their original location. The stones in the western wall were placed in a ditch excavated some 10–15 cm into the ground and were leaning against a low inner wall of turf, which unfortunately could only be recognized in short stretches along the central part of the wall.

Two rows of vertically placed flagstones originally divided the interior of the structure lengthways. In the following this feature will be referred to as the 'mid-passage-framing'. Large parts of the eastern mid-passage-framing were still preserved, while the stone lining in the western section was badly disturbed, with only six stones still lying in their original position (Figure 10.4). The southern end of the western side was completely deprived of stones, but traces of the mid-passage-framing were seen in the form of a narrow low trench, approximately 4 m long, in which stones were probably set. The average width of the mid-passage was about 80 cm. The stones used for the construction of the mid-passage-frame were mainly oblong pieces of granite, ranging in length from 35 to 60 cm, with one stone being about 90 cm long.

In the northern part of the mid-passage an area about 1 m² was paved with flagstones. On both sides of the axial feature a large number of slab stones were found, often lying in stacks of up to seven to eight. The slab stones seemed to be placed at random, with some resting on thin layers of humus, indicating that they did not form a part of the structural design of the areas between the mid-passage and the walls. The slab stones are more likely to have been part of a pavement covering the interior of the axial feature – a possibility strengthened by the fact that when placed side by side they covered an area of approximately 11.5 m², roughly corresponding to the sise of the space represented inside the axial feature.

The inside of the mid-passage had only a 2–3 cm thick layer of vegetation resting directly on a layer of gravel. Apart from a few retouched flakes, bone, antler and tusk fragments, the upper

Figure 10.4 The mid-axial passage.

part of the gravel layer seemed sterile, but under 5–15 cm of gravel two rows of pits were found along the inner edges of the mid-passage-framing and a third row was found on the central axis.

The well-preserved pits along the mid-passage-framing were shaped like boxes that were rectangular to trapezoid in outline, and from approximately 10 x 18 cm to 20 x 32 cm in size. The pits were dug down some 7–10 cm into the sub-soil and each box was shaped by a stone slab placed flat in the bottom, while the sides were plastered with one or more slabs set on edge. The pits seems to have been placed in sets, with the majority of these spaced some 90–140 cm from the middle of one pit to the next (Figure 10.5).

A surprising feature of these sets is that their bottom stone slabs also had features in common with each other, in that the same type of stone was used in each pit. One had a grey soapstone-like bottom stone while another has reddish sandstone. Other stone types used were banded gneiss, grey sandstone and red granite. All these types of stone can be found in the vicinity of the site, mainly in the low hills to the north, south and east. A vertical cross-sectioning of the pits did not give any clear image of the original shape prior to the placing of the bottom and side stones, as no organic material was found on the sides or under the stones.

Our suggestion is that these stone pits served as foundations for a number of long and narrow stones found tipped over in connection with six of the pits. In most cases the base of these 40–70 cm long stones fitted exactly into the pits, and even though preservation conditions were excellent none of the pits contained whalebones or pieces of wood indicating that they should have had a function as foundation pits for roof-carrying posts. At the end of the excavation we were left with some 53 oblong stones that were found in or close to the mid-passage. These oblong stones are very similar to the stones found making up the mid-passage-

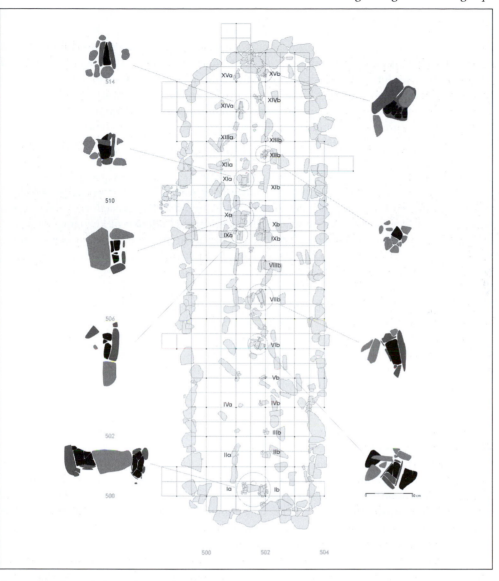

Figure 10.5 General plan with stone-lined pits.

frame. We therefore suggest that some 28 of the oblong stones were originally placed in the mid-passage-frame, while the remaining nineteen were used as uprights in the stone-lined pits on the inside of the framing.

A third row of pits without stones was found along the central axis of the mid-passage at the same level as the upper part of the stone lined pits. The eight 2–3 cm deep pits were seen as small concentrations of charcoal. The distance between the charcoal concentrations ranges from 125 cm to 240 cm and they are more evenly spaced in the northern half of the mid-passage, suggesting that one or two pits are missing in the southern half.

The areas on both sides of the central axis revealed a very thin cultural layer which in most parts did not exceed 5 cm in depth, and had accumulated directly on the gravel subsoil. The number of artefacts in the structure is generally low. Inside the axial feature some seven flakes, one harpoon head, a copper harpoon blade and a fragment of a biface were found, while the surrounding areas contained about 970 flakes, some 49 formed lithic artefacts, and around twenty formed and recognizable artefacts of organic material. The largest quantities of finds came in the form of very small flakes from the re-sharpening of bifaces, blades and harpoon heads. Among the formed artefacts, blades and bladeknives comprise by far the largest categories (36 pieces out of 50 total). In addition, thirteen harpoon heads – non-functional miniature harpoon heads and full-sized functional harpoon heads, one of which had facial features – constitute 72 per cent of the recognizable artefact types made of organic material.

The most numerous finds category consisted of flakes, for the most part under 5 mm in diameter. They were mainly found in seven relatively tight concentrations along the outside of the mid-passage on both sides, ranging in size from 1 to 3 m². The general impression is that the spread of flakes was probably produced through a limited number of knapping sequences, representing one or a few episodes. The overall distribution of the flakes, as well as other artefacts, point to some sort of wall-effect between the mid-passage and the areas on both sides, as only seven of 976 flakes were found inside the mid-passage (Figure 10.6).

Despite several test pits dug on both the western (towards the coast) and eastern side of the longhouse, we only found a limited amount of bone material and lithic waste, and did not succeed in defining a regular midden area in proximity to the structure.

A heavily vegetated small area with no structures was found 10 m north of the longhouse. An excavation here revealed an approximately 5 cm thick layer of brown humus and gravel with a substantial amount of bones (mainly walrus), a few flakes and a harpoon head of walrus tusk. The debris accumulated in this area seems to originate from a more conventional midden area of approximately 25 m² on the edge of a plateau just above it. In the upper midden area several walrus bones could be seen on and in the vegetation.

To the south-west, below the edge of a large outcrop, five huge stone enclosures were situated. The walls were constructed of larger stones and measured approximately 1.5 x 4 m. They were interpreted as caches for walrus carcasses.

To the north-east some ten structures were situated scattered over a distance of roughly 50 m. Each consisted of two to three flagstones in line, framed by two parallel slab rows and covered by a flagstone. Nothing can be said about their function. West of the megalith structure, three remains of small indeterminable features were observed.

A total of eight rows of hearths were located around the longhouse. The rows were from 15 to 33 m long and contained eight to ten hearth units. Even though differences could be seen between the rows, the majority of the hearth units consisted of a broad slabstone flanked on two sides by upright blocks, while several smaller slabs formed a storage platform on one or both sides. In two cases the rows formed double, parallel lines: one row being constructed as mentioned above, while the others were constructed as simple hearths, i.e. a vertical flagstone surrounded by round, head-size stones. In two other cases, the hearth units were directly connected to each other and framed by two parallel rows of stone. In one of the largest and heaviest rows, a lid was placed on top of the two upright sides.

Several hearth units in one of the rows had a small round stone placed on top of the central flagstone; its function is unknown. This phenomenon has however also been observed at Late Dorset sites in Canada, and it has been proposed that they are 'closing stones' placed there when the site was abandoned. Although the hearth rows are in principle constructed in the same way, there is much to indicate that they were not built at the same time. There is, for example, a striking difference in the state of preservation and the degree of overgrowth from row to row.

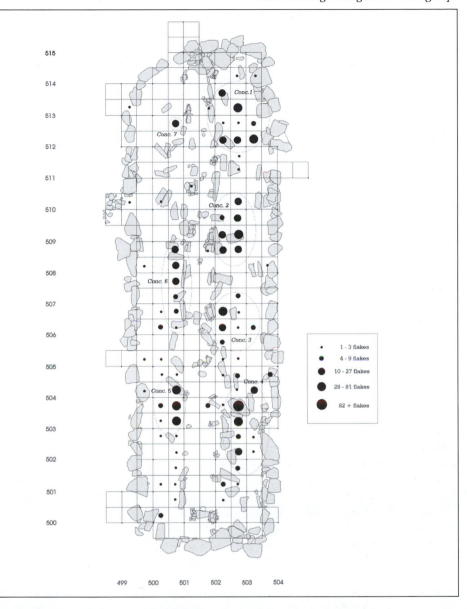

Figure 10.6 Distribution of flakes in the megalithic structure.

Five hearths of a different type were excavated. Two did not produce any material, while two hearths produced a limited amount of burnt material. Finally, one hearth produced substantial amount of burnt wood, bones and moss. No artefacts were found in connection with the excavations.

To summarize the investigations at the site, we may stress that at present three so-called longhouses are known from Greenland, located in the Hatherton Bay area. Late Dorset sites are exclusively found in the Thule District, i.e. from the southern part of Washington Land to the northern part of Melville Bay. Admittedly, only a limited amount of surveys have been undertaken both in the Thule District and in the areas south and north thereof (Andreasen 2000). With the evidence at hand the presently known distribution of sites seems to indicate that the Greenland sites should be seen as an integrated part of a regional Late Dorset group, with its most extensive settlement in the general area of Bache Peninsula, Ellesmere Island, only some 50 km west-north-west of Hatherton Bay (Schledermann 1990).

All the hearth rows described above contained between eight and ten hearth units and may perhaps indicate the presence of eight to ten families using the site, and the same goes for the number of fire-places and axial charcoal pits in the main longhouse structure as suggested by Schledermann on the basis of his work on Ellesmere Island (1990). This relationship leads us to assume that this longhouse probably should be perceived as a highly developed form of hearth row rather than an actual dwelling. Arguing further along these lines, it may explain not only the representation of both organic and lithic artefact types – the opposite of what is normally found in dwellings – but also the constructional details, such as the construction of the axial feature with its colonnade of upright stones (Figure 10.7).

Judging both by the position of the pits found in the central axis of the mid-passage – under the 5–15 cm of 'sterile' gravel – and the radiocarbon datings, the longhouse may have had its origin as an actual hearth row, later transformed into the structure presently seen. The burnt material in the pits would then be the limited remains of the original hearth row. The same course of development can perhaps been seen in the Ellesmere Island longhouses, as no well-defined hearths, only small concentrations of charcoal and burnt bone, were found in the excavated longhouses (Schledermann 1990).

Furthermore, the lack of artefacts and the very limited amount of burnt material found in all

Figure 10.7 The megalithic structure with the authors' reconstruction of the colonnade of upright stones.

but one of the hearth rows (in spite of excellent preservation conditions) lead us to believe that hearth rows did not serve as places of everyday cooking. Rather, they can be seen as symbolic fire-places within the framework of an occasional communal gathering, perhaps with the women gathered around the outside hearth rows and the men inside, as suggested by the types of artefact found inside the longhouse.

We therefore argue that there is good reason to replace the term 'longhouse' with the term 'Arctic megalithic structure', indicating a more non-utilitarian function or more specifically, a form of symbolic representation of communal gatherings and spiritual activities. The impression of a non-utilitarian function for the Greenland megalithic structure is reinforced by the almost complete lack of artefacts in the mid-passage, as indicated by the clear wall-effect which indicates that some sort of cover had separated it from the surrounding areas.

Other writers (Maxwell 1985; McGhee 1996; Plumet 1985; Schledermann 1990) have noted that the longhouses probably had a strong non-utilitarian aspect to them, emphasizing their use as places for short-term gatherings, much the same as the *aasiviks*, the summer gatherings of the historical Inuit. It also seems to be commonly agreed that the longhouses never have had a common roofing, although it is suggested that each family raised a tent inside the structure (Damkjar 2000).

If the number of hearths can be taken as an indication of the number of families at the site, we suggest that around fifty people were gathered corresponding to the number of people living in two small winter settlements (cf. McGhee 1996: 206). One of these may have been one of the settlements in Hatherton Bay. If we assume that each hearth-unit represents one family, there is a surprising stability in the number of people using in site through the approximately 300 years we assume it has been used. This may indicate that the site was visited by a relatively stable group residing in the area over several centuries, perhaps occasionally meeting with the groups in the area of Bache Peninsula on Ellesmere Island with respect to Hatherton Bay.

A general weakness of the excavations on the site in Hatherton Bay is the limited excavation of the areas between the structures. In the time available to us for fieldwork we chose to prioritise a total excavation of the inside of the megalithic structure, and were thus unable to reach a more complete understanding of the site as a whole. Excavation between the structures may very well reveal a large number of *structures latentes* that may be a key to the function of these types of site.

SHAMANISM AND COSMOLOGY

Among the architectual traits at the megalithic site, the mid-axial construction and the fire-places appear as something different from the structures known from subsequent Neo-Eskimo sites. Nevertheless, the mid-axial or mid-passage phenomenon has been a very stable feature in dwellings of the eastern Arctic since the emergence of the first Palaeo-Eskimos in the later half of the third millennium BC (Knuth 1967) and continued as such during the following ca. 3,500 years. As they were the first humans to enter these then-virgin hunting fields, they were assumed to have brought the idea for the division of the dwelling with them from outside. The archaeological data point to the west, to Alaska where the Denbigh culture has been defined as the basis of the Palaeo-Eskimo tradition (Giddings 1964). But in this part of the palaeo-Eskimo Arctic we lack evidences of the mid-axial structure in sites investigated.

Looking for similar structures, Knuth (1967: 47ff.) has drawn attention to western Eurasia, especially the Sámi (Lapp) lands in northern Fenno-Scandia and the Kola Peninsula, where dwellings occur with a mid-axial structure described and depicted in eighteenth-century ethnographic sources. The descriptions come very close to the Palaeo-Eskimo dwellings, and in

On linguistic evidence the Samoyed-Finno-Ugric split occurred about 2,000 years ago, but it is a matter of ongoing debate as to how long the Sámi have spoken a Finno-Ugric language, and perhaps they represent a still earlier northern population that had shifted to a Uralic language (Fortescue 1998: 182). With regard to the situation in the eastern region, and the problem as to when the first Palaeo-Eskimos appeared on the shores of the Bering Strait, we do not know if they represent the immediate linguistic ancestors of the modern Inuit. However, the language they spoke would in all likelihood have been an offshoot of the same Uralo-Siberian complex, and the date of their appearance may be considered against recent estimates of the approximately 4,000 years that have elapsed since the Aleut and Eskimo began to go their own ways (cf. Fortescue 1998: 188; Fiedler 1992: 151).

On the evidence mentioned above we may maintain that the introduction of the mid-axial structure and its shamanistic elements expressed vestiges of a cosmology of common Uralo-Siberian origin, which appeared when newcomers arrived in western Eurasia and the eastern North American Arctic some 2,000 and 4,000 years ago respectively.

CONCLUSION

Our chapter has focused on the shamanism of the Late Dorset, aspects of which we argue can be interpreted from a recently excavated Greenlandic megalithic structure. Such structures, often labelled as longhouses despite their strong non-utilitarian aspect, have been reported from the greater part of the easternmost Arctic. Although long dwelling-houses are known from the Dorset culture (though details of them have not been published – see Rowley and Rowley 1997: 274), something different took place in the eastern Arctic with the introduction of the megalithic structures described.

The reason for its appearance has been explained with reference to external factors deriving both from changes in nature and from new population events in the west. Coping with these challenges, the Dorset people came increasingly to rely on the strength of their cultural tradition. Collective efforts were invested in the construction of megalithic structures, the function of which was shamanistic and comparable to the later neo-Eskimo *qassi*, the men's house (cf. Gulløv 1988).

The maritime adapted neo-Eskimos, who reached the eastern Arctic sometime in the early second millennium AD, can be seen for the first time in the archaeology of the western shores of the Bering Strait where their sites are dated to the beginning of our era. We can also see continuing cultural influence from further south within Asia, as far at least as the Amur, and from Iron Age China beyond. The split between the recent Yupik and Inuit Eskimo languages probably has its roots in these events (cf. Fortescue 1998; McGhee 1988).

Hereafter, the mid-axial feature with its reference to the river as a route from life to death was no longer seen as an element in the dwelling structures of the neo-Eskimos. However, this Palaeo-Siberian idea probably lies behind the treatment of the dead as observed as late as the early eighteenth century in Greenland: when somebody died in a house, the body was not be taken out through the entrance passage customarily used by the inmates, but instead through the window; if a death occurred in a tent, then the corpse was removed through the rear (Egede 1925: 376).

Though the 'Dorset culture' is an archaeological construction, the Tunit people have to be taken seriously as a prehistoric reality, as they became a part of the Inuit cultural tradition in the eastern Arctic. The scenario described above is open to radical revision if we do not accept this to be the case.

REFERENCES

Andreasen, C. (2000) 'Palaeo-Eskimos in northwest and northeast Greenland', in M. Appelt, J. Berglund and H.C. Gulløv (eds) *Identities and Cultural Contacts in the Arctic,* Copenhagen: Danish Polar Center.

Anisimov, A.F. (1963) 'The shaman's tent of the Evenks and the origin of the shamanistic rite', in H.N. Michael (ed.) *Studies in Siberian Shamanism,* Toronto: University of Toronto Press.

Appelt, M. and Gulløv, H.C. (eds) (1999) *Late Dorset in High Arctic Greenland,* Copenhagen: Danish Polar Center.

Arneborg, J. and Gulløv, H.C. (eds) (1998) *Man, Culture and Environment in Ancient Greenland,* Copenhagen: Danish Polar Center.

Arutiunov, S.A. (1988) 'Even: reindeer herders of eastern Siberia', in W.W. Fitzhugh and A. Crowell (eds) *Crossroads of Continents. Cultures of Siberia and Alaska,* Washington, DC: Smithsonian Institution Press.

Boas, F. (1964) *The Central Eskimo,* Lincoln: University of Nebraska Press.

Damkjar, E. (2000) 'A survey of Late Dorset longhouses', in M. Appelt, J. Berglund and H.C. Gulløv (eds) *Identities and Cultural Contacts in the Arctic,* Copenhagen: Danish Polar Center.

Dumond, D.E. (1987) 'A re-examination of Eskimo-Aleut prehistory', *American Anthropologist* 89(1): 32–55.

Egede, H. (1925) *Det gamle Grønlands ny Perlustration 1741.* Meddelelser om Grønland 54, Copenhagen: Commission for Scientific Research in Greenland.

Fiedler, S.J. (1992) *Prehistory of the Americas,* Cambridge: Cambridge University Press.

Fitzhugh, W.W. (1997) 'Searching for the Grail: virtual archeology in Yamal and circumpolar theory', in R. Gilberg and H.C. Gullv (eds) *Fifty Years of Arctic Research. Anthropological Studies from Greenland to Siberia,* Copenhagen: National Museum of Denmark.

Fortescue, M. (1988) *Eskimo Orientation Systems,* Meddelelser om Grønland, Man and Society 11, Copenhagen: Commission for Scientific Research in Greenland.

—— (1998) *Language Relations across Bering Strait. Reappraising the Archaeological and Linguistic Evidence,* London: Cassell.

Giddings, J.L. (1964) *The Archeology of Cape Denbigh.* Providence, RI: Brown University Press.

Gulløv, H.C. (1988) 'Where is the Greenlandic qassi? – a study of settlement structures', *Folk, Journal of the Danish Ethnographic Society* 30: 181–200.

—— (1997) *From Middle Ages to Colonial Times. Archaeological and Ethnohistorical Studies of the Thule Culture in South West Greenland 1300–1800 AD,* Meddelelser om Grønland, Man and Society 23, Copenhagen: Commission for Scientific Research in Greenland.

—— (2000) 'Natives and Norse in Greenland', in W.W. Fitzhugh and E. Ward (eds) *Vikings: The North Atlantic saga,* Washington, D.C.: Smithsonian Institution Press.

Jenness, D. (1925) 'A new Eskimo culture in Hudson Bay', *Geographical Review* 15(3): 428–37.

Knuth, E. (1967) *Archaeology of the Musk-ox Way,* École Pratique des Hautes Études, Contributions du Centre d'Études Arctiques et Finno-Scandinaves 5, Paris: Sorbonne.

McGhee, R. (1988) 'A scenario for Eskimo-Aleut prehistory', in R. Shaw, R. Harritt and D.E. Dumond (eds) *The Late Prehistoric Development of Alaska's Native People,* Alaska Anthropological Association Monograph Series 4, Anchorage: Aurora.

—— (1996) *Ancient People of the Arctic,* Vancouver: University of British Columbia Press.

Mason, O.K. (2000) 'Archaeological Rorschach in delineating Ipiutak, Punuk and Birnirk in NW Alaska: masters, slaves or partners in trade?', in M. Appelt, J. Berglund and H.C. Gulløv (eds) *Identities and Cultural Contacts in the Arctic,* Copenhagen: Danish Polar Center.

Maxwell, M.S. (1985) *Prehistory of the Eastern Arctic,* New York: Academic Press, Inc.

Meldgaard, J. (1955) 'Dorset kulturen. Den Dansk-amerikanske ekspedition til Arktisk Canada 1954', *Kuml* 158–77.

Olsen, B. (1994) *Bosetning og samfunn i Finnmarks forhistorie,* Oslo: Universitetsforlaget.

Pitul'ko, V. (1991) 'Archeological data on the maritime cultures of the west Arctic', *Fennoscandia Archaeologica* 8: 23–34.

Plumet, P. (1985) *Archéologie de l'Ungava: le site de la Pointe aux Bélougas (Qilalugarsiuvik) et les maisons longues dorsétiennes,* Paléo-Québec 18, Montréal: Université du Québec à Montréal.

—— (1989) 'Le foyer dans l'Arctique', *Actes du Colloque de Nemours 1987, Mémoires du Musée de Préhistoire d'Ile de France* 2: 313–25.

Chapter Eleven

Special objects – special creatures: Shamanistic imagery and the Aurignacian art[1] of south-west Germany

Thomas A. Dowson and Martin Porr

In the summer of 1931 a German archaeologist by the name of Gustav Riek began excavating deposits at Vogelherd cave in the Swabian Mountains of south-west Germany. During the excavation he recovered a number of small ivory statuettes in layers of Aurignacian age (*c.*32,000 BP), the best known of which is the Vogelherd horse (Figure 11.1). The analysis of these statuettes is said to have captured Riek for the rest of his life (Wagner and Wehrberger 1994: 13). Since Riek's excavations at Vogelherd, two other caves in the Swabian Mountains, Hohlenstein-Stadel (1935–9 and 1956–60; Wetzel 1961) and Geißenklösterle (1974–83 and 1985–9; Hahn 1988) have revealed further statuettes dating to the Aurignacian. Altogether sixteen identifiable carved statuettes of Aurignacian age have been recovered from all three sites. The ^{14}C and AMS dates obtained from the two subsequent series of excavations confirmed Riek's interpretation of the dating of the Vogelherd statuettes.

Riek's initial finds at Vogelherd greatly influenced the character of subsequent Palaeolithic research in south-west Germany. The various excavations of Palaeolithic sites undertaken in the last sixty or so years in the Swabian Mountains, mostly concentrating on cave deposits, were supported largely as a result of Riek's recovery of the Swabian statuettes from Vogelherd. For Germany and Central Europe, at least, this art was and still is widely recognised as the 'earliest evidence of artistic expression' (Müller-Beck and Albrecht 1987 – our translation) which in turn strongly shaped the interpretation of the statuettes in German archaeology.

Figure 11.1 The Vogelherd horse. Length *c.*48 mm (reproduced here with the permission of the Institut für Ur- und Frühgeschichte, Abteilung Ältere Urgeschichte und Quartärökologie, Universität Tübingen).

PREVIOUS INTERPRETATIONS OF THE SWABIAN STATUETTES

For Gustav Riek, writing in the 1930s, the exclusive reproduction of animals we find in the Swabian statuettes provided conclusive evidence for both the characterisation of Aurignacian communities and the prominence and prestige that hunting held within those communities. Aurignacian 'man' was first and foremost a hunter, and 'the power of the hunter was celebrated in artistic expression' (Riek 1934: 297 – our translation). Later, in the 1980s, it was primarily the antiquity of these statuettes that led Müller-Beck to place this art at the origin of humanity's technical competency. For Müller-Beck the statuettes represent the first expressions of humanity's ability and desire to explain the environment (1987: 17). In a striking diagrammatic representation of this position, Müller-Beck places the Vogelherd horse at the origins of such technical advances as the printed page, the radio and the television. It was through these statuettes that Aurignacian peoples are said to have obtained information and learnt things about their environment which enabled them to produce the necessary resources for their continued existence. Interpretations such as these, either of European Palaeolithic art in general or more specifically the Swabian statuettes, are no longer tenable (for discussions of these interpretative strategies see, for example, Rector 1985; Ucko 1987; Conkey 1997; Tomásková 1997; Dowson 1998).

More recently, Joachim Hahn has analysed these objects in a more sophisticated manner. Not only did he explore the taphonomy, the supposed stylistic conventions and the functions of these objects, he has also ventured ethological interpretations drawing on identifiable behavioural features the artists carved. For Hahn, the art provided a code for a complex set of visual messages which centred around an ideology of power and strength, possibly having a pedagogical function (Hahn 1986, 1993). And, much like Riek's pioneering work, Hahn's book *Kraft und Aggression – Die Botschaft der Eiszeitkunst im Aurignacien Süddeutschlands?* ('Power and aggression: The message of the Aurignacian art of Southwest Germany?') has became one of the best-known archaeological publications in recent years from this region.

In the wider context of European Palaeolithic art research, however, these statuettes have been largely overshadowed by the seemingly more spectacular parietal art of France and, to a lesser extent, Spain. The large bulls in Lascaux or the delicately shaded bison from Altamira have been continuously presented as much more visually arresting than the small, albeit exceptionally carved, Swabian statuettes. These figurines simply do not compare to the prehistoric grandeur of the Magdalenian art of France and Spain, and the geographical location of such 'spectacular' sites as the painted caves enables the creation of a history of art that begins in Lascaux and ends in the Louvre. Consequently, the inclusion of the Swabian statuettes in international discussions merely serves to illustrate two, somewhat mundane points: first, these objects provide empirical evidence for the apparent antiquity of mobiliary art, and second, they also provide evidence for its regional distribution.

Interestingly, on another level the Swabian statuettes do not fit into certain preconceived ideas about the development of Palaeolithic art. Since its 'discovery', research on the Upper Palaeolithic art of Europe has been informed by Eurocentric and stereotypical ideas that the intellectual West holds to be true for the history of art as well as for the history of humanity. The Upper Palaeolithic art of Europe, located in the 'prehistoric' period of conventional histories of art, has become the obvious candidate for the origin of the Western artistic tradition itself. This 'prehistoric art' has its own internal development over thousands of years, moving from simple, crude markings in the Aurignacian to surprisingly spectacular images, such as those found in Magdalenian Lascaux. Within this scheme of thinking the Swabian statuettes are an anomaly. They are undoubtedly very well carved, showing considerable artistic/technical expertise, but they are also amongst the oldest – they should not be so 'well done' according to a traditional art historical approach. Consequently, they are sometimes acknowledged as a challenge to accepted wisdom (see, for example, Clottes 1993), but that challenge is only ever nominal and passive. The statuettes are all but dismissed, never actually playing an active role in our academic and popular constructions of Upper Palaeolithic art in Europe. Outside the Palaeolithic archaeology of Central Europe, certainly up until the mid 1990s, these statuettes did not feature in any sustained discussion (see also Hahn 1986: 39).

However, with the discovery in 1994 of Grotte Chauvet (in the Ardèche region of France), the statuettes have been receiving added attention (see, for example, Clottes 1996, 1998), the reasons for which are two-fold. First, the paintings in Chauvet have been dated to the Aurignacian, around 31,000 years ago, making them more or less the same age as the statuettes. Second, there are many paintings in Chauvet that depict felines and other dangerous animals: the same has long been noted in the Swabian statuettes. In fact, this repertoire of animal imagery for both Chauvet and the Swabian assemblage compares well with other supposed Aurignacian sites in the Dordogne region of France, which have as many as three times more dangerous animals than later Gravettian sites in the same region (Delluc and Delluc 1991). What was once a unilinear trajectory 'from Lascaux to the Louvre' is currently being replaced with a longer sequence that begins with Chauvet. Again, the Swabian statuettes merely provide empirical, corroborating evidence for what is observed in Franco-Cantabrian Palaeolithic art; never are they empowered to actively influence or determine interpretative trends. The Swabian statuettes continue to be of merely passing interest, perpetuating a Francocentric perspective on the origins of art. This represents another example of how 'art' objects such as the Swabian statuettes – like the figurines of Willendorf and Dolni Vestonice – have been 'lift[ed] effortlessly out of their local settings into a pan-European tradition of symbolic expression' (Tomásková 1997: 281).

In this chapter we start from a position that does *not* see the Swabian statuettes as art objects in a generally pan-European (and specifically Franco-Cantabrian) Palaeolithic artistic tradition, with further links to the position that the latter holds in the history of art. Ucko (1987) has forcefully argued against the concept of a linear evolution of prehistoric art from simple to complex imagery, suggesting that it is highly likely that there were in fact different, perhaps contemporary, traditions of artistic practice in the Palaeolithic of Europe. However, specific analyses of Palaeolithic art to take such a conclusion into account have not been forthcoming (but see Tomásková 1997). We propose to offer such an analysis here, emphasising that a more specific study of the kind that we devote to the Swabian statuettes does not simply offer insights into the diversity of artistic practice during the Palaeolithic in Europe, but rather – if followed up elsewhere – will go some way to providing an alternative to the unilinear version of the history of art that is currently widely accepted, and hence continuously reinforced.

We theorise the meaning and social role of the Swabian statuettes in a specific, regional and local context, and advance an interpretation of them by drawing on an understanding of shamanism. Over the last decade or so the shamanistic interpretation of Upper Palaeolithic art has developed considerably. In 1988 two papers were published which gave this approach a new direction and a firmer methodological basis. One attempted to find a link between bird ethology and certain images of birds in Upper Palaeolithic cave art (Davenport and Jochim 1988), while the other explored a neuropsychological link between the visions seen in an altered state of consciousness and Palaeolithic imagery (Lewis-Williams and Dowson 1988). What was once an off-the-cuff explanatory remark on certain enigmatic images has now developed into a more theoretically and methodologically rigorous interpretative framework (see, for example, Lewis-Williams 1991, 1997a, 1997b; Dowson 1998; Lorblanchet and Sieveking 1997). In this chapter we explore both the ethological and neuropsychological aspects of the Aurignacian art of south-west Germany. In so doing, we do not simply offer speculations on the 'meaning' of these statuettes, but more specifically we construct an informing context, which then enables us to begin an exploration of their role in negotiating social interaction.

THE AURIGNACIAN ART OF SOUTH-WEST GERMANY

The Aurignacian technocomplex is generally recognised as the oldest period of the Upper Palaeolithic in Europe. The Aurignacian is exclusively associated with anatomically modern *Homo sapiens*, and two modern skulls were recovered from the Aurignacian deposits of Vogelherd (see Riek 1934: 302–8). Most of the sites with Aurignacian deposits in the Upper Danube area are cave sites, situated in different tributary valley systems. Art objects were excavated in three sites situated in the Achtal and the Lonetal: Vogelherd, Hohlenstein-Stadel and Geißenklösterle (Hahn 1983: 276; 1993: 230). At Vogelherd conventional radiocarbon dating yielded results from 23,060 to 31,900 BP years for the Aurignacian levels (Hahn 1986: 11; 1993: 230). The Aurignacian level at Hohlenstein-Stadel was dated by conventional ^{14}C methods to 31,750 ± 1150–650 BP (H-3800–3025) and by AMS to 32,000 BP ± 550 (ETH-2877) (Hahn 1995: 88; see also Hahn 1993: 231). Datable material from the upper Aurignacian level, containing the statuettes, at Geißenklösterle has produced a large number of AMS dates which fall between 32,300 ± 700 (OxA-5708) and 36,800 (1000 (OxA 4595), with a mean value at 33,500 ± 350 (Hahn 1995: 88–90; Richter *et al.* 2000: 86).

The Aurignacian in south-west Germany has come to be regarded as a regional unit because of different features that make up the artefact inventories. Both stone and organic artefacts show a patterning that can be distinguished from other regions in Europe. For example, the extensive use of mammoth ivory for the production of rods, pendants and batons is exceptional. Furthermore, among the ivory beads is a stylistic form that has to date only been found in this region. Finally, the occurrence of the Aurignacian figurative mobiliary art in this region is unique (Hahn 1986: 25; see also Hahn 1977, 1987). From the three sites mentioned, there are twenty-one identifiable and five unidentifiable objects. Of the identifiable objects seventeen are figurative, the others being a stone pendant, an oval bone retoucher, an engraved large mammalian bone and a painted stone from Geißenklösterle. In the following discussion we focus on the figurative objects.

The statuettes are generally rather small, around 5 cm in length. Only the 'anthropomorph' from Hohlenstein-Stadel is exceptional in this regard (296 mm in height). All but one of the statuettes were manufactured from locally available mammoth ivory; the other, the mammoth half relief from Vogelherd, was made from mammoth bone. There are both animal and anthropomorphic figurines. The animals carved are exclusively large, terrestrial mammals, such as felines, bears, mammoths, bovines and a possible rhinoceros. The species diversity of the carved animals represents only a fraction of the animals present in the faunal assemblages recovered from all three sites (Hahn 1986: 156–60), indicating an intentional rather than a random choice of subject matter. The specific ways in which the Aurignacian artists chose to carve their animal and anthropomorphic statuettes also indicate that further choices were considered in producing these objects.

The carving of the animals' heads always displays the obvious facial features such as the mouth, ears and eyes. In certain instances a distinctive expression is included. The body of the carved animal is usually well represented, and in some examples perhaps somewhat exaggerated. Musculature is often present as the bodies emphasise full, rounded forms. In contrast to this, the extremities, as in the hooves and feet, are reduced in size or sometimes not included.

Because the omissions are not the product of taphonomic processes, and very slender forms can in fact be carved in ivory, the artists must have intentionally chosen not to include hooves and feet. The significance of this feature needs to be considered in any discussion. Finally, the animals are always symmetrical along the longitudinal axis; in each case the legs are parallel to each other (Hahn 1993: 232).

The anthropomorphic representations, on the other hand, were clearly created with a different set of decisions. The heads are either schematic, without facial expressions at all, or they are animal heads displaying all facial features, as in the human-lion statuette from Hohlenstein-Stadel (Figure 11.2). The body is either shortened or left in natural proportions. The limbs are also generally represented naturalistically, apart from the statuette from the Vogelherd level IV, which has no limbs at all (Hahn 1986: 154–5; 1993: 233).

The detailed and obviously intentional ways in which the Swabian artists chose to depict their subjects allows an interpretation of the facial expressions and postures and to identify behavioural expression. In two of the lion statuettes the neck and head form a horizontal line, while the ears are twisted backward (Figure 11.3; Hahn 1993: 234). Lions during aggressive or threatening behaviour typically adopt this posture. Two of the lion statuettes, the single head from Vogelherd (Figure 11.4) and the therianthrope from Hohlenstein-Stadel (Figure 11.2) exhibit an alert face indicated by the cocked ears and closed mouth. Similarly, the bear from Geißenklösterle (Figure 11.5) is standing in an upright position with extended arms, which is typical of a threatening or attacking position. Finally, the unusual position of the Vogelherd horse (Figure 11.1) has been identified as one of a stallion impressing females. Hahn (1993: 235) concludes that although 'the number

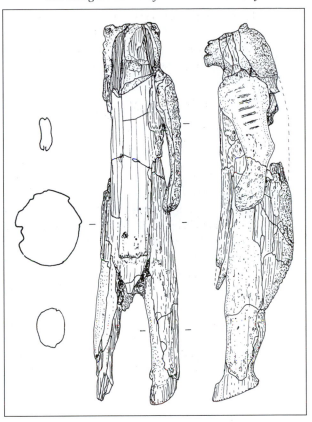

Figure 11.2 The reconstructed human-lion statuette from Hohlenstein-Stadel. Height *c.*296 mm (after Hahn 1986: Tafel 17).

Figure 11.3 A lion statuette from Vogelherd with pointed ears. Note also the patterning of the dots and long incisions. Length *c.*57 mm (reproduced here with the permission of the Institut für Ur- und Frühgeschichte, Abteilung Ältere Urgeschichte und Quartärökologie, Universität Tübingen).

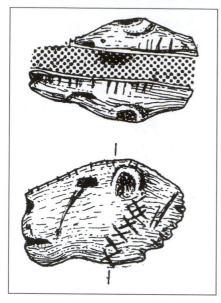

Figure 11.4 The head of a lion from Vogelherd. Note the erect ears and small incsions at the neck. Length *c.*30 mm (after Hahn 1986: Tafel 15).

of Aurignacian mobiliary art objects is too small to offer any significant quantitative values, the number of postures which deviate from ordinary neutral ones seems rather high'. As the statuettes show a selection in favour of strong and large animals, carved with powerful expressions and postures of aggression, strength and alertness, the statuettes reinforce notions of power and strength (Hahn 1993: 240). As yet, no distinguishing behavioural features have been identified in the statuettes of mammoths. Nonetheless, they do represent a strong and powerful animal.

Having discussed the ethological characteristics of these statuettes we now turn to consider other features that, we argue, point to hallucinatory origins. In the Swabian statuettes, there are two features we draw attention to in this context. The first is the human-lion statuette from Hohlenstein-Stadel (Figure 11.2), and the second are the geometric patterns incised on the surface of these statuettes (see, for example, Figs 11.3 and 11.6). Despite the fact that we are arguing for hallucinatory/neuropsychological interpretations already offered for Upper Palaeolithic art in general, here we explore the detailed nature of hallucinatory imagery in these objects to make specific, not general interpretations.

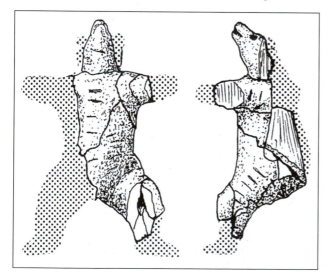

Figure 11.5 A bear statuette from Geißenklösterle in an aggressive posture. Height *c.*49 mm (after Hahn 1986: Tafel 22).

Although in a poor state of preservation, there is no doubt that the so-called 'lion-man' from Hohlenstein-Stadel is a conflation of both human and feline, possibly lion, anatomies. The head is clearly that of a large feline while the body and the posture are anthropomorphic. The extremities do not resemble human hands or feet but rather the paws of a feline. Hahn (1994: 103) was quite explicit in claiming that nothing supports the assertion that this statuette might represent a human wearing a mask, as has often been suggested for depictions similar in character found in the Palaeolithic cave art in such sites as Les Trois Frères and Gabillou.

A number of researchers have interpreted these parietal images as sorcerers in costume, some going so far as to compare them with Witsen's often reproduced picture of a Siberian shaman (e.g. in Clark 1971). More recently, research drawing neuropsychological accounts of altered states of consciousness has suggested that these human-animal images are graphic representations of experiences where humans feel they are transforming into animals during deeper stages in their altered states of consciousness (Lewis-Williams and

Dowson 1988; Clottes and Lewis-Williams 1996). The transformation into an animal is in fact one of the most frequently reported hallucinatory experiences of deeper stages of altered states of consciousness. In one such report a person said:

> I thought of a fox, and instantly I was transformed into that animal. I could distinctly feel myself a fox, could see my long ears and bushy tail, and by a sort of introversion felt that my complete anatomy was that of a fox.
>
> (Siegel and Jarvik 1975: 105)

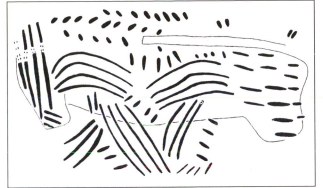

Figure 11.6 A schematic rendition of a more complex motif of multiple arcs, zigzags and notches on a statuette from Vogelherd. Length of statuette *c*.63 mm (after Marshack 1976: 276).

The Hohlenstein-Stadel human-lion is a clear example of such an experience. This interpretation is further supported by the somewhat peculiar posture of the statuette and the position of the feet or paws, which do not allow the statuette to stand upright on its own. The posture of the 'lion-human', and the way in which its 'feet' are carved, gives the distinct impression that it is 'hovering' or 'suspended' above the ground. A sense of floating is yet another widely reported hallucinatory experience of altered states of consciousness. Two different and universally accepted hallucinatory experiences – the transformation of a human into an animal, and the sense of floating – are included in this particular statuette and thus point to an interpretation that is informed by experiences obtained in altered states of consciousness.

Moving on, we now turn to the geometric patterns incised on the otherwise naturalistically carved animal statuettes. The designs consists of dots, straight and curved lines, angles, and small crosses. They are cut in rows or in more complex patterns such as grids and, in one case, a more complex motif made up of multiple arcs, zigzags and dots (Figure 11.6). Shorter notches tend to emphasise the legs and their muscles, as well as the neck (as in Figure 11.4) and the back, while longer incisions are found on the torso of the statuettes (as in Figure 11.3). Series of parallel rows of dots tend to run along the axis of the statuette (again, also in Figure 11.3).

These patterns have been interpreted as a technique for indicating natural markings such as fur colour or fur length (Wagner 1981). Dismissing such an explanation and drawing an analogy with Australian Aboriginal art, Hahn (1986) has suggested these patterns could refer to the animals' skeletal features. The geometric designs themselves, and more importantly their repeated distribution on the bodies, suggest this interpretation is not plausible either. In any event, we reject this sort of simple, look-alike method of analogical argument (see Lewis-Williams 1991: 150–1). The geometric patterns are clearly not realistic, representing neither internal nor external characteristics of the anatomy of the carved animals.

A much more plausible interpretation, one that relies on far less assumptions about Aurignacian peoples' artistic abilities and sensibilities, is that these geometric patterns represent the entoptic phenomena seen in almost all altered states of consciousness. Further, and more significantly, a characteristic of hallucinations experienced during deeper stages of trance is that they tend to be superimposed on and intimately associated with iconic imagery. We suggest, then, that Aurignacian artists used the geometric patterns to show that these statuettes were not simply carvings of animals people might have encountered in their day-to-day lives. Rather,

Age: Recent Trends, 30–41. Sheffield: Department of Archaeology and Prehistory, University of Sheffield.

—— (1994) *Fragments from Antiquity: An Archaeology of Social Life in Britain, 2900–1200 BC*, Oxford: Blackwell.

Bloch, M. (1974) 'Symbols, song, dance and features of articulation. Is religion an extreme form of traditional authority?', *Archives Européennes de Sociologie (European Journal of Sociology)* 15: 55–81.

Bradley, R. (1989a) 'Deaths and entrances: a contextual analysis of megalithic art', *Current Anthropology* 30(1): 68–75.

—— (1989b) 'Darkness and light in the design of megalithic tombs', *Oxford Journal of Archaeology* 8(3): 251–9.

—— (1998) 'Ruined buildings, ruined stones: enclosures, tombs and natural places in the Neolithic of south-west England', *World Archaeology* 30(1): 13–22.

—— (2000) *An Archaeology of Natural Places*, London: Routledge.

Bradley, R., Phillips, T., Richards C. and Webb, M. (2001) 'Decorating the houses of the dead: incised and pecked motifs in Orkney chambered tombs', *Cambridge Archaeological Journal* 11(1): 45–67.

Carpenter, E. (1973) *Eskimo Realities*, New York: Holt, Rinehart and Winston.

Chatwin, B. (1987) 'Dreamtime', *Granta* 21: 39–79.

Classen, C., Howes, D. and Synott, A. (1994) *Aroma: The Cultural History of Smell*, London: Routledge.

Dams, L. (1984) 'Preliminary findings at the "Organ" sanctuary in the Cave of Nerja, Malaga, Spain', *Oxford Journal of Archaeology* 3(1): 1–14.

Davidson, J.L. and Henshall, A.S. (1989) *The Chambered Cairns of Orkney*, Edinburgh: Edinburgh University Press.

—— (1991) *The Chambered Cairns of Caithness*. Edinburgh: Edinburgh University Press.

Devereux, P. and Jahn, R.G. (1996) 'Preliminary investigations and cognitive considerations of the acoustical resonances of selected archaeological sites', *Antiquity* 70: 665–6.

Dronfield, J. (1995a) 'Subjective vision and the source of Irish megalithic art', *Antiquity* 69: 539–49.

—— (1995b) 'Migraine, light and hallucinogens: the neurocognitive basis of Irish megalithic art', *Oxford Journal of Archaeology* 14(3): 261–75.

—— (1996) 'Entering alternative realities: cognition, art and architecture in Irish passage-tombs', *Cambridge Archaeological Journal* 6(1): 37–72.

Eliade, M. (1964) *Shamanism: Archaic Techniques of Ecstasy*, London: Routledge and Kegan Paul.

Eogan, G. (1986) *Knowth and the Passage-tombs of Ireland*, London: Thames and Hudson.

Evans, M.J. (1976) 'Physiological and psychological effects of infrasound at moderate intensities', in W. Tempest (ed.) *Infrasound and Low Frequency Vibration*, London: Academic Press.

Feld, S. (1982) *Sound and Sentiment: Birds, Weeping, Poetics and Song in Kaluli Expression*, Philadelphia: University of Pennsylvania Press.

—— (1996) 'A poetics of place: ecological and aesthetic co-evolution in a Papua New Guinea rainforest community', in R.F. Ellen and K. Fukui (eds) *Redefining Nature: Ecology, Culture and Domestication*, Oxford: Berg.

Fleming, A. (1973) 'Tombs for the living', *Man* 8(2): 177–93.

Gage, J., Jones, A., Bradley, R., Spence, K., Barber, E.J.W. and Taçon, P.S.C. (1999) 'What meaning had colour in early societies?', *Cambridge Archaeological Journal* 9(1): 109–26.

Gell, A. (1995) 'The language of the forest: landscape and phonological iconism in Umeda', in E. Hirsch and M. O'Hanlon (eds) *The Anthropology of Landscape: Perspectives on Space and Place*, Oxford: Clarendon Press.

Gibson, J.J. (1966) *The Senses Considered as Perceptual Systems*. Boston: Houghton Mifflin Company.

Gräslund, B. (1994) 'Prehistoric soul beliefs in northern Europe', *Proceedings of the Prehistoric Society* 60: 15–26.

Huntington, R. and Metcalf, P. (1991) *Celebrations of Death: The Anthropology of Mortuary Ritual*, Cambridge: Cambridge University Press.

Jackson, A. (1968) 'Sound and ritual', *Man* 3(2): 293–9.

Kawada, J. (1996) 'Human dimensions in the sound universe', in R.F. Ellen and K. Fukui (eds) *Redefining Nature: Ecology, Culture and Domestication*, Oxford: Berg.

Lessa, W.A. and Vogt, E.Z. (1979) *Reader in Comparative Religion: An Anthropological Approach*, New York: HarperCollins.

Lewis, I.M. (1971) *Ecstatic Religion: An Anthropological Study of Spirit Possession and Shamanism*, Harmondsworth: Penguin Books.

—— (1996) *Religion in Context: Cults and Charisma*. Cambridge: Cambridge University Press.

Lewis-Williams, J.D. and Dowson, T.A. (1993) 'On vision and power in the Neolithic: evidence from the decorated monuments.', *Current Anthropology* 34(1): 55–65.

Lund, C. (1981) 'The archaeomusicology of Scandinavia', *World Archaeology* 12(3): 246–65.

Lynch, F. (1973) 'The use of the passage in certain passage graves as a means of communication rather than access', in G. Daniel and P. Kjærum (eds) *Megalithic Graves and Ritual*, Copenhagen: Jutland Archaeological Society.

MacGregor, G. (1999) 'Making sense of the past in the present: a sensory analysis of carved stone balls', *World Archaeology* 31(2): 258–71.

MacKie, E.W. (1997) 'Maeshowe and the winter solstice: ceremonial aspects of the Orkney Grooved Ware culture', *Antiquity* 71: 338–59.

Megaw, J.V.S. (1960) 'Penny whistles and prehistory', *Antiquity* 35: 6–13.

—— (1968) 'Problems and non-problems in palaeo-organology: a musical miscellany', in J.M. Coles and D.D.A. Simpson (eds) *Studies in Ancient Europe*, Leicester: Leicester University Press.

—— (1984) 'The bone ?flute', in W.J. Britnell and H.N. Savory (eds) *Gwernvale and Penywyrlod: Two Neolithic Long Cairns in the Black Mountains of Brecknock*, Cambrian Archaeological Monographs No. 2.

Mills, S. (2000) 'An approach for integrating multisensory data: the examples of Sesklo and the Teleorman Valley', in C. Buck, V. Cummings, C. Henley, S. Mills and S. Trick (eds) *U.K. chapter of computer applications and quantitative methods in archaeology*, Oxford: British Archaeological Reports.

Needham, R. (1967) 'Percussion and transition', *Man* 2(4): 606–14.

Neher, A. (1961) 'Auditory driving observed with scalp electrodes in normal subjects', *Electroencephalography and Clinical Neuropsychology* 13(3): 449–51.

—— (1962) 'A physiological explanation of unusual behaviour in ceremonies involving drums', *Human Biology* 34: 151–60.

Nussbaum, D.S. and Reinis, S. (1985) *Some Individual Differences in Human Response to Infrasound*, Institute for Aerospace Studies, report 282, Toronto: University of Toronto.

O'Kelly, M.J. (1982) *Newgrange*. London: Thames and Hudson.

Parker Pearson, M. and Richards, C. (1994) 'Architecture and order: spatial representation and archaeology', in M. Parker Pearson and C. Richards (eds) *Architecture and Order: Approaches to Social Space*. London: Routledge.

Pocock, D. (1981) 'Sight and knowledge', *Transactions, Institute of British Geographers (New Series)* 6: 385–93.

—— (1988) 'The music of geography', in D. Pocock (ed.) *Humanistic Approaches in Geography*. Department of Geography Occasional Publication (New Series) 22. Durham: Durham University.

—— (1989) 'Sound and the geographer', *Geography* 74(1): 193–200.

—— (1993) 'The senses in focus', *Area* 25(1): 11–16.

Pollard, J. and Gillings, M. (1998) 'Romancing the stones: towards a virtual and elemental Avebury', *Archaeological Dialogues* 5(2): 143–64.

Porteous, J.D. (1990) *Landscapes of the Mind: Worlds of Sense and Metaphor*, Toronto: University of Toronto Press.

Potapov, L.P. (1978) 'The shaman drum as a source of ethnographical history', in V. Diószegi and M. Hoppál (eds) *Shamanism in Siberia*, Budapest: Akadémiai Kiadó.

Purser, J. (1997) *The Kilmartin Sessions: the Sounds of Ancient Scotland*, Compact disc produced by the Kilmartin House Trust, Argyll: KHT CD1.

RCAHMS (1946) *Orkney and Shetland 2: Orkney*, Edinburgh: Royal Commission on the Ancient and Historical Monuments of Scotland.

Renfrew, C. (1979) *Investigations in Orkney*, London: Society of Antiquaries.

Reznikoff, I. and Dauvois, M. (1988) 'La dimension sonore des grottes ornées', *Bulletin de la Société Préhistorique Française* 85(8): 238–46.

Richards, C. (1992) 'Doorways to another world: the Orkney-Cromarty chambered tombs', in N. Sharples and A. Sheridan (eds) *Vessels for the Ancestors: Essays on the Neolithic of Britain and Ireland*, Edinburgh: Edinburgh University Press.

—— (1993) 'Monumental choreography: architecture and spatial representation in Late Neolithic Orkney', in C. Tilley (ed.) *Interpretative Archaeology*, Oxford: Berg.

—— (1996a) 'Monuments as landscape: creating the centre of the world in late Neolithic Orkney', *World Archaeology* 28(2): 190–208.

—— (1996b) 'Henges and water: towards an elemental understanding of monumentality and landscape in Late Neolithic Britain', *Journal of Material Culture* 1(3): 313–36.

Riordan, J. (1989) *The Sun Maiden and the Crescent Moon: Siberian Folk Tales*, Edinburgh: Canongate.

Rodaway, P. (1994) *Sensuous Geographies*, London: Routledge.

Rundstrom, R.A. (1990) 'A cultural interpretation of Inuit map accuracy', *Geographical Review* 80(2): 155–68.

Scarre, C. (1989) 'Painting by resonance', *Nature* 338: 382.

Schafer, R.M. (1977) *The Tuning of the World*, Toronto: McClelland and Stewart.

—— (1993. *Voices of Tyranny, Temples of Silence*, Indian River, Ontario: Arcana Editions.

Seeger, A. (1994) 'Music and dance', in T. Ingold (ed.) *Companion Encyclopedia of Anthropology*, London: Routledge.

Sherratt. A. (1991) 'Sacred and profane substances: the ritual use of narcotics in later Neolithic Europe', in P. Garwood, D. Jennings, R. Skeates and J. Toms (eds) *Sacred and Profane: Proceedings of a Conference on Archaeology, Ritual and Religion*, Monograph 32. Oxford: Oxford University Committee for Archaeology.

Sommarström, B. (1989) 'The Sami shaman's drum and the holographic paradigm discussion', in M. Hoppál and O. von Sadovsky (eds) *Shamanism Past and Present, Part 1*, Budapest: Ethnographic Unit, Hungarian Academy of Sciences.

Suedfeld, P. (1980) *Restricted Environmental Stimulation*, New York: John Wiley and Sons.

Tandy, V. and Lawrence, T.R. (1998) 'The ghost in the machine', *Journal of the Society for Psychical Research* 62: 360–4.

Thomas, J. (1990) 'Monuments from the inside: the case of the Irish megalithic tombs', *World Archaeology* 22(2): 168–78.

—— (1993a) 'The politics of vision and the archaeologies of landscape', in B. Bender (ed.) *Landscape: Politics and Perspectives*, Oxford: Berg.

—— (1993b) 'The hermeneutics of megalithic space', in C. Tilley (ed.) *Interpretative Archaeology*, Oxford: Berg.

—— (1999) *Understanding the Neolithic*, London: Routledge.

Tilley, C. (1994) *A Phenomenology of Landscape*, Oxford: Berg.

—— (1996) 'The power of rocks: topography and monument construction on Bodmin Moor', *World Archaeology* 28(2): 161–76.

Tuan, Yi-Fu. (1974) *Topophilia*, Eaglewood Cliffs: Prentice-Hall.

—— (1979) 'Sight and pictures', *Geographical Review* 69(4): 413–22.

Tuzin, D. (1984) 'Miraculous voices: the auditory experience of numinous objects', *Current Anthropology* 25(5): 579–96.

Vitebsky, P. (1995) *The Shaman*, London: Little, Brown and Company.

Walter, V.J. and Walter, W.G. (1949) 'The central effects of rhythmic sensory stimulation', *Electroencephalography and Clinical Neuropsychology* 1: 57–86.

Watson, A. and Keating, D. (1999) 'Architecture and sound: an acoustic analysis of megalithic monuments in prehistoric Britain', *Antiquity* 73: 325–36.

—— (2000) 'The architecture of sound in Neolithic Orkney', in A. Ritchie (ed.) *Neolithic Orkney in its European Context*, Cambridge: McDonald Institute for Archaeological Research.

Whittle, A. (1996) *Europe in the Neolithic: The Creation of New Worlds*. Cambridge: Cambridge University Press.

Zuckerman, M. (1969) 'Hallucinations, reported sensations, and images', in J.P. Zubek (ed.) *Sensory Deprivation: Fifteen Years of Research*, New York: Appleton-Century-Crofts.

Chapter Thirteen

An ideology of transformation: Cremation rites and animal sacrifice in early Anglo-Saxon England

Howard Williams

INTRODUCTION

Over the last two centuries, numerous studies have tried to reconstruct the character of the religious beliefs and rituals of the Anglo-Saxon kingdoms prior to their conversion to Christianity during the seventh century AD. In recent years too there have been published works dedicated to identifying the character of early medieval pagan beliefs (Hines 1997; Griffith 1996; Jolly 1996; Owen 1981; Wilson 1992; on the conversion see Mayr-Harting 1972 and Higham 1997). Paganism has been sought in the literary evidence such as the writings of Northumbrian monk the Venerable Bede, who mentions the existence of a pagan priest, a sanctuary and ceremonies linked to the agricultural cycle (Hines 1997: 379; see also North 1997). A range of other sources including hagiographies, homilies, poems (such as *Beowulf*) and healing charms have all been mined for pagan survivals and pagan-Christian syncretism (Glosecki 1988, 1989; Jolly 1996; Meaney 1989; Robinson 1993). Place-name studies have also been used to ascertain pagan beliefs and places of worship (Gelling 1978; Meaney 1995; Wilson 1992). However, the only contemporary evidence comes from archaeological research. Images on metalwork and pottery have been interpreted in terms of pagan mythologies (Chadwick Hawkes *et al.* 1965; Myres and Green 1973; Reynolds 1980; Wickham-Crowley 1992; Wilson 1992), while certain excavated structures have been interpreted as pagan shrines and temples (Blair 1995; Hope-Taylor 1977: 154–69). However, it is most common for interpretations of Anglo-Saxon paganism to focus upon the large corpus of excavated graves dating to the fifth to seventh centuries AD. Objects found in funerary contexts have been seen as having magical or amuletic functions (Meaney 1981; Wilson 1992). The mortuary rites themselves, such as the use of cremation or the provision of grave goods and burial mounds, are often thought to indicate pagan practices and/or beliefs in the afterlife (Reynolds 1980; Wilson 1992). Finally, some studies have attempted to identify pagan ritual specialists from their distinctive grave furniture (Dickinson 1993a; see also Knüsel and Ripley 2000; Wilson 1992).

Despite these many approaches, Anglo-Saxon scholars are often cautious, sceptical and sometimes openly critical of these attempts to reconstruct Anglo-Saxon paganism, not only from sources derived from the later, Christian Anglo-Saxon period, but also from early Anglo-Saxon archaeological evidence (e.g. Hines 1997: 385–91). For the burial evidence, the complex local and regional variability evident in excavated Anglo-Saxon cemeteries is often taken as evidence that pre-Christian religion was not a static, uniform and enduring phenomenon but varied within and between communities, perhaps according to social and political structures (Filmer-Sankey 1992; see also Wood 1995). An alternative view of this mortuary variability is that religious affiliations were impermanent or had little direct relationship to mortuary behaviour. Instead, mortuary practices are regarded as a context for social, political and ideological activity, rather than explicitly religious beliefs and practices (see Hedeager 1992; Hines 1997: 383). For example, the validity of inferring religious affiliation on the basis of the provision of grave goods, body posture or the orientation of graves has come under serious and critical scrutiny, particularly in relation to Christianisation (Boddington 1990; Schülke 1999; Young 1977, 1999). A related perspective is seen in the argument that only through interaction with the Church did mortuary practices take on an overtly and belligerently pagan character (Hines 1997: 387). At the cemetery of Sutton Hoo, mortuary practices have been interpreted as part of an ideological resistance to the Kentish and Merovingian agents of Christianisation in early seventh-century East Anglia (Carver 1992, 1998). More frequently, in the last two decades the majority of studies of burial archaeology have avoided the question. The pagan status of the graves is either regarded as an implicit assumption that requires little further study, or else the character of paganism is thought to be not worthy of study or beyond the scope of archaeological enquiry. Instead, discussions have focused on the social context of ritual practices and ritual deposition while remaining circumspect concerning their specific religious connotations (e.g. Härke 2000; Lucy 1998, 2000). Hence recent studies have focused instead upon the inference of social organisation, structures and identities from the symbolism and variability of mortuary practices (Crawford 1998; Härke 1992, 1997a; Huggett 1996; Lucy 1998; Pader 1982; Stoodley 1999, 2000). In addition, debates have raged around the scale and character of Germanic migration and the nature of ethnicity by focusing on the burial data (e.g. Hamerow 1994; Härke 1990, 1997b; Lucy 1998, 2000). Much of this discussion has taken place in relation to inhumation graves, although the study of the cremation rites of early medieval England has followed comparable trends (see Crawford 1997; Hills 1993, 1999a; Richards 1984, 1987, 1992, 1995; Ravn 1999; for review of this issue see Williams 2001a).

While these discussions of social structure, ethnicity and, to some extent, symbolism and ideology are important and valuable, they have shifted the focus of enquiry away from the religious and cosmological qualities that burial rites may simultaneously hold. This might be seen in the context of Anglo-Saxon archaeology's traditional focus upon issues deemed appropriate by historians (such as migration and kingdom formation) as well as a collective realisation of the many inherent difficulties in discussing Anglo-Saxon religion and ritual. For example, when discussing Anglo-Saxon cremation rites, consideration of their symbolic and religious meanings has been limited to their social function (see Williams 2001a). In early medieval Europe cremation is regarded as the archetypal pagan rite: for example, the Capitularies of Charlemagne against the Old Saxons show that cremation rites could be regarded by Christians as pagan (King 1987: 205; see also Effros 1997). Yet *how* were they pagan? To date, there has been no detailed consideration of the precise ways in which the form and content of cremation and post-cremation rites could be linked to pre-Christian ideologies, cosmologies and world views. It is argued here that this is a weakness of current perspectives, since it is only through an appreciation of the religious values, symbols and metaphors of mortuary practices than we can adequately appreciate the importance and efficacy of cremation within the ethnic, social and political structures of the fifth to seventh centuries AD (see Andrén 1993; Härke 1997b; Hedeager 1998, 1999; Williams 1998, 1999, 2000, 2001b).

In order to pursue this argument, the chapter focuses upon one aspect of the cremation rite – the sacrifice of animals – to draw out some themes that may indicate links between the cremation and post-cremation treatment of the dead and pre-Christian ideologies that may have shamanistic connotations. Despite the many difficulties involved, this chapter argues that cremation rites constituted part of a wider 'ideology of transformation' in early Anglo-Saxon England that served to forge individual and community links with the supernatural, to define religious and social identities and to articulate myths of origin.

CREMATION PRACTICES AND ANIMAL SACRIFICE IN EARLY ANGLO-SAXON ENGLAND

Firstly, let us briefly review the archaeological evidence for animal sacrifice in early Anglo-Saxon cremation rites. The excavation of cremation burials of the early Anglo-Saxon period has taken place since the nineteenth and twentieth centuries (e.g. Myres and Green 1973; Williams 2001a). However, it is only recently that attention has turned to the study of the cremation rite itself rather than the form and decoration of the urns frequently used to contain the cremains (Myres 1969, 1977a). This knowledge has been derived from the detailed study and publication of large, well-excavated cemeteries. Notably, the excavation and post-excavation analysis of the cemetery of Spong Hill with over 2,500 cremation burials has greatly increased the sample of published graves (Hills 1977; Hills and Penn 1981; Hills, Penn and Rickett 1987, 1994). Other important cemeteries include those at Newark and Sancton (Kinsley 1989; Timby 1993). In turn, this research has made possible the systematic osteological analysis of cremated remains (Bond 1993, 1994, 1996; McKinley 1993, 1994; for early studies see Wells 1960 and Wilkinson 1980). There remains huge potential in future research: in particular, excavations directed by Kevin Leahy at Cleatham in Lincolnshire produced 1,014 cinerary urns that would be an ideal project for future osteological analysis (Leahy 1998). However, the information collated so far allows us to reconstruct, in broad terms, the sequence of cremation rites in the fifth to seventh centuries AD.

As in many societies, the cremation of the dead was only one stage of a complex ritual (Figure 13.1). Before cremation, we can assume that the body was prepared for the pyre with artefacts and clothing in a manner comparable to inhumation graves. After being consumed by the flames, the remains were usually collected and placed in ceramic vessels, although occasionally bronze or organic containers were used. We can identify a considerable variety in the burial rites, both within the same cemeteries and between different cemeteries and regions. For example, the ceramic urns used to contain the cremated remains are extremely varied in terms of both their form and decoration (Myres 1977a; Richards 1984, 1987; see below, pp. 199–200). The spatial organisation and context of the rite also differs between cemeteries and regions. Cremation is found alongside inhumation rites in most areas. In eastern England between the middle fifth century and the early seventh century AD, cremation cemeteries (where inhumation was either rare or absent) were much larger than broadly contemporary inhumation cemeteries (where cremations are few or absent). These large cremation cemeteries may have served as central burial places for several communities who may have been dispersed over a wide region (e.g. Hills 1977; Kinsley 1989; Leahy 1998; McKinley 1994; Myres and Green 1973; Timby 1993). In southern England and the West Midlands, cremation rites were employed in different ways. Large, predominantly cremation cemeteries are absent, but at some sites cremation is found alongside contemporary inhumation graves in comparable numbers; such sites are consequently labelled 'mixed-rite' cemeteries (e.g. Cook and Dacre 1985; Down and Welch 1990; see Williams 2001a).

One of the most important contributions of osteological studies has been the realisation that animal sacrifice was much more common in cremation rites than had previously been thought

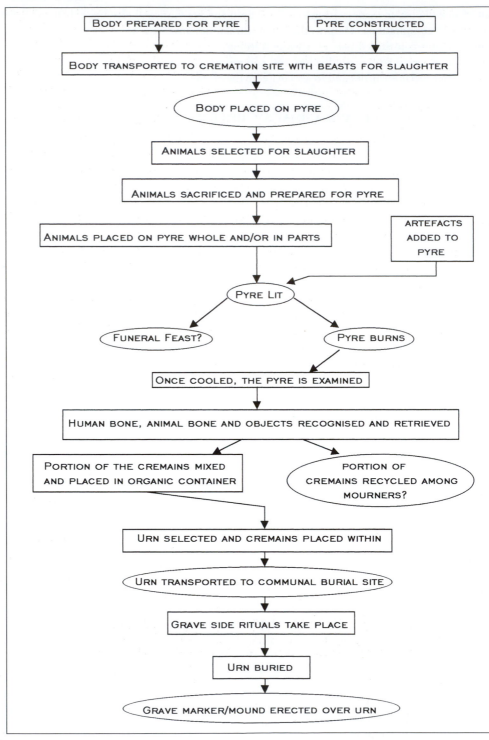

Figure 13.1 The conjectural and simplified sequence of rites during early Anglo-Saxon cremation practices informed by archaeological and osteological evidence.

possible (Bond 1994: 121; McKinley 1994; Richards 1987: 125). The sites of Spong Hill and Sancton are particularly important, given the high quality of the excavation and post-excavation analyses. At these sites, almost half the cremation burials contained animal remains (46.4 per cent of graves at Spong Hill – McKinley 1994: 92) suggesting that animal sacrifice was a widespread aspect of the funerary rites. Given that animal bones could have been missed when retrieving bone from the pyre, or missed by archaeologists during analysis, the overall percentage of funerals involving animal sacrifice and burial may have been far higher. A range of animal species have been recognised, although the cremation rite prevents a species-specific identification in the majority of instances. When species identification is possible, the bones of horse, sheep/goat, pig, cattle and dog have been found in a series of combinations. Infrequent occurrences included the bones of birds, deer, fox, fish, beaver and hare, while bear claws may suggest that occasionally the hides of this animal were placed on the pyre with the dead (McKinley 1994: 92). Horse and sheep/goat are by far the most common species. At both Spong Hill and Sancton, Julie Bond argues that horses were probably the most frequently sacrificed species, though the fact that the remains of sheep/goat are more diagnostic in the heavily fragmented cremated bone assemblages has produced the impression that these are the most common species (Figs 13.2 and 13.3). At the unpublished cemetery of Elsham, Richards (1987) noted that sheep/goat were the most frequent species.

A variety of evidence suggests that animals held a special importance in the cremation process. Firstly, while animal sacrifice is also found in association with inhumation graves, particularly in eastern England, it is much less common (see below, p. 201). Even if similar numbers of animals were sacrificed at the funerals of individuals disposed of by inhumation, they were not buried in the graves with the dead. It therefore seems as if a special link between animals and the dead was constructed through the cremation rite, in a way not replicated in the

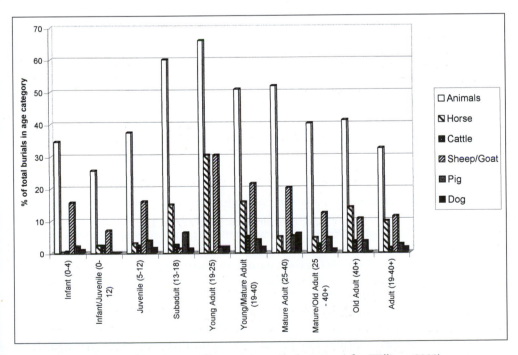

Figure 13.2 Aged burials from Spong Hill containing animal remains (after Williams 2000).

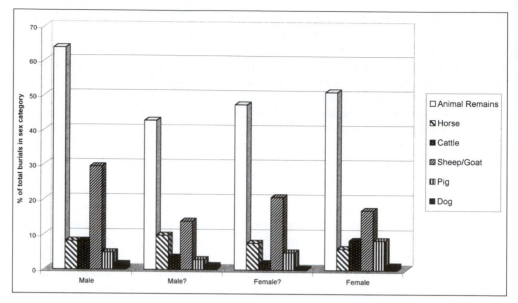

Figure 13.3 Sexed burials from Spong Hill containing animal remains (after Williams 2000).

inhumation rite. Furthermore, the species selected for sacrifice do not appear to fully reflect the economy of early Anglo-Saxon England. Bone assemblages from settlements are dominated by sheep/goat, and these are also frequent in cremation cemeteries. However, whereas the remains of horse and dog are often included in cremation burials they are extremely rare on settlements (Crabtree 1995: 23–5; Richards 1992: 139).

Animals were probably sacrificed for funerary feasting, but this does not seem to have been the primary concern in their slaughter. Even though there is widespread evidence of butchery, the motivation seems to be for the beasts to accompany the deceased through the ritual process (Richards 1987: 125). The animals' flesh may have been partly consumed by mourners, perhaps as an important ritual act, yet the close relationship between the dead and animal bones may have been an equally important stimulus for the sacrifice. Pigs and sheep/goat seem to have been butchered and placed on the pyre as joints of meat. They may have therefore provided food for the mourners and the dead, but also associated the dead with any special qualities or attributes that these animals may have been believed to have. However, at Sancton and Spong Hill, Julie Bond has observed that in many cases dogs, horses and cattle accompanied the deceased as whole animals. Few butchery marks were found on the bones of these species, suggesting that although they may have been dismembered to make cremation easier, they were not prepared for consumption and most animal parts were represented in the burial (Bond 1993: 304; 1994: 126, 128; 1996: 83). This also contrasts with the Spong Hill settlement site where there is evidence that horses as well as cattle were prepared for consumption (Bond 1994: 123). Therefore, as Julian Richards has cogently argued, feasting was a secondary consideration and does not explain the close association of animals and people throughout the funerary process (Richards 1987, 1992).

So, animals are particularly associated with cremated remains, and the species selected for funerary sacrifice differ from those present in and around settlements. Their relationship with the cremated dead is further emphasised by the fact that Julian Richards (1987) and Mads Ravn (1999) have identified a number of links between the identity of the deceased as revealed by osteological and artefact data, and the species of animals interred with the dead. For instance, adults, and adult males in particular, were more frequently buried with animal remains (McKinley 1994: 99; Richards 1992: 139; see also Williams 2000: figs 2 and 3). Young adults are particularly linked with the provision of animal remains, although all categories of the dead could receive animal sacrifices (Figure 13.2). Overall, male graves contain more animal remains than female graves, although both males and females could receive the same range of animal species (Figure 13.3). Using correspondence analysis, Ravn identifies even closer associations between a particular group of adult males with martial equipment, buried with horses and with urns adorned with animal-shaped stamps (1999, and see below, pp. 200–1). Hills (1999a) also sees animal remains, especially horses, as more common in wealthy cremation graves at Spong Hill, and at this site, horses are uncommon in infant and juvenile burials.

These observations suggest that different species and combinations of species may have formed part of a complex symbolic system for signalling the identity of the dead, including elements of status, gender and age categories (Richards 1987, 1992). However, two qualifications are required. First, despite these correlations the ubiquity of the rite across cremation cemeteries must also be recognised. While the sacrifice of animals may have been used by mourners to articulate their identity, status and wealth as well as that of the deceased, animal sacrifice was not an exclusive concern of a warrior elite (*contra* Ravn 1999). For example, while horses may be more common in male adult graves, they are not found exclusively in such contexts. Second, the inclusion of animal remains on the pyre and throughout the rest of the ritual process suggests that much closer relationships were being articulated between animals and the dead person. Animals were not simply placed on the pyre, they were consciously retrieved and placed in an urn with human remains and artefacts. This relationship suggests something more than the animals acting as status and identity symbols: it may instead indicate that the cremation and post-cremation treatment of animals and people was intended to forge a link between the two, as they were both transformed and altered by the technologies and practices of the funeral itself. In other words, the aim of the animal sacrifice may not have been to 'represent' the deceased's social identity, but to contribute to its transformation and reconfiguration.

Consequently, cremation rites set up symbolic associations between animal species and the physical remains of the dead through the ritual process. In Anglo-Saxon cremation burials, the dead and animals underwent the same transformation by fire, perhaps on the same pyre. Their bones were retrieved, combined and buried in the same urns, almost as if the identity of the dead, constructed through the funeral, incorporated elements of both human and animal. Furthermore, animal accessory vessels have been identified at Spong Hill and Sancton. These are burials of animal remains in cinerary urns placed adjacent to human cremation burials. Here, horse is predominant but usually combined with other species (McKinley 1994: 93). It seems as if the analogy of person and animal is taken one stage further in this case. Faunal remains are accorded the same respect as the human occupant of the grave and given their own cinerary urn. In a few cases, they are even given their own grave goods.

CONTEXT AND INTERPRETATION: ANIMALS AND FUNERALS IN ANGLO-SAXON ENGLAND

Let us now turn to the wider context of animals and death as revealed in early Anglo-Saxon archaeological evidence. Animals are not only found in cremation urns; on occasions they are depicted on them, particularly on urns dated to the sixth century (Fig. 13.4). Again, a variety of species are portrayed, including horses, sheep and deer in both stamped and inscribed

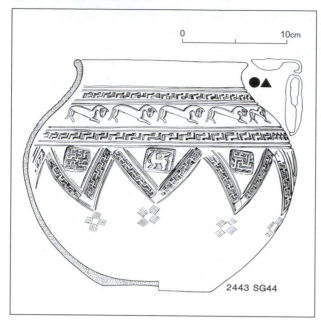

Figure 13.4 Urn from burial 2443 from Spong Hill (after Hills, Penn and Rickett 1987: 133, drawn by Kenneth Penn and reproduced by kind permission of Norfolk Museum and Archaeology Service).

decoration (Capelle 1987; Eagles and Briscoe 1999; Hicks 1993; Hills 1983; Myres and Green 1973: fig. 4). Horses are the most commonly portrayed beasts among the stamped designs (Eagles and Briscoe 1999: 101), but there are also mythical creatures including the 'wyrm' designs on some urns (Lethbridge 1951). These portrayals represent distinctive animals, but there are also more abstract designs that have been seen by J.N.L. Myres as zoomorphic (Myres 1977b). On a few urns, the linear, inscribed ornamentation may have been employed intentionally to give impression of eyes or a crested animal body with hair (Myres 1977b). Sometimes the plastic decoration (bosses and knobs) on urns are framed by stamped patterns and dots that may have meant to be regarded as eyes. Some of these interpretations are questionable, but among the more convincing examples are two urns from Newark, one depicting two birds on the lid of an urn (now lost), and another with a series of bosses shaped as animals (or perhaps portraying bear skins; Kinsley 1989). In all cases, the aim seems not simply to present the animals in a realistic way, but to portray them wholly or in part in an idealised, sometimes abstract form (see also Richards 1992: 139). Admittedly these vessels form only a small proportion of the total number of cinerary urns, but they hint at more sophisticated relationships between the deceased and the animal because they are evoked *on* as well as *in* the urns. Indeed, the animals on the urn may be regarded as symbolically 'framing' and 'containing' the dead (see Hills 1999b).

Julian Richards has discussed how animal symbolism also extends to the metalwork found in fifth and sixth century graves (1992: 137–41). From eastern England the most commonplace female brooch type from cremation and inhumation cemeteries, the cruciform brooch, often has a beast's head as its foot, sometimes resembling a horse or serpent with flaring nostrils (Åberg 1926: 28–56; Hines 1984; Richards 1992). Sometimes the animal-headed brooch feet are themselves used as pottery stamps on cinerary urns (Briscoe 1985; Richards 1992). It may also be worth noting that stamped decoration would often be applied with bone tools, perhaps a further way in which animals were associated with the funerary context (Richards 1995: 60). Such acts may help to set up numerous allusions between people's bodily attire and animal identities. A range of artefacts from southern and eastern England are decorated with Salin's Style 1 animal art, in which the themes of transformation and ambiguity loom large (Dickinson 1993b and forthcoming; Leigh 1984; Kristofferson 1995). As David Leigh has discussed, animals are depicted that, when viewed from a different perspective or angle, constitute a human face or mask (Leigh 1984: 39; see also Hawkes 1997: 332–3). So, we have a number of themes. Not only are animals important in their depiction as well as their sacrifice during funerary display, but the art and cremation seem to have served parallel functions. Both the portrayal of animals and the cremation of sacrificed beasts served to transform animals, and mingle or confuse their forms with those of people.

It is in these same regions of eastern England that animals are found whole or in part together with inhumed individuals (Vierck 1971; Wilson 1992: 97–103). The frequency is nowhere near as high as in the cremation graves, but once again a wide range of species occur, with the horse again being prevalent. As in cremation burials, horses are more likely to be inhumed next to adult male individuals. On other occasions they are placed in relative isolation within the cemetery (Dickinson and Speake 1992: 108–12; Vierck 1971; Kinsley 1993: 58–61; Serjeantson 1994: 66–8). They are usually found whole, as with the recent discovery of a horse with a male weapon burial from Lakenheath in Suffolk. However, individual body parts have also been discovered. Some of these might represent joints of meat, while others, such as the horses' heads retrieved from the Great Chesterford cemetery, and an articulated foreleg from Broughton Lodge, may suggest more ritualised acts of deposition (Evison 1994: 31–5; Filmer-Sankey 1992; Kinsley 1993: 46; Serjeantson 1994: 66–70).

However, even in these cases the association with cremation is not far away. Animal sacrifice seems much more common in eastern England where cremation is most prevalent (Vierck 1971), and cremation was employed in many of the same cemeteries where inhumed horses are found. Elsewhere, symbolic or partial cremation accompanies sacrificed animals. At Wanlip, Leicestershire, a man and horse were inhumed on a layer of charcoal and ash (Liddle 1980: 18) while a horse at Great Chesterford showed signs of partial cremation (Serjeantson 1994: 68). Similar rites occur for both cremated and inhumed animals. For instance, the decapitation of the horse at West Heslerton parallels evidence for the same practice from a cremation burial at Sancton (Bond 1993: 304; Powlesland and Haughton 1986). This suggests a ritualised element to the slaughter of these animals (assuming that decapitation can hardly have been the easiest or quickest means of killing a horse). It is important to note that this relationship between horses and burial continues but changes its context into the early seventh century. They are found at high-status barrow burials such as the cremation graves beneath mounds 3 and 4 at Sutton Hoo, and also inhumed beneath mound 17 (Bond 1996; Carver 1998). Horse bones were also retrieved from the cremation barrow burial at Asthall in Oxfordshire (Dickinson and Speake 1992: 110–12). Clearly animal sacrifice was still an important visual and symbolic element of these complex and theatrical elite mortuary rites (Carver 1998; Williams 2001b).

To date there have been few direct interpretations of the specific relationship between cremation rites and animal sacrifice in early Anglo-Saxon England. Julie Bond, Catherine Hills (1999b), Julian Richards (1987, 1992) and Mads Ravn (1999) have all noted the importance of animal sacrifice as a statement of wealth and status, reflecting the social identity of the deceased. The rite of animal sacrifice is believed to allow us to identify aspects of early Anglo-Saxon social structure and cultural connections between eastern 'Anglian' England and the homelands of the Anglo-Saxons on the Continent. Crabtree (1995) and Richards (1992) also regard animal sacrifice as a symbolic act related to wider religious and ideological programs in society. Richards (1992) suggests a totemic function for particular animal species as denoting certain social categories. Crabtree (1995) also sees the sacrifice of whole animals in the broader context of other animal remains used in funerary contexts: the provision of food offerings, animal bone amulets and artefacts made from animal bone. While I would concur with these views as not only sensible but appropriate given the available evidence, these explanations remain partial. No attempt is made to explain why certain animals were appropriate for symbolising wealth and social identity, as opposed to other material resources available in society. Nor is there any attempt to address specifically the relationship between animals and the cremation process: the ritual transformation of the dead by fire from one social, cosmological and ontological state to another. I wish to build on these important discussions by suggesting that shamanistic themes of transformation and journeying might explain the particular form and content of cremation rites and animal sacrifice.

DEATH, ANIMALS AND SHAMANISM: ANTHROPOLOGICAL PARALLELS

It might be relevant to discuss two forms of analogy to help place this interpretation in its wider context. Firstly we can discuss the known significance of animal sacrifice at funerals in societies where shamanism is practised. Anthropological accounts provide us with a broader perspective in understanding the social, cultural and religious attitudes of people towards animals and the significance of animal sacrifice in particular (e.g. Ingold 1986). There are many difficulties in archaeologists using ethnographic analogies from societies in different parts of the globe, and assuming that the same meanings and associations motivated comparable formal behaviour (see Hodder 1982). Unfortunately, the character of the fragmented ethnographic literature for this topic makes it inevitable that discussions do not focus on a contextual use of analogy from a single community but draw upon the accounts from a number of different societies (see Ingold 1986). However, they may still provide some evidence to support the interpretation of early Anglo-Saxon animal sacrifice suggested above. In particular, the ethnographic evidence does seem to show that the sacrifice and close physical association of animals with the corpse can relate to metaphors of soul journeying and shamanistic transformations.

First, let us briefly consider some relationships between shamanic rituals and death rituals. Shamans are involved in death in a variety of ways. As healers they attempt to prevent death, through intercession, journeying and combat with supernatural forces. In some cultures they are prohibited from funerals because shamanistic seances can bring back the dead (e.g. Bogoras 1911: 520), but in many societies they are among the ritual specialists involved in funerary rites. In other cultures they can be the masters of mortuary ceremonies (e.g. Nebesky de Wojkowitz 1951). As Mircea Eliade has noted, in many shamanistic societies the shaman's journey to supernatural realms often involves travelling along the same routes as the dead are believed to take, and the shaman's journey can be regarded as a symbolic death (Eliade 1964, 1977: 17). While in healing shamans may rescue the spirit of their patient *from* the afterlife, following death they often act as psychopomps, directing the dead *to* the afterlife. These ideas are widespread and may set up a recursive relationship between shamanic journeys and a society's perceptions and knowledge of mythical funerary geographies. In some societies, shamanic rituals take place at the burial site, and the bones of the dead are incorporated into seances and rites because of their power over the living (Kan 1989). Furthermore, shamans form a very special category of the dead and may be likened to the dead during life (Kan 1989: 119–20; Vitebsky 1995: 94–5). Indeed, shamanic initiations often involve a symbolic and sometimes violent death through dismemberment, or devouring by animal spirits, followed by the symbolic reassembly and rebirth of the body (Glosecki 1989; Vitebsky 1995: 59–63).

Consequently, we can see a number of relationships between shamanic and funerary rites. Both can be perceived as a journey, and both involve death and regeneration articulated in terms of disassembly and dissolution followed by reconstitution (Czaplicka 1914: 181; Humphrey and Onon 1996; see Bloch and Parry 1982). As Piers Vitebksy shows for the Sora of Orissa, shamanism can be central to the ways in which memories of the dead are configured, and cosmologies are made (Vitebsky 1993). It is hardly surprising that in some societies at least, such as the Tlingit of the American Northwest Coast, direct analogies are made between the shaman's initiation – involving 'death' and the subsequent disarticulation and rearticulation of the shaman's body – and the cremation and post-cremation treatment of the dead (Kan 1989: 51, 105–6).

Could animal sacrifice relate to this relationship between shamanic rituals and death rituals? It is frequently noted that shamans evoke animals in a variety of ways during their rituals, including the mimicking of animals or their sacrifice (e.g. Czaplicka 1914: 240; Eliade 1964: 190). Animals can act as intermediaries with the supernatural or as steeds on journeys to other realms. As mentioned above, animal spirits are also believed to choose the shaman and to devour him or her, disassembling and reassembling the shaman's bones according to a defined order during initiation (Glosecki 1989: 24). In the funerary rites of some societies where shamanism is a central practice, it therefore appears that animal sacrifice at funerals can be considered to enable the dead to undergo their proper transformation. A variety of metaphors may be suggested, and the animal may be regarded as a sacrificial substitute for the deceased, as a steed, as a guide, or perhaps as the 'soul' of the deceased itself.

Such associations of animal sacrifice with cremation rites can be found in many societies around the world. In 'tribal' India for instance, there are accounts of animal sacrifices punctuating and articulating the social, cosmological and ontological transformation of the dead among the Khasis of Bengal (Gurdon 1914; Århem 1989), the Todas (Rivers 1906; Walker 1986) and the Sora of Orissa (Vitebsky 1993, 1995). Animal sacrifice seems also to be a consistent feature of funerals in Siberian societies where shamanism is a prominent form of religious belief and experience. Among the Buryat, people were often cremated together with a horse, and three days later the remains were collected into a sack and placed in a hole in a pine tree (Czaplicka 1914: 156). Two reindeer are slaughtered and placed on the pyre among the Chuckchee (Bogoras 1911), and a similar fate befell the reindeer that drew the sledge to the cremation site among the Koryak (Jochelson 1908: 111). In each case, the animals employed are undergoing the similar roles to the animal helpers in the culture's shamanic rituals. Among the Yakut (who bury their dead), Sumner recorded that animals sacrificed at the funeral were the steeds of the dead riding to the next world (1901: 98–104). The Gilyak of Sakhalin and the lower Amur sacrificed dogs while the cremation pyre burned, with the animals' heads turned in the direction that their spirit should send a message to the next world. They were then eaten at the pyre site (Black 1973: 71). The Gilyak perceived a special affinity between people and dogs, which are the only domestic species and believed to be mediators with the divine (Black 1973: 89–93). Humphrey and Onon discuss a similar conception among the Daur Mongols: an old, castrated horse of the deceased is saddled outside the house from which a string 'rein' is attached to the dead person's body. It is then killed and its heart, liver, lungs and spleen removed and placed beside the coffin. The animal is believed to be the soul's mount on the journey to the afterlife (Humphrey and Onon 1996: 195). All these societies practice shamanic rites, with beliefs in soul journeying and close animal–people relationships in death. Just as the shaman rides on an animal, or changes into an animal for a journey to other realms, so the sacrifice of animals allows the same transformation for the dead.

None of these societies practice behaviour identical to that found in early Anglo-Saxon England. However, these examples clearly bring home the powerful symbolic importance that animal sacrifice can hold in facilitating the proper transition and reconfiguration of the dead through funerary rites. Such cases illustrate that, rather than simply being a convenient means of disposing of the deceased's moveable wealth and providing food for the mourners, the sacrifice of animals within the cremation ceremony can be seen in relation to animistic and shamanistic ways of viewing the world, in which rituals renegotiate animal–person relations.

DEATH, ANIMALS AND SHAMANISM: SCANDINAVIAN SOURCES

Scandinavian sources provide much more evidence of the relationships between animals and death, through a shamanistic 'ideology of transformation' (there are many publications on the topic of *seiðr* – the possible Norse shamanism – of which some relevant English-language examples include: Ellis 1943; Ellis Davidson 1964, 1981, 1988, 1993; Buchholz 1971; Dronke 1997 (trans.); Eliade 1964; DuBois 1999; Glosecki 1989; Grambo 1989; Price 2000, 2001). These accounts provide a second source of analogy for our consideration.

Numerous animals have associations with death, the dead and what appear to be shamanistic rituals in Scandinavian sources, but the horse in particular clearly had sacred and funerary associations in pagan mythology (Ellis Davidson 1988: 49–57). Snorri tells us that Baldr's horse was led to the funeral pyre and sacrificed, suggesting that this was an integral part of funerary practices (*The Prose Edda*, Faulkes 1987: 50), while two horses are sacrificed in Ibn Fadlan's account of a Viking Rus funeral (Jones 1968). We also learn elsewhere of horse sacrifice, how horses sacred to Freyr were kept near his temples and that live horses were valued in augury and divination (Flint 1991: 266). They were sacrificed and eaten during religious festivals and, and once sacrificed, their heads raised on poles could be invested with magical power (a practice related in *Egils saga Skallagrímssonar,*Fell 1975: 100).

Óðinn's horse Sleipnir may represent an instance of the horse conceived as a shamanic animal (Eliade 1964; Ellis Davidson 1964: 142; Price 2000, 2001) With eight legs and runes carved on his teeth, he carried Óðinn to the entrance of Hel in order to gain wisdom and knowledge from the seer's grave, and also bore his son Hermodr to Hel to seek the resurrection of his brother Baldr (*The Prose Edda*, Faulkes 1987: 50; *The Poetic Edda* – Larrington 1996: 243). These qualities are not restricted to the steed of Óðinn, as Baldr rides to Hel on the horse sacrificed at his funeral and the horse of Freyr has the ability to take Skirnir on a journey to Giantland to woo Gerðr for his master (*The Poetic Edda*, Larrington 1996: 63). In these cases, horses are vehicles of journeying between worlds and hence communication with the dead.

There are also hints that animals could be integral to the nature of the social person during life, and were thus particularly important at the time of death. Horses and other domestic animals could have been regarded as guardians, external souls of individuals and shaman's familiars. The term *fylgja* found in Scandinavian tradition relates the concept that animals could be the fetches or 'souls' of individuals, equivalent to animal guardians (Glosecki 1989: 183). They are often seen in dreams and omens, and could include a wide variety of animals depending upon the personality of the deceased (e.g. Turville-Petre 1964: 229, 227–30). These ideas are taken to extremes with the idea that individuals could shape-shift into an animal form that represents an extension of the social person. Thus the bear heroes of Scandinavian tradition not only have the attributes of bears, but in some stories can go into a trance in order to emerge in their bear form to fight in battle (as in *Hrólfs saga Kraka*, Jones 1961: 313).

These concepts of shape-shifting and soul journeys in the form of animals seem to extend to the dead themselves, for even the souls of the dead are sometimes depicted as animals in the saga literature (Ellis Davidson 1981). For instance, in *Eyrbyggja Saga* Thorolf Twist-Foot returns after his death to haunt the farmstead near to which he had been buried. He is exhumed and his body dragged to a small knoll by the sea (*Eyrbyggja Saga*, Pálsson and Edwards 1972: 95). This is effective for a time, but then he begins haunting again. This time, his body is once more exhumed, cremated, and the ashes scattered on the foreshore. However, a cow with a broken leg (like Thorolf himself) licks the stone where the ashes were scattered and eventually gives birth to a brutally uncontrollable bull. This animal eventually kills Thorodd, the new owner of the farmstead, and disappears forever into a nearby river (*Eyrbyggja Saga,* Pálsson and Edwards

1972: 155–60). This hints that spirits of the dead could be conceived as taking on animal forms (Ellis Davidson 1981). Inescapably this literature is medieval in date, and written in a thoroughly Christian context with an idealised and romantic vision of the pagan past. Despite this, these sources represent more subtle associations between the dead and animals that broaden the possibilities for understanding the evidence from early Anglo-Saxon graves to include themes of soul journeying, shape-shifting and transformation.

DEATH AND ANIMALS: ANGLO-SAXON WRITTEN AND PICTORAL SOURCES

From Anglo-Saxon culture there are hints that animals held more than an economic and functional value, and may have been the focus of a range of religious values, superstitions and prohibitions. For instance, the Venerable Bede informs us that cattle were sacrificed as a part of pagan seasonal ceremonies (Hines 1997; Wilson 1992), and that the pagan priest Coifi was prohibited from riding a stallion (*Historia Ecclesiastica* II 13, Sherley-Price 1955; but see North 1997). Certain activities, such as horse racing, were deemed unseemly for men of God (*Historia Ecclesiastica* V 6, Sherley-Price 1955) but not necessarily pagan, although horses were still the focus of cultural practices abhorred by papal legates to England in the eighth century (Meaney 1981: 132). Further hints that horses in particular had a special religious status as well as cultural importance come from the equine names of the mythical heroes Hengist and Horsa (Yorke 1997). The poem *Beowulf* depicts horses as important participants of funerary rites, even though this source cannot be regarded as a direct portrayal of pre-Christian burial ritual (*Beowulf* lines 3168–77, Alexander 1973; *contra* Ellis Davidson 1993: 135). There are however, two sources that hint at a tradition linking horses with death. The late Saxon 'charm for a Sudden Stitch', begins:

> Loud were they, lo, loud, when they rode over the burial mound;
> they were fierce, when they rode over the land.
>
> (Griffith 1996: 189; Jolly 1996: 139)

The charm depicts the causes of an illness as riders traversing a barrow. Whatever the creatures imagined were, the link between the horse, the supernatural and the burial mound is apparent. In this context, the early eighth-century Franks' casket is interesting. The whale-bone casket is adorned with carvings which, at the centre of a scene on one end of the box, portray a horse that according to Leslie Webster embodies the themes of death, wilderness and exile (Webster 1999). Despite being constructed in a Christian context, it seems that the pagan scenes were deliberately selected and juxtaposed against Roman and Christian images, hence the front of the casket depicts Wayland the Smith in his forge (a scene from a pagan story with shamanistic elements known from later Scandinavian sources – Dronke 1997) being placed next to the Adoration of the Magi (Webster 1999). Following Webster, we can regard the scene on the right hand end as one of pagan significance in which a horse and a bird are associated with a burial mound covering a person. Meanwhile, a creature that may resemble a horse – half-animal, half-human – also sits on a barrow. The runes around the scene refer to this beast as 'Hos on the sorrow-mound' (Webster 1999; see also Semple 1998). It requires special pleading to use these fragments of evidence to reconstruct the importance of animals in funerary rites of the fifth and sixth centuries, but they at the very least suggest that animals, horses in particular, were the focus of religious and cultural values beyond their value as moveable wealth. In turn, this provides a context where we can imagine their potential importance in the symbolism of funerary rites.

—— (1999a) 'Did the people of Spong Hill come from Schleswig-Holstein?' *Studien Zur Sachsenforschung* 11: 145–54.

—— (1999b) 'Spong Hill and the Adventus Saxonum', in C.E. Karkov, K.M. Wickham-Crowley and B.K.Young (eds) *Spaces of the Living and the Dead: An Archaeological Dialogue,* Oxford: Oxbow.

Hills, C. and Penn, K. (1981) *The Anglo-Saxon Cemetery at Spong Hill, North Elmham. Part II: Catalogue of Cremations,* East Anglian Archaeology 11, Dereham: Norfolk Archaeological Unit.

Hills, C., Penn, K. and Rickett, R. (1987) *The Anglo-Saxon Cemetery at Spong Hill, North Elmham. Part IV: Catalogue of Cremations,* East Anglian Archaeology 34, Dereham: Norfolk Archaeological Unit.

—— (1994) *The Anglo-Saxon Cemetery at Spong Hill, North Elmham. Part V: Catalogue of Cremations,* East Anglian Archaeology 67, Dereham: Norfolk Archaeological Unit.

Hines, J. (1984) *The Scandinavian Character of Anglian England in the Pre-Viking period,* Oxford: British Archaeological Reports.

—— (1997) 'Religion: the limits of knowledge', in J. Hines (ed.) *The Anglo-Saxons from the Migration Period to the Eighth Century: An Ethnographic Perspective,* Woodbridge: Boydell.

Hodder, I. (1982) *The Present Past,* London: Batsford.

Hope-Taylor, B. (1977) *Yeavering: An Anglo-British CEntre in Early Northumbria,* London: Dent.

Huggett, J. (1996) 'Social analysis of early Anglo-Saxon inhumation burials: archaeological methodologies', *Journal of European Archaeology* 4(3): 337–65.

Humphrey, C. and Onon, U. (1996) *Shamans and Elders: Experience, Knowledge and Power among the Daur Mongols,* Oxford: Oxford University Press.

Ingold, T. (1986) *The Appropriation of Nature,* Manchester: Manchester University Press.

Jochelson, W. (1908) *The Koryak,* Publications of the Jesup North Pacific Expedition, Vol. VI, New York: American Museum of Natural History.

Jolly, K.L. (1996) *Popular Religion in Late Saxon England. Elf Charms in Context,* Chapel Hill: University of North Carolina Press.

Jones, G. (tr.) (1961) *Eirik the Red and Other Icelandic Sagas,* London: Oxford University Press.

—— (1968) *A History of the Vikings,* Oxford: Oxford University Press.

Kan, S. (1989) *Symbolic Immortality, The Tlingit Potlatch of the Nineteenth Century,* Washington, DC: Smithsonian Institution Press.

King, P.D. (ed.) (1987) *Charlemagne: Translated Sources,* Kendal: Privately printed.

Kinsley, A.G. (1989) *The Anglo-Saxon Cemetery at Millgate, Newark-on-Trent, Nottinghamshire,* Nottingham: University of Nottingham.

—— (1993) *Broughton Lodge. Excavations on the Romano-British Settlement and Anglo-Saxon Cemetery at Broughton Lodge, Willoughby-on-the-Wolds, Nottinghamshire 1964–8,* Nottingham: University of Nottingham.

Knüsel, C. and Ripley, K. (2000) 'The Berdache or Man-Woman in Anglo-Saxon England and early medieval Europe?', in A. Tyrrell and W. Frazer (eds) *Social Identity in Early Medieval Britain,* Leicester: Leicester University Press.

Kristoffersen, S. (1995) 'Transformation in Migration Period animal art', *Norwegian Archaeological Review* 28(1): 1–18.

Larrington, C. (tr.) (1996) *The Poetic Edda,* Oxford: Oxford University Press.

Leahy, K. (1998) 'Cleatham, North Lincolnshire: the 'Kirton-in-Lindsey' cemetery', *Medieval Archaeology* 42: 94–5.

Leigh, D. (1984) 'Ambiguity in Anglo-Saxon Style I art', *Antiquaries Journal* 64: 34–42.

Lethbridge, T.C. (1951) *A Cemetery at Lackford, Suffolk,* Cambridge: Cambridge University Press.

Liddle, P. (1980) 'An Anglo-Saxon cemetery at Wanlip, Leicestershire', *Transactions of the Leicestershire Archaeological and Historical Society* 55: 11–21.

Lucy, S. (1998) *The Early Anglo-Saxon Cemeteries of East Yorkshire,* Oxford: British Archaeological Reports.

—— (2000) *The Anglo-Saxon Way of Death,* Stroud: Sutton.

Mayr-Harting, H. (1972) *The Coming of Christianity to Anglo-Saxon England,* London: Batsford.

McKinley, J. (1993) 'Cremated bone', in J. Timby (ed.) 'Sancton I Anglo-Saxon cemetery. excavations carried out between 1976 and 1980', *Archaeological Journal* 150: 243–365.

—— (1994) *The Anglo-Saxon Cemetery at Spong Hill, North Elmham. Part VIII: The Cremations,* East Anglian Archaeology 69, Dereham: Norfolk Museum Service.

Meaney, A. (1981) *Anglo-Saxon Amulets and Curing Stones,* Oxford: British Archaeological Reports.

—— (1989) 'Women, witchcraft and magic in Anglo-Saxon England', in. D. Scragg (ed.) *Superstition and Popular Medicine in Anglo-Saxon England,* Manchester: Manchester Centre for Anglo-Saxon Studies.

—— (1995) 'Pagan English sanctuaries, place-names and hundred meeting places', in W. Filmer-Sankey and D. Griffiths (eds) *Anglo-Saxon Studies in Archaeology and History* 8, Oxford: Oxford University Committee for Archaeology.

Myres, J.N.L. (1969) *Anglo-Saxon Pottery and the Settlement of England,* Oxford: Clarendon Press.

—— (1977a) *A Corpus of Anglo-Saxon Pottery of the Pagan Period,* Cambridge: Cambridge University Press.

—— (1977b) 'Zoomorphic bosses on Anglo-Saxon pottery', *Studien zur Sachsenforschung* I: 281–93.

Myres, J.N.L and Green, B. (1973) *The Anglo-Saxon Cemeteries of Caistor-by-Norwich and Markshall, Norfolk,* London: Society of Antiquaries.

Nebesky de Wojkowitz, R. (1951) 'Ancient funeral ceremonies of the Lepchas', *Eastern Anthropologist* 5: 27–40.

North, R. (1997) *Heathen Gods in Old English Literature,* Cambridge: Cambridge University Press.

Owen, G.R. (1981) *Rites and Religions of the Anglo-Saxons,* New York: Barnes & Noble.

Pader, E.J. (1982) *Symbolism, Social Relations and the Interpretation of Mortuary Remains,* Oxford: British Archaeological Reports.

Pálsson, H. and Edwards, P. (tr.) (1972) *Eyrbyggja Saga,* Harmondsworth: Penguin.

Piggott, S. (1962) 'Heads and hoofs', *Antiquity* 36: 110–18.

Powlesland, D. and Haughton, C. (1986) 'Excavations at Heslerton, North Yorkshire, 1978–82', *Archaeological Journal* 143: 53–173.

Price, N.S. (2000) 'Drum-Time and Viking Age: Sámi-Norse identities in early medieval Scandinavia', in M. Appelt, J., Berglund and H.C. Gulløv (eds) *Identities and Cultural Contacts in the Arctic,* Copenhagen: National Museum of Denmark and Danish Polar Center.

—— (2001) 'The archaeology of seiðr: circumpolar traditions in Viking pre-Christian religion', in C. Dempsey (ed.) *Proceedings of the Viking Millenium International Symposium,* St John's: Parks Canada.

Ravn, M. (1999) 'Theoretical and methodological approaches to Migration Period burials', in M. Rundkvist (ed.) *Grave Matters. Eight Studies of First Millennium AD Burials in Crimea, England and Southern Scandinavia,* Oxford: British Archaeological Reports.

Reynolds, N. (1980) 'The King's whetstone, a footnote', *Antiquity* 54: 232–7.

Richards, J.D. (1984) 'Funerary symbolism in Anglo-Saxon England: further social dimensions of mortuary practices', *Scottish Archaeological Review* 3: 42–55.

—— (1987) *The Significance of Form and Decoration of Anglo-Saxon Cremation Urns,* Oxford: British Archaeological Reports.

—— (1992) 'Anglo-Saxon symbolism', in M. Carver (ed.) *The Age of Sutton Hoo,* Woodbridge: Boydell.

—— (1995) 'An archaeology of Anglo-Saxon England', in A. Ausenda (ed.) *After Empire: Towards an Ethnology of Europe's Barbarians,* Woodbridge: Boydell.

Rivers, W.H.R. (1906) *The Todas,* London: Macmillan.

Robinson, F. (1993) *The Tomb of Beowulf and Other ESsays on Old English,* Oxford: Blackwell.

Schülke, A. (1999) 'On Christianization and grave-finds', *European Journal of Archaeology* 2(1): 77–106.

Semple, S. (1998) 'A fear of the past: the place of the prehistoric burial mound in the ideology of middle and later Anglo-Saxon England', *World Archaeology* 30(1): 109–26.

Serjeantson, D. (1994) 'The animal bones', in V. Evison (ed.) *An Anglo-Saxon Cemetery at Great Chesterford, Essex,* CBA Research Report 91, London: Council for British Archaeology.

Sherley-Price, L. (tr.) (1955) *Bede: Ecclesiastical History of the English People,* Harmondsworth: Penguin.

Stoodley, N. (1999) *The Spindle and the Spear,* Oxford: British Archaeological Reports.

—— (2000) 'From the cradle to the grave: age organization and the early Anglo-saxon burial rite', *World Archaeology* 31(3): 456–72.

Sumner, W.G. (1901) 'The Yakut', *Journal of the Royal Anthropological Institute* 31: 65–110.

Timby, J. (1993) 'Sancton I Anglo-Saxon cemetery. Excavations carried out between 1976 and 1980', *Archaeological Journal* 150: 243–365.

Turville-Petre, E.O.G. (1964) *Myth and Religion of the North,* London: Weidenfeld.

Vierck, H. (1971) 'Pferdegräber im Angelsächsichen England', in M. Müller-Wille (ed.) Pferdegrab und Pferdeopfer im frühen Mittelalter', *Berichten v.d. Rijksdienst v.h. Oudheidkundig Bodemonderzoek 1971:* 189–99, 218–20.

Vitebsky, P. (1993) *Dialogues with the Dead – The Discussion of Mortality among the Sora of Eastern India,* Cambridge: Cambridge University Press.

—— (1995) *The Shaman,* London: Macmillan.

Walker, A.R. (1986) *The Toda of Southern India: A New Look,* Delhi: Hindustan Publishing Corporation.

Webster, L. (1999) 'The iconographic programme of the Franks Casket', in J. Hawkes and S. Mills (eds) *Northumbria's Golden Age,* Stroud: Sutton.

Wells, C. (1960) A Study of Cremation, *Antiquity* 34: 29–37.

Wickham-Crowley, K. (1992) 'The birds on the Sutton Hoo instrument', in C. Neuman de Vegvar and R. Farrell (eds) *Sutton Hoo: Fifty Years After,* Miami: American Early Medieval Studies.

Wilkinson, L. (1980) 'Problems of analysis and interpretation of skeletal remains', in P. Rahtz, T. Dickinson and L. Watts (eds) *Anglo-Saxon Cemeteries 1979,* Oxford: British Archaeological Reports.

Williams, H. (1998) 'Monuments and the past in early Anglo-Saxon England', *World Archaeology* 30(1): 90–108.

—— (1999) 'Placing the dead: investigating the location of wealthy barrow burials in seventh century England', in M. Rundkvist (ed.) *Grave Matters. Eight Studies in First Millennium AD Burials in Crimea, England and Southern Scandinavia,* Oxford: British Archaeological Reports.

—— (2000) '"Burnt Germans in the age of iron": Early Anglo-Saxon mortuary practices and the study of cremation in past societies', Unpublished Ph.D thesis, Reading: University of Reading.

—— (2001a) '"The remains of pagan Saxondom"? The study of Anglo-Saxon cremation rites', in S. Lucy and A. Reynolds (eds) *Death and Burial in Early Medieval Britain.,* Leeds: Society of Medieval Archaeology.

—— (2001b) 'Death, memory and time: a consideration of mortuary practices at Sutton Hoo', in C. Humphrey and W. M. Ormrod (eds) *Time in the Medieval World,* Woodbridge: York Medieval Press/Boydell & Brewer.

Wilson, D. (1992) *Anglo-Saxon Paganism,* London: Routledge.

Wood, I.N. (1995) 'Pagan religion and superstitions east of the Rhine from the fifth to the ninth century', in A. Ausenda (ed.) *After Empire: Towards an Ethnology of Europe's Barbarians,* Woodbridge: Boydell.

Yorke, B. (1997) 'Fact or fiction? The written evidence for the fifth and sixth centuries AD', in W. Filmer-Sankey and D. Griffiths (eds) *Anglo-Saxon Studies in Archaeology and History* 6, Oxford: Oxford University Committee for Archaeology.

Young, B. (1977) 'Paganisme, christianisation et rites funéraires Mérovingiens', *Archéologie Médiévale* 7: 5–81.

—— (1999) 'The myth of the pagan cemetery', in C.E. Karkov, K. Wickham-Crowley and B.Young (eds) *Spaces of the Living and the Dead: An Archaeological Dialogue.* Oxford: Oxbow.

Chapter Fourteen

Waking ancestor spirits: Neo-shamanic engagements with archaeology

Robert J. Wallis

[T]he Pagan renaissance is obvious. Bookstores are full of books on the ancient native religions. In Great Britain, you cannot avoid the Pagan network. They even have university professors who are openly Pagan. In Iceland, Paganism became an official religion in 1973. Everywhere in Europe…[w]itness the return of the Druids, the shamans and the priests of the Gods.

(Christopher Gerard, cited by Henry 1999: 3)

[W]e moderns have nothing whatsoever of our own; only by replenishing and cramming ourselves with the ages, customs, arts, philosophies, religions, discoveries of others do we become anything worthy of notice.

(Nietzsche 1983 [1874]: 79, cited by Jakobsen 1999: 147–8)

INTRODUCTION

The subject of this chapter contrasts markedly with other contributions to this volume. Rather than exploring shamanisms of the past, I discuss contemporary – neo-shamanic – readings of those shamanisms. Neo-shamanism is a spiritual path among Westerners that utilises aspects of indigenous shamanism and representations of shamanism in the past, for personal and communal spiritual empowerment. This may sound like quite an *interesting* subject, but hardly *central* to the concerns of an 'archaeology of shamanism'. However, I seriously question the view that dismisses neo-shamanic interactions with archaeology as simply 'fringe' or 'eccentric'. Specific instances, from rituals and protests at archaeological sites to reconstructions of Viking and Celtic 'shamanism', require that archaeologists are aware of and involved with the political and ethical sensitivities of neo-shamanism. More than an afterthought, an 'add-on', supplemental to the main area of discussion, neo-shamanism must be taken seriously. And rather than beginning with shamanism in the past, an archaeology of shamanism necessarily begins with neo-shamanism, in the present.

AUTOARCHAEOLOGY

I came to this study as a trained archaeologist, but also with a personal involvement in neo-shamanism. This has created many tensions for me, tensions that I am forced to resolve on a day-to-day basis. Most of all, my 'coming out' as a so-called 'neo-shaman' is controversial. But where conventional anthropologists might promptly reject my ethnography based on my being 'native', recent movements in ethnography confront the fallacy of the insider–outsider dichotomy (see, for example, papers in Young and Goulet 1994). This fledgling 'experiential anthropology' challenges those anthropologists concerned with going native to alter their view. Their fear is a colonialist hangover, a fear of descent into 'savagery'. Experiential anthropology deconstructs the paralogism of absolute 'objectivity' and 'detachment', and replaces them with the nuanced understandings the 'insider's' view can bring. In challenging the impasse of going native, my theoretical and methodological considerations may be broadly characterised as 'post-modern', traversing specific concepts of alternative archaeologies (see, for example, Denning 1999), post-colonial discourse (see, for example, Ashcroft *et al.* 1998), queer theory (see, for example, Dowson 1998), and multi-sited ethnography (Marcus 1995). These ideas coalesce into what I call an 'autoarchaeology' in which self-reflexively considering and taking into account our own socio-political locations and motivations is crucial to understanding the past, to 'queering' archaeology (Wallis 2000).

As an autoarchaeologist I am being up-front about my own standpoint. If, as an archaeologist, I were to explore neo-shamanism without acknowledging my own involvement, or if, with an active role in neo-shamanism I downplayed my archaeological training, I would be compromising my integrity in both these 'worlds'. Autoarchaeology facilitates an ongoing addressing and redressing of my own partiality, my own perspective, in a politically explicit way that does not claim dubious credentials of objectivity and impartiality. Indeed, rather than threatening my academic credentials, I think they would be seriously open to question if I ignored or left unsaid my experiential, 'insider' approach for fear of ostracism. My intention is that such political explicitness actually promises a far more open-minded discussion. In making explicit my own positionality however, I in no way wish to imply that I have a moral high ground over other researchers, since my work is simply one way of telling. My aim is to get people who may currently think neo-shamanism has nothing to do with them, to think again, and to thereby open up dialogue between the disparate interest groups.

NEO-SHAMANISM AND CONTEMPORARY PAGANISM

Archaeology has yet to recognise the implications neo-shamanism has for its ideas and subjects of study. Archaeologists tend to dismiss neo-shamanism as 'fringe' and regard the New Age, Paganism, and neo-shamanism – as with all alternative archaeology – negatively (but see Finn 1997; Denning 1999). This neglect of research is unprecedented and does not reflect an insignificant research area. Neo-shamanic engagement with the past is considerable and accelerating, thereby implicating and requiring the attentions of archaeologists. Neo-shamans approaching shamanisms in the past are most often contemporary Pagans, who fall into three categories (in order of popularity): Wicca (contemporary witchcraft), Druidry and Heathenry. Wicca (derived from the Anglo-Saxon *wicca*, possibly meaning witch) is an initiatory religion in which practitioners revere divinity in nature as manifest in the polarity of a goddess and god (with female often privileged over male). It has been considerably influenced by shamanism, for mention of it appears in many core texts (see, for example, Farrar and Farrar 1984; Starhawk 1989). Some Wiccans even term their religion 'Shamanic Wicca', 'Shamanic Craft' and 'Wiccan-shamanism' (see, for example, Adler 1986: 430–4; Luhrmann 1989: 134, 329). Practices such as inducing trance, working magic, divination, interacting with spirits and animal familiars, and healing via supernatural means, are certainly reminiscent of many shamanistic practices.[1] Of interest to archaeology is the way in which Wicca often claims descent from prehistoric European shamanisms. This idea was popularised in the first part of the last century by Margaret Murray whose first book *The Witch Cult in Western Europe* (1921) argued 'the victims of the early modern witch trials had been practitioners of a surviving pagan religion' (Hutton 1999: 194–5). Her second contribution, *The God of the Witches* (1933), 'asserted the doctrine that the horned god of the greenwood had been the oldest deity known to humans, and traced his worship across Europe and the Near East, from the Old Stone Age to the seventeenth century' (Hutton 1999: 196).

The more feminist and goddess-oriented branches of Wicca, by virtue of a common ancestry, in many ways resonate with the Goddess movement. Goddess spirituality has been heavily influenced by the work of Marija Gimbutas (see, for example, Gimbutas 1974), for whom the famous Turkish site of Çatal Hüyük is a goddess site *par excellence* (see, for example, Jencson 1989; Meskell 1995; Hutton 1997). The current engagements between adherents to Goddess spirituality and archaeologists there are somewhat strained, due to conflicting approaches and interpretations. Despite Hodder's claims for a self-reflexive archaeological process at the site that accommodates both archaeological strategies and alternative goddess views (see, for example, Hodder's website: http://catal.arch.cam.ac.uk/ [accessed 17 August 2000]), other archaeologists see the practice being far removed from the ideal (see, for example, Hassan 1997).

Indeed, Meskell argues that the differences between Pagans and academics are so fundamental that there is little room for fruitful negotiation (Meskell 1999). Of course this realisation should not promote avoidance of the issues, and as I shall demonstrate, there are various instances where productive dialogues have flourished. It is interesting to note at this juncture that Gimbutas was not the first to suggest Goddess interpretations of archaeological data. Hutton suggests the most obvious precedents were Margaret Murray who, 'whole-heartedly endorsed the idea that the prehistoric European and Mediterranean world had worshipped a single supreme female deity' (Hutton 1999: 273), and Jacquetta Hawkes who portrayed Neolithic European communities as living in harmony with the earth and worshipping a single mother-goddess that personified nature (Hutton 1999: 278–9). Hutton (1999: 280) goes on to point out that such figure-heading archaeologists as O.G.S. Crawford, Vere Gordon Childe and Glyn Daniel declared 'their belief in the veneration of a single female deity by New Stone Age cultures' (see, for example, Crawford 1957; Childe 1958; Daniel 1958). Clearly, while some archaeologists today may do their best to forget it, their predecessors are strange but intimate bedfellows with neo-shamanic approaches to the past, a past that cannot be ignored because of its repercussions in the present.

Druidry is a case in point. It is perhaps, after Wicca, the second most popular branch of contemporary Paganism in Britain today. As is well known, Druids are inspired by the Iron Age druids and all things 'Celtic' that are perceived to relate to them, from medieval and romantic literature, to archaeology and the legacy of early antiquarians such as William Stukeley, a.k.a. 'Archdruid Chyndonax' (Sebastion 1990: 97–8). A number of authors consider the relations between druids past and Druids present (see, for example, Piggott 1968; Green 1997; Jones 1998), but while Modern Druids endure as an object of ridicule among most archaeologists, the negative stereotypes are transforming. The idea that Druids claim descent from ancient Iron Age orders, for instance, is increasingly being replaced – among both Druids and academics – by a recognition that Druidry is very much a tradition situated in the modern era (see, for example, Harvey 1997). Even so, its antiquity is at least as old as archaeology (Hutton 1997) and the two are indeed, 'blood brothers' (Sebastion 2000).

Like Wicca and Goddess spirituality, Druidry is markedly influenced by shamanism. This is particularly evident in the work of John Matthews who interprets the medieval Welsh manu-scripts attributed to the Bard Taliesin according to shape-shifting and other 'Celtic' shamanistic metaphors (see, for example, Matthews 1991). These interpretations are controversial (see, for example, Jones 1998), since the poems' reliability and chronology is notoriously problematic (see, for example, Hutton 1991) and juxtaposition of the terms Celtic and Shaman appears anachronistic. It is neo-shamanic representations of the past such as this, however, that usurp academic publications in the popular realm. While Matthews claims scholarly objectivity, other Druids, such as Tim Sebastion of the Secular Order of Druids (SOD), are unashamedly romantic (see, for example, Sebastion 1990). He is a shield knight of the Loyal Arthurian Warband and is, like his liege King Arthur Pendragon, 'accepted as the reincarnation of one of the Knights of the Round Table' (Sebastion 2000). The aims of these Druids for the future of archaeological sites are often highly pragmatic, such as the Solstice Project's plans to reconstruct Avebury's Sanctuary and so employ the local unemployed and detract attention away from Stonehenge as a festival site (Sebastion 2000). Indeed where ancient sites, especially Stonehenge, are concerned, the Druids are increasingly being viewed as equals by archaeologists (and the heritage managers) (see, for example, Bender 1998).

The presence of neo-shamanism in Druidry is also made clear by my discussions with Philip 'Greywolf' Shallcrass (Joint-Chief of the British Druid Order). Not only does Greywolf claim to interact with spirits and a spirit world for healing and empowerment (as shamans do), and to have been 'chosen' by them (rather than he choosing to communicate with them, as is typical of most neo-shamans), but he also reconstructs 'native British' sweat lodges (for an archaeological reconstruction, see Barfield and Hodder 1987) and conducts rituals at ancient sites including Stonehenge and Avebury (Figure 14.1). He is also heavily involved in negotiations with English Heritage over access to Stonehenge and, more controversially, the reburial of skeletal remains likely to be excavated during the Stonehenge Management Plan (Wallis 2000). Such issues may bring the alternative Other too close for comfort for many conservative archaeologists, but where such dialogue promotes positive compromise on both sides of the equation, rather than the violence of previous years (such as the 1985 summer solstice 'Battle of the Beanfield' near Stonehenge in which so-called 'New Age travellers' were forced into confrontations with police), the outcome can only point towards beneficial negotiations in the future. This sort of inter-action contrasts markedly with the example of 'Kennewick Man' in the USA, where debates have recently raged over a 9,000-year-old skeleton found in Washington state (see, for example, Radford 1998). Under NAGPRA (Native American Graves Protection and Repatriation Act 1990), Native Americans demanded the ancestral remains be reburied with appropriate ritual. Some archaeologists believe that rather than being Native American, the bones may be ancient European in origin, and have requested time for further analysis. The 'Asatru Folk Assembly', a right-wing Heathen organisation, then argued that if the remains are European then as a traditional European religion, they should have exclusive rights to the bones. As a result, both Native Americans and the Asatru Folk Assembly were allowed to conduct ceremonies over the bones. This situation exemplifies how archaeologists cannot ignore neo-shamanism, cannot neglect the sensitive political outcomes of their 'objective' scientific research.

CASE STUDY 1

Speaking with the Viking dead – Heathen neo-shamanism

The Asatru Folk Assembly is part of – albeit an atypical right-wing aspect that does not typify the movement as a whole – the third popular branch of paganism known to its practitioners variously as Heathenism, Heathenry, Odinism, Asatru ('allegiance to the gods'), or more loosely the 'Northern' tradition. Contemporary Heathens utilise Norse and Icelandic literature and mythology, Viking and Anglo-Saxon Migration Period history and archaeological sources, and

Figure 14.1 A large procession of Druids at Avebury Henge. They are led by Greywolf, Joint-Chief of the British Druid Order.

all things with a Germanic and Heathen theme, to revive and reconstruct a contemporary religion. In the same vein as other Pagan traditions, Heathenry takes many forms and there are a variety of functioning groups worldwide. Smaller localised groups known as 'Hearths' meet together and are comparable with a Wiccan 'Coven' or Druidic 'Grove'. Harvey's (1997) discussions mark the most comprehensive and erudite survey of Heathenism to date. He suggests practitioners are steadily growing in numbers and the practices are advancing in 'coherence' (Harvey 1997: 53). There is no need for me to replicate what Harvey details, but there is a great deal of room to explore the shamanistic elements in Heathenry. These, in similarity with Wicca and Druidry, are mostly only touched on by other ethnographers of the traditions and are of considerable significance to archaeologists.

Shamanism permeates Heathenry more than any other contemporary Pagan tradition, perhaps because more associations between the two have been suggested (whether correctly or not) in the historic and archaeological record (see, for example, Simek 1993). Numerous aspects of the god Odin and goddess Freyja for instance, may display aspects of shamanism, particularly their associations with '*seiðr*'. *Seiðr* is an obscure practice of 'magic' in the sources that is often disreputable or related to sorcery, and various academics argue that *seiðr* was a shamanic technique (see, for example, Ellis Davidson 1993: 137). I have met numerous Heathen shamanistic and/or seiðr practitioners in the UK and USA; for instance 'Runic' John, from Lancashire, whose patron deity is Woden[2] and who gives 'rune readings' and 'shamanic healing'.

Figure 14.2 'Runic' John, Heathen neo-shaman, completing a shamanic healing. John has extracted a malignant spirit from the patient and is slamming it into the ground where it will be absorbed into Helheim, a Heathen term for the realm of the Lower World in Nordic cosmology. On the ground in front of him is his shamanic rattle, and he wears Thor's hammer around his neck.

When conducting runic divinations for clients, John says that he enters a trance in which Woden sits behind him and covers his right eye with his hand (in Norse mythology, Odin sacrifices an eye to gain wisdom). At this point, John knows he has the 'sight' to be able to read the runes. In Figure 14.2 John is seen sending a malignant spirit into the earth where it will be absorbed and recycled, having just extracted it from a patient. And in Figure 14.3, John is possessed by Odin during a public ritual, stood rigid and transfixed by the ecstatic inspiration of

Figure 14.3 'Runic' John is possessed by the spirit of the god Woden, in a public shamanic ritual.

the god. Moments later, John shape-shifted into a wild boar in the spirit world (an experience he later recounted) and to the surprise of onlookers, fell to hands and knees and charged around grunting and snorting, nose to the ground, churning up dust.

John is a highly idiosyncratic Heathen shaman, typical of the individualised and eclectic nature of neo-shamanism today. A more widely publicised and popular technique is that of seiðr (see, for example, Lindquist 1997) practised by among others, the Hrafnar community in San Francisco led by Diana Paxson. The best recorded ancient instance of *seiðr* is in the *Saga of Eiríkr the Red* (see, for example, Magnus Magnusson and Hermann Pálsson 1965), in which a seeress or *völva* performs a 'seance' for a Greenlandic community suffering a famine. Many features of this tale may, according to neo-shamans and academics alike, hint at shamanistic practices. The *völva* eats a strange porridge before the ritual, containing the hearts of various creatures. She wears unusual clothing such as a black lambskin hood lined with cat's fur and cat skin gloves. Furthermore, a pouch at her waist contains various (unstated) charms, perhaps similar to those found in a pouch at the Fyrkat site, Denmark including the bones of birds and small mammals, and entheogenic henbane seeds (Price, pers. comm.). She also holds a long staff topped with a brass knob that is studded with stones and she sits on a ritual platform with a cushion of hen-feathers beneath her. Viewed shamanistically, the items of dress may indicate the *völva's* relationships to her spirit-helpers, and her characteristic staff may act as a connection with the earth, or it may symbolise the world tree Yggdrasil. However, this view is at variance with some academic (non-practitioner) interpretations (see Price in press). Thus attired, the seeress's *seiðr* proceeds: the verses that enable the spirits to be present are sung or chanted, and in communication with that realm, the *völva* prophesies a better future for the community and for each person who asks her questions. Contemporary seiðr-workers use sources such as this to reconstruct and revive the *seiðr* seance.

The saga literature is also used by Heathens to reconstruct what may have been Nordic 'possession' practices. The impetus for this practice arose, Paxson told me, when a deity first possessed a *völva* during a seiðr session, an unexpected happening that required some explanation and contextualisation. Diana researched the historic sources and believes she has found examples of possession in the Norse texts, particularly the earlier material. A possible example is in the *Saga of King Óláfr Tryggvason* (*Flateyjarbók* 1, see Guðbrandur Vigfússon and Unger 1860–8) in which an idol of Freyr travels around the country in a wagon, accompanied by his 'wife', a priestess (*gyðja*). The hero of the tale, Gunnar, fights with the idol and takes its place, whereupon the Swedes are well pleased that the god can now feast and drink, and are even more pleased when his 'wife' becomes pregnant! The tale is written from the perspective of the Norwegians, and if read at face value is a gibe at the gullibility of the heathen Swedes who believe Gunnar's impersonation of Freyr to be real. If the saga is approached as a possible example of possession however, as Paxson would suggest, then it may have been common practice among the Swedes for a person to take on the form of a deity and let the deity speak through them. In this case Gunnar is the 'shaman', or whoever else was accompanying the *gyðja*, before being usurped by him: Gunnar's struggle with Freyr would actually be a fight with the previous shaman.[3] Having come across this literature, Paxson also noticed that traditional shamanic societies often incorporated possession into their rites (see, for example, Lewis 1989). To build on the fragmentary Nordic evidence with contemporary possession techniques, Diana studied the increasingly popular practice of Umbanda, in Brazil. Essentially, she combined an ethnographic analogy with Old Norse sources to reconstruct a Heathen Possession technique. Whatever misgivings archaeologists and other academics with interests in the past may have – with a perceived 'inappropriate' 'appropriation' of ethnographic analogy and 'misreading' of the literary sources – these reconstructions of seiðr and possession are deeply empowering for the contemporary practitioners.

CASE STUDY 2

Waking prehistoric ancestors – neo-shamanism at ancient sites

Neo-shamanic engagements with the past are most direct at archaeological sites. In many ways these are explicitly shamanic. The goddess-oriented megalithic gazetteer to Britain by Julian Cope (1998) for instance, recommends that visitors to Avebury should 'always hold shamanic experiments' (Cope in Thompson 1998: 12). To give some bearing on why and how neo-shamans are involved with archaeological sites, Greywolf told me:

> Druids like to make ritual at ancient stone circles since there is a strong feeling that they are places where communion with our ancestors may be made more readily than elsewhere . . . I am drawn to Avebury . . . because it is my heartland . . . the place where I feel most spiritually 'at home'.

> (Greywolf, pers. comm.)

At Avebury and similar sites, from other Later Neolithic stone circles to Iron Age Hillforts, Greywolf and his kind make ritual at the eight Pagan festivals that celebrate the wheel of the year.[4] At such events various rituals and festivities occur, including handfasting (marriage), and child-naming ceremonies (baptism). Increasing numbers of people like Greywolf make pilgrimages to ancient places each year. A Bournemouth University survey of Avebury's visitors recorded that 16 per cent of them expressed spiritual motivation as their reason for visiting (Calver 1998). This number surges to represent a clear majority around the Pagan festivals. Such intimate relationships with Neolithic remains have resulted in certain management, presentation and conservation issues for the site curators.

A good, recent example (besides the better-known problems at Stonehenge), concerns the events surrounding the excavation of 'Seahenge', a small Bronze Age timber circle discovered in 1999 at Holme-Next-The-Sea on the east coast of England. The expropriation of such monuments, ownership of and management of the past, and rights of access, involves many interest groups, from archaeologists (including academic archaeologists, field archaeologists, museum workers and site managers) and anthropologists, to students of religion and history, local groups, and even politicians and the police. Yet neo-shamans and their peers are not addressed seriously in site management strategies, and furthermore, the political nature of site presentation has not been adequately examined. The situation at the timber ring at Holme-Next-The-Sea is exemplary of the increasingly activist positions neo-shamans are assuming in relation to archaeological sites. It also shows how the aims of the interest groups can be successfully negotiated.

Perplexed by the 'meaning' of this idiosyncratic monument, a neo-shaman says she 'didn't feel any particular energy coming from it', and wonders, 'maybe it'll come to me in a dream?' (Brown 1998: 15). Meanwhile, the national archaeological agency English Heritage initially determined to record the circle and then allow it to be eroded by the sea; it was thought too expensive to be preserved. A campaign was co-ordinated by local people, archaeologists and neo-shamanic persons (including Clare Prout of the mostly Pagan organisation Save Our Sacred Sites) to excavate and remove the henge from the threats of the sea, preserve it, and then place it on display. Owing to destructive conditions and the close proximity of flocks of wading birds, the display could not be *in situ*; indeed, the original location of the monument would have been some 30 miles inland. Local people were also concerned the display would end up too far from Holme, with a subsequent loss of their heritage, and therefore tourism. English Heritage's dendrochronological tests then followed, involving use of a chainsaw, a process that greatly upset the groups wanting to preserve the henge. *The Times* reported that protesters turned up to halt the excavations (documented by the popular British television programme Time Team); Druids claimed that the henge's location on a ley line meant that it should not be moved lest its spiritual essence be lost (Morrison 1999: 20). In the early hours of a June morning English Heritage came to finish the job – with bulldozers – in what was called a 'Dawn Raid' (*Sacred Hoop News* 1999 25: 8), only to face protesting Druids and others prepared to stand their ground. One sat on the central upturned tree (suggested by some to be a shamanic sky burial site) playing a didgeridu. This confrontation 'sent shock waves across the pagan and shamanic communities not only in Britain but also the US' (*Sacred Hoop News* 1999 25: 8). As with the example of Stonehenge, archaeologists are viewed very negatively at such times, 'as manifestations of imperialism' and 'an uncaring discipline, typical of a dominant elitist society' (Ucko 1990: xv). In the end, 'Seahenge' was excavated and 'preserved', and Time Team made a reconstruction of the monument. By and large, the Time Team programme demonstrated that the Druidic perspective was marginalised. Simply put, their claims on the monument were not taken seriously (cf. Plouviez 2000).

The happenings at this most recently discovered and probably highly significant ancient site – (interpretations range from shamanic sky burial site to fish trap) – exemplify the increasing tension that exists between site custodians and groups opposing their protocols, including local people and neo-shamans.[5] New situations seem to be emerging all the time: from the recent disagreements between Pagans, heritage managers and Christians over the erecting of a new monolith at Mayburgh stone circle in north-west England, to successful neo-shamanic and local objections to the planned removal of two standing stones in the Avebury region in Wiltshire (as discussed on the Stones and Nature Religions Scholars email discussion lists). Indeed, there appear to be increasing tensions amongst archaeologists too. A recent article in *British Archaeology*, by its editor Simon Denison, expresses discontent about the way 'Seahenge' was 'yanked out of the sands': 'The excavation . . . was destruction, nothing short of vandalism' (Denison 2000: 28. See also 'Letters' in *British Archaeology* 53: 24–5). Holme-Next-The-Sea compares with Stonehenge as a site of serious political contestation between heritage managers and alternative interest groups. However, the situation is most certainly not just doom and gloom, as I next discuss.

SEEING TOWARDS 'EXTRA PAY' FOR SHAMANISMS, PRESENT AND PAST

Neo-shamanic approaches to various aspects of the past, from Druidic and Viking reconstructions to engagements with archaeological sites, should clearly be of considerable interest to archaeologists and other academics with concerns over how the past is approached and represented. This interest should not only be of 'concern', however, since there are some distinctly positive neo-shamanic interactions with the past that give what Harvey (1997: chapter 7) calls 'extra pay'[6] to shamanisms past and present. A first example is where neo-shamans actively and positively engage in archaeological site management processes. At 'Seahenge', Clare Prout joined David Miles (Chief Archaeologist, English Heritage), Druid protestors, archaeologists and other interest groups in a discussion on how to address the tense situation. She claims that through this dialogue 'we got a fabulous result' (pers. comm.),[7] though of course there will always be people who disagree: where Prout and English Heritage wanted to excavate and preserve the monument, other Druids demanded it be left *in situ*. Despite the conflicts, the example of 'Seahenge' shows how disputes *can*, largely, be resolved. For the most part, respectful and diplomatic negotiations between the interest groups appear to reap positive results, 'perhaps to the extent that Seahenge will be the last disturbance of a sacred site without prior consultation and compromise' (Bannister 2000: 13). Interestingly, by the end of the dispute, many of the archaeologists who initially wrote off the Druids stated that in retrospect they wished they had got them on board. By getting involved in protest and negotiation, and by thereby challenging the negative stereotypes of themselves, neo-shamans are, I argue, giving 'extra pay' to shamanism, since it is used as a force for change and social critique, rather than a trendy word and bandwagon. In so doing, they are also giving extra pay to the archaeological sites they spiritually respect.

The issue of seiðr in Heathenism provides a second example of 'extra pay', when its practitioners undergo experiences that challenge Western worldviews. Some Heathen neo-shamans in Britain and North America, in contrast to being 'safe' and 'Westernised',[8] confront and challenge conservatism both in Heathenism and wider society. Heathenry writ large is a conservative new religion with moral, ethical and spiritual values adhering to 'middle' England and America. 'Traditional' family values are sacred and the issue of same-sex relations remains controversial. Associations with nationalism, racism and homophobia do not typify Heathenism,[9] but the unfortunate history of associations between Viking religions and Nazism this century is seized upon by contemporary groups motivated by far-right politics. They, in turn, are picked out by the tabloid press so that the liberal attitudes of others are eclipsed. Seiðr practices among liberal-minded Heathens are not always regarded favourably by the rest of the Heathen community because many of them find notions of 'spirits' and practices involving direct communications with deities and the ancestors to be extremely dubious, verging on the blasphemous (Blain pers. comm.; see also Blain and Wallis 2000). Nevertheless, Diana Paxson of the Hrafnar community told me that seiðr is becoming increasingly popular.

At the time of the Icelandic Sagas, *seiðr* was a disreputable practice (with an obvious knock-on effect today among the Heathens who use these Old Norse sources), and the working of magic was generally held to be antisocial behaviour. *Ergi* is an enigmatic term used in the myths and sagas to describe a male *seiðr*-worker or *seiðmaðr*. Loki the Trickster deity, for instance, calls Odin (a warrior god) *ergi* when he practises *seiðr* techniques he learned from the goddess Freyja (*Lokasenna* 24, in *The Poetic Edda* ed. and tr. Dronke 1997: 338). *Ergi* may refer to an 'effeminate man' or to being 'unmanly', and as widespread academic opinion has it, to passive male homosexuality, reflecting the pejorative sentiments surrounding a man or god who practises 'women's magic'. *Seiðr* and *ergi* contrast significantly to the sort of 'strong warrior' male role model deemed conventional and desirable during the unpredictable and uncertain times of Viking migration and conflict.

Their shamanic experiences have led many contemporary seiðr-workers to re-appraise the negative associations of *seiðr* and *ergi*. They suggest that in earlier times, certainly before Christian prejudice, *seiðr* may have been a more acceptable practice. Nordic society may have been more 'shamanistic' and the status of a *seiðmaðr* and his *ergi* might even compare with the shaman *berdache* in some Native American societies (for discussions of *berdache* see, for example, Roscoe 1991; Whitehead 1993). In similarity to *seiðr* and *ergi*, *berdache* is a loaded term, a colonial construction that imposed Eurocentric understandings of gender and sexual relations onto indigenous cultures. In contrast to Western values, *berdache*-type shamans (see, for example, Czaplicka 1914), gender-crossing priests such as some Hindu *hijras* (see, for example, Nanda 1993a, 1993b), multiple gender conceptions (see, for example, Herdt 1996), and same-sex relations (see, for example, Sparkes 1998), are cross-culturally consistent. This consistency deconstructs the simplistic Western conflation of gender and sex. Rather than the binary 'two-spirited people' (see, for example, papers in Jacobs *et al.* 1997), 'changing ones' (Roscoe 1998) may be the most applicable replacement for '*berdache*'. As evidence for changing ones in ancient northern Europe, Heathens may cite Saxo Grammaticus who remarks on the *berdache*-type priests or 'wives' of Freyr (a male 'fertility' god) at Uppsala in Sweden. Saxo describes the hero Starkaðr as being 'disgusted with the womanish body movements' of the priests of Freyr, and the 'soft tinkling of bells' (*Gesta Danorum,* Book 6, tr. Ellis Davidson and Fisher 1998: 172). Elsewhere, Tacitus (*Germania* 43) describes Germanic priests dressed in women's clothing. Furthermore, some burial evidence may point towards changing ones in Anglo-Saxon society (Wilson 1992: 96–7; Clark-Mazo 1997: 11), although it is of course imperative that Western conceptions of gender are not imposed on artefact assemblages.

Simply by practising seiðr today then, neo-shamans engage in a dissonant act that receives prejudice from within their own spiritual community and from wider culture. Paxson suggested the 'opening up' of oneself psychically to be successful in seiðr can be regarded as a female ability rather than a male one, and only certain men generally want to be involved with seiðr because of this, these most often being gay men. The high proportion of gay men in the Hrafnar community is quite unrepresentative of Heathenry in general, so the combination of gay men and seiðr places Hrafnar further into a marginal category in Heathenry, perhaps reflective of its geographical location in liberal San Francisco. Being gay and practising seiðr presents a significant challenge to conventional Heathenry and the normative West. Not all men practising seiðr however, are gay. Over time, Diana says more 'straights' have begun to practice seiðr. For heterosexual male seiðr-workers, experiences with seiðr also challenge conventional classifications of gender with a domino effect for other masculist Western attitudes. Bil is a seiðr-worker in New Mexico who works with the dying to ease their spiritual transition and has various 'ghosts' as spirit-helpers. He points out that:

> My sexuality is heterosexual. I was never approached by the ghosts who follow me to change that in any way. I was, however, severely 'lambasted' for carrying too much of a 'macho attitude' and was forced to make changes in that area – so much so, that folks often wonder, now, if I am homosexual or not. They usually figure it out soon enough when they meet my family and friends. My eccentricity doesn't stem from sexuality or sexual preference but mainly from the fact that I have no emotional reactions any longer (I have emotions; I just don't demonstrate reaction with them, that's all).
>
> (Blain and Wallis 2000)

And, Jordsvin has clearly been deeply affected by seiðr when he argues:

> The concept of sexual orientation *per se* is a modern one. There do seem to be references in the lore connecting men who do seiðr with men who have sex with men, more specifically, men who are in the receptive role during such activities. Obviously, this should not be an excuse for bigotry against gay people today. Gay men and women seem often to show a knack for seiðr, but heterosexual men can and do learn it and do it quite well.
>
> (Blain and Wallis 2000)

In a similar vein, 'James', a newcomer to seiðr practices living in Britain, has experiences that challenge various normative Western sensory and ideological perceptions. He says:

> Ergi mainly fits with my rituals with Freyja, rituals of possession . . . I think many people (especially men) would find seiðr disturbing because of how it makes them feel (apart from the radical change into shamanic consciousness), going beyond stereotypes of male, female, gay, etc. For me, seiðr with Freyja allows an integrating understanding of what it is to be male, female and other multiple possibilities. That is empowering and affects how I live with my reality, world, local and spiritual communities. It changes who I am.
>
> (Blain and Wallis 2000)

Harvey (1997: 122; see also 1998) asserts that working in environmental education comprises one example of how neo-shamanism embodies a postmodern critique of society and thereby gives 'extra pay'. I agree, and argue that seiðr-work and its subsequent disputing and altering of normative Western stereotypes similarly represents a significant disruption of, and protest to, modernity. Dowson argues 'the very practice of archaeology provides the foundations of social and epistemological privilege by authorizing a heterosexual history of humanity' (1998: 4). Conservative Heathens follow this line and cultivate their perceived closeness to their ancestors by assuming ancient Heathen communities consisted of heterosexual family units as we largely have them today. In direct contrast, the seiðr-workers I have discussed use their experiences to provide an alternative history of seiðr that challenges conventional understandings of the past. Where many archaeologists unconsciously underwrite homophobia in their reification of familial units and heterosexual relations, gay and straight seiðr-workers disrupt these biases, interpreting the past in ways beyond normative archaeology. They 'actively challenge the manner in which epistemological privilege is negotiated in archaeology' (Dowson 1998: 4). In their engagements with shamanic practice, they also challenge both the atheistic stance of contemporary society and the aversion to interactions with spirits in their Heathen communities.

These seiðr-workers are not simply going on shamanic trips for fun or profit, as the critics of neo-shamanism largely suggest, but are radically reorienting their worldviews. In terms of consciousness alterations, gender conceptions, sexual orientation and community interactions, these neo-shamans are more like some indigenous shamans. I argue rather than 'appropriating' aspects of indigenous shamanisms, or shamanism in the past, these neo-shamans give significant 'extra pay' to shamanisms past and present. They accord with Taussig's (1987) astute understanding of shamanism as being embedded in an intrinsically socio-political process that destroys any belief – neo-shamanic or academic – in shamanism solely as a safe or benevolent phenomenon. Taussig argues the shamanic career and its rituals are open-ended, there is always a tension in the air, an aura of unpredictability. Rather than there being a strictly followed narrative pattern and a cathartic shamanic 'healing', the nature of shamanism is consistently undetermined and without certain or known outcomes, as Western observers would like to see. The ritual may be unsuccessful, disputes may not be resolved, the shaman's spirits may depart and the career end abruptly. This ongoing nature of unpredictability waxes and wanes alongside the desired catharsis and constancy all people and their societies want, just as shamans themselves often struggle with malevolent and benevolent spirits, sorcery and healing. Where shamanic vocations are culturally constituted, the shamanic world itself is also intrinsically political and in perpetual change. Recognising the uncertainty of the shamanic office allows Taussig to deconstruct the 'classic' Western model of shamanism in which shamans are perceived to be largely male, dominating figures who control social relations and charismatically master their communities. The intrinsic uncertainty of shamanism suggests this image is a fabrication by Western observers imposing their masculist ideals inappropriately. The same image is also reified by those neo-shamans who portray shamanism as being safe, controllable and desirable. Seiðr neo-shamanism, in sharp contrast, typifies Taussig's assertion that shamanism is a deeply political phenomenon, with the potential for 'dismantling all fixed notions of identity' (Taussig 1989: 57). As changing ones, seiðr-workers give extra pay to shamanism by permeating the perceived academic boundaries between 'shamanism' and 'neo-shamanism', by being more like indigenous shamans. They also positively give extra pay to neo-shamanism itself, empowering the term and associated practices in ways beyond the negative stereotypes critics impose on them.

CONCLUSION

Any discussions of neo-shamanism must inevitably consider issues of the invention of tradition and the authenticity of reconstructions of the past. In this chapter I have tried to demonstrate that neo-shamans are not somehow misinterpreting the past where archaeologists 'know best'. While some neo-shamans may be 'inventing' some rather outlandish interpretations, such as the Asatru Folk Assembly's claims on Kennewick Man, accusing these and other neo-shamans of 'inventing' tradition is deeply problematic. As Herzfeld states:

> such terms as the 'invention of tradition' . . . suggest the possibility of an ultimately knowable historic past. Although traditions are invented, the implicit argument suggests, there ought to be something else that represents the 'real' past. But if any history is invented, all history is invented. We should not view one kind of history as more invented than others, although its bearers may be more powerful and therefore more capable of enforcing its reproduction among disenfranchised classes.
>
> (Herzfeld 1991: 12)

Moreover, to assume these practitioners are merely 'pretending' when they reconstruct these religions would be naïve and would not take their beliefs seriously (see, for example, Salomonsen 1999). Re-enactors of the past are often very passionate about the authenticity of their reconstructions, but in contrast neo-shamans are reconstructing the past in and for the present, for personal and communal spiritual empowerment. The authenticity of the reconstruction is not the main issue, merely its relevance and pragmatism for the practitioners. Of course the question is inappropriate anyway: 'authentic in relation to what?' – archaeological interpretations, that are themselves ever-changing, transient, subject to fashions and fads?

Archaeologists may be custodians of the past, those most often with direct access to its remains and whose interpretations of it are perceived publicly to be scientific fact. But archaeologists are not owners of the past and do not have exclusivity to the market of ideas that interpret it. This is made blatantly clear by the multitude of books on Celtic shamanism, seiðr magic, and so on, that far outsell academic publications. As Hutton argues,

> It is a classic case of a situation in which the experts are feeding the public with information while leaving it free to make such imaginative reconstructions as it wishes…Druids [and other neo-shamans] are well placed to take advantage of it…indeed, it is almost a duty on their part to do so, for the more people who are involved in the work, and the broader the range of plausible pictures imagined, the healthier the situation.
>
> (Hutton 1996: 23)

If this bookish equation alone does not encourage archaeologists to engage with neo-shamans, then where neo-shamans are prominent in direct action at ancient sites, archaeologists are under an even greater obligation to engage with them. To quote Hutton again, where he specifically remarks on Tim Sebastion's SOD:

> [W]hether or not outsiders may approve of the politics of SOD, God and Law, they have to be taken seriously. Their campaign has posed valid questions about the control and responsibility of the Nation's past, which eventually provoked a major debate among archaeologists. By 1992, 25 of the latter, many of them celebrities, were prepared to write a letter to the Guardian condemning the policy of English Heritage. . . . Between them they

have made a distinctive contribution to the history of religion and magical culture in Britain, and another to the history of politics. It is an impressive dual achievement, in such a few years, for movements which so clearly address problems specific to modernity, yet do so in terms of images drawn from the remote past.

(Sebastion 2000)

Rather idiosyncratically, my role as an autoarchaeologist spans both these worlds of archaeology and neo-shamanism. I aim to have negotiated these worlds in this chapter, and promoted a dialogue between 'orthodox' and 'alternative' interest groups that is positive, tolerant and reciprocal. Only by pursuing an open-minded exploration of neo-shamanism is it possible to appreciate that beyond engaging with archaeology in an 'eccentric' and confrontational way, there are neo-shamans that are actively engaging in positive dialogues with archaeologists and heritage managers. There are others who, in contrast to many neo-shamans, avoid romanticising and appropriating indigenous shamanism, and who are well aware of the sensitivities of their practices, so embedding them in specific social relations. According to Dowson's 'elements of shamanism', they *are* shamans. These considerations of neo-shamanism are pertinent but controversial in current archaeology and anthropology. I hope this discussion makes plain to the various interest groups that neo-shamanism has very much to do with *us*. Such a strategy, alongside my advocating 'an archaeology of *neo-shamanism*', seems timely. If neo-shamanism continues to be side-lined as insignificant, then as archaeologists of shamanism we will be reifying academic exclusivity, ignoring the central role of neo-shamanism in influencing our understandings of shamanism. But most of all, we will be neglecting our responsibilities as autoarchaeologists. That is, being explicit about our own socio-political motivations for undertaking an archaeology of shamanism in the first place.

NOTES

1 As an aside, in his definitive historical work on 'Modern Pagan Witchcraft' Hutton mentions a nineteenth-century Welsh cunning man who may have got the idea for his costume from accounts from 'Siberian tribal shamans' (Hutton 1999: 90).

2 Odin has linguistic variations including: ON Óðinn, OE Woden, OF Wodan OHG Wutan, Wuotan.

3 On the other hand, or in addition – for each interpretation is not mutually exclusive – Blain (pers.comm.) suggests the possibility that a 'spirit-marriage' is described, similar to the Siberian shamanic examples (Czaplicka 1914), with the wife as the 'shaman': she has a spirit-spouse, Freyr, and a human-spouse, Gunnar, which is customary for the Swedes but is incomprehensible to the Norwegians who assume Gunnar must be impersonating Freyr. And if Freyr is said to speak, this must 'really' be Gunnar speaking, rather that the *gyðja* relaying Freyr's messages.

4 The eight Pagan festivals mark and celebrate the seasonal changes seen in nature during the ever-turning 'wheel of the year'. There is an emphasis on the agricultural cycle and adherents use these times to connect with the land, reflect on how the changes in nature reflect changes in self and community, observe long-term patterns of stability and change, and to make ritual and celebration. The following dates are somewhat arbitrary since they may depend on planetary alignments, the proximity of sunrise and sunset, and the festivals tend to last for some days. In order: Samhain (Halloween) 31 October, Yule (Winter solstice) 21 December, Imbolc 2 February, Spring equinox 21 March, Beltane (May Day) 1 May, Summer solstice 21 June, Lammas 31 July, Autumnal equinox 21 September. For full discussion of their meanings, see Harvey 1997.

5 It is germane to note how the English Heritage view of the Holme-Next-The-Sea affair differs from that of neo-shamans. In *Heritage Today* (Issue 47, September 1999) the glossy magazine for English Heritage members, English Heritage are presented as having a common-sense approach (excavating the timbers as quickly as possible for preservation) in contrast to the rather hysterical responses of Druids and other neo-shamans. In their favour though, it is encouraging to see David Miles (English Heritage Chief Archaeologist) responding to the interests of alternative groups with an open mind. He

was keen to put the point to me, when we met at the European Association of Archaeologists' annual meeting, that English Heritage's aim is not the museumification of the landscape. Rather, they have the difficult job of balancing the needs of preservation with the promotion of public interaction.

6 The term Harvey chooses to employ hints at a fiscal return from neo-shamans to indigenous shamans. In reality this is not solely the case, indeed there are many ways neo-shamans give extra pay to shamanism that have nothing to do with money. Despite the connotations of capitalism and a patronising 'pat on the back' of indigenous shamans that may be perceived in the term 'extra pay', I can think of no better way of describing the process in operation, so have chosen to continue using the term here. There are numerous ways neo-shamans can be seen to be returning benefits to shamanism, such as using the term sensitively, raising awareness of the injustices faced by indigenous communities, and undergoing experiences that are acutely comparable to indigenous shamanism.

7 Similar 'fabulous results' have emerged at Stonehenge, which was open to all for the 2000 summer solstice.

8 Elsewhere I (Wallis In press), among others (see, for example, Harvey 1997; Jakobsen 1999), have pointed out certain problems with aspects of neo-shamanism, such as its universalising of shamanism in a fashion typical of occidental homogeneity, and reducing of shamanic experience to psychological archetypes, both of which avoid what Brown (1989) calls the 'dark side of the shaman'.

9 Certain groups however, such as the Odinic Rite and Hammarens Ordens Sallskap in Britain, and the Asatru Folk Assembly in the USA, are ostensibly concerned with 'blood and soil' issues though they try to avoid being explicitly racist, nationalist (British and/or European) and homophobic.

REFERENCES

Adler, M. (1986) *Drawing down the Moon: Witches, Druids, Goddess-worshippers and other Pagans in America Today*, Boston: Beacon Press.

Ashcroft, B., Griffiths, G. and Tiffin, H. (1998) *Key Concepts in Post-colonial Studies*, London: Routledge.

Bannister, V. (2000) 'A load of old rubbish', *Pagan Dawn: The Journal of the Pagan Federation* 135 (Beltane): 12–13.

Barfield, L. and Hodder, M. (1987) 'Burnt mounds as saunas, and the prehistory of bathing', *Antiquity* 61: 370–9.

Bender, B. (1998) *Stonehenge: Making Space.* Oxford: Berg.

Blain, J. and Wallis, R.J. (2000) 'The "ergi" seidman: Contestations of gender, shamanism and sexuality in northern religion, past and present', *Journal of Contemporary Religion* 15(3): 395–411.

Brown, M. (1998) 'Henge of the sea', *Sacred Hoop* 24: 15.

Brown, M.F. (1989) 'Dark side of the shaman', *Natural History* (November): 8–10.

Calver, S. (1998) *Avebury Visitor Research 1996–1998.* Report on behalf of the National Trust, Bournemouth: Bournemouth University.

Childe, V.G. (1958) *The Prehistory of European Society*, Harmondsworth: Penguin.

Clark-Mazo, G. (1997) 'Shamanism or "bad bones"?: Comments on the International Medieval Conference', *Pagan Dawn: the journal of the Pagan Federation* 125: 11.

Cope, J. (1998) *The modern antiquarian: a pre-millennial odyssey through megalithic Britain*, London: Thorsons.

Crawford, O.G.S. (1957) *The Eye Goddess*, London: Phoenix House.

Czaplicka, M.A. (1914) *Aboriginal Siberia: A Study in Social Anthropology*, Oxford: Clarendon Press.

Daniel, G. (1958) *The Megalith Builders of Western Europe*, London: Hutchinson.

Denison, S. (2000) 'Issues: One step to the left, two steps back', *British Archaeology* 52: 28.

Denning, K. (1999) 'Archaeology and alterity', unpublished paper presented in the 'Method and theory 2000' session at the Society for American Archaeology 64th Annual Meeting, Chicago.

Dowson, T.A. (1998) 'Homosexualitat, teortia queer i arqueologia' ['Homosexuality, queer theory and archaeology'] *Cota Zero* 14: 81–7 (in Catalan with English translation).

Dronke, U. (ed. and tr.) (1997) *The Poetic Edda. Vol. II Mythological Poems*, Oxford: Oxford University Press.

Ellis Davidson, H. (1993) *The Lost Beliefs of Northern Europe*, London: Routledge.

Ellis Davidson, H. and Fisher, P. (eds and tr.) (1998) *Saxo Grammaticus: The History of the Danes. Books I-IX*, Woodbridge: Brewer.

Farrar, J. and Farrar, S. (1984) *The Witches' Way: Principles, Rituals and Beliefs of Modern Witchcraft*, London: Robert Hale.

Finn, C. (1997) 'Leaving more than footprints: modern votive offerings at Chaco Canyon prehistoric site', *Antiquity* 71: 169–78.

Gimbutas, M. (1974) *The Goddesses and Gods of Old Europe: Myths and Cult Images*, London: Thames and Hudson.

Green, M. (1997) *Exploring the World of the Druids*, London: Thames and Hudson.

Guðbrandur Vigfússon and Unger, C.R. (eds) (1860–8). *Flateyjarbok: en samling af norske konge-sagaer med indskudte mindre fortællinger om begivenheder i og udanfor Norge samt Annaler 1–3*, Kristiania: no publisher.

Harvey, G. (1997) *Listening People, Speaking Earth: Contemporary Paganism*, London: Hurst and Co.

—— (1998) 'Shamanism in Britain today', *Performance Research* 3(3): 16–24.

Hassan, F.A. (1997) 'Beyond the surface: comments on Hodder's "Reflexive excavation methodology"', *Antiquity* 71: 1020–5.

Henry, H. (1999) 'Trends: pagan powers in modern Europe', *Hinduism Today International* (July): 1–3.

Herdt, G. (1996) 'Mistaken sex: culture, biology and third sex in New Guinea', in G. Herdt (ed.) *Third Sex Third Gender: Beyond Sexual Dimorphism in Culture and History*, New York: Zone Books.

Herzfeld, M. (1991) *A Place in History: Social and Monumental Time in a Cretan Town*, Oxford: Princeton University Press.

Hutton, R. (1991) *The Pagan Religions of the Ancient British Isles: Their Nature and Legacy*, Oxford: Blackwell.

—— (1996) 'Introduction – who possesses the past?', in P. Carr-Gomm (ed.) *The Druid Renaissance*. London: Thorsons.

—— (1997) 'The Neolithic Great Goddess: a study in modern tradition', *Antiquity* 71: 91–9.

—— (1999) *Triumph of the Moon: A History of Modern Pagan Witchcraft*, Oxford: Oxford University Press.

Jacobs, S., Thomas, W. and Lang, S. (1997) (eds) *Two-spirit People: Native American Gender, Sexuality, and Spirituality*, Illinois: University of Illinois Press.

Jakobsen, M.D. (1999) *Shamanism: Traditional and Contemporary Approaches to the Mastery of Spirits and Healing*, Oxford: Berghahn Books.

Jencson, L. (1989) 'Neopaganism and the Great Mother Goddess', *Anthropology Today* 5(2): 2–4.

Jones, L. (1998) *Druid, Shaman, Priest: Metaphors of Celtic Paganism*, Enfield Lock: Hisarlik Press.

Lewis, I.M. (1989) *Ecstatic Religion: A Study of Shamanism and Spirit Possession*, London: Routledge.

Lindquist, G. (1997) *Shamanic Performance on the Urban Scene: Neo-shamanism in Contemporary Sweden*, Stockholm Studies in Social Anthropology 39, Stockholm: University of Stockholm.

Luhrmann, T. M. (1989) *Persuasions of the Witches' Craft: Ritual Magic in Contemporary England*, Cambridge, Mass.: Harvard University Press.

Magnus Magnusson and Hermann Pálsson (1965) *The Vinland Sagas: The Norse Discovery of America*, London: Penguin.

Marcus, G.E. (1995) 'Ethnography in/of the World System: the emergence of a multi-sited ethnography', *Annual Review of Anthropology* 24: 95–117.

Matthews, J. (1991) *Taliesin: Shamanism and the Bardic Mysteries in Britain and Ireland*. London: Aquarian.

Meskell, L. (1995) 'Goddesses, Gimbutas and "New Age" archaeology', *Antiquity* 69: 74–86.

—— (1999) 'Feminism, paganism, pluralism', in A. Gazin-Schwartz and C. Holtorf (eds) *Archaeology and Folklore*, London: Routledge.

Morrison, R. (1999) 'Mad dogs and Englishmen . . .', *The Times* 22.06.99.

Murray, M.A. (1921) *The Witch-cult in Western Europe: A Study in Anthropology*, Oxford: Clarendon Press.

—— (1933) *The God of the Witches*, London: Sampson Low.

Nanda, S. (1993a) 'Hijras: an alternative sex and gender role in India', in G. Herdt (ed.) *Third Sex Third Gender: Beyond Sexual Dimorphism in Culture and History*, New York: Zone Books.

—— (1993b) 'Hijras as neither man nor woman', in H. Abelove, M.A. Barde and D.M. Halperin (eds) *The Lesbian and Gay Studies Reader*, London: Routledge.

Nietzsche, F. (1983) [1874] 'On the uses and disadvantages of history for life', in F. Nietzshe *Untimely Meditations*, Cambridge: Cambridge University Press.

Piggott, S. (1968) *The Druids*, London: Pelican.

Plouviez, J. (2000) 'Debating Seahenge – archaeology and emotion', i *Rescue News* 81: 3.

Price, N.S. (in press) *The Viking Way: Religion and War in Late Iron Age Scandinavia*, Uppsala: Uppsala University Press.

Radford, T. (1998) *Equinox: Homicide in Kennewick*, London: Channel Four Television.

Roscoe, W. (1991) *The Zuni Man-woman*, Albuquerque: University of New Mexico Press.

—— (1998. *Changing Ones: Third and Fourth Genders in North America*. London: Macmillan.

Salomonsen, J. (1999) 'Methods of compassion or pretension? Anthropological fieldwork in modern magical communities', *The Pomegranate: a new journal of neo-pagan thought* 8: 4–13.

Sebastion, T. (1990) 'Triad /I\: the Druid knowledge of Stonehenge', in C. Chippendale, P. Devereux, P. Fowler, R. Jones and T. Sebastian (eds) *Who Owns Stonehenge?*, Manchester: Batsford.

—— (2000) 'Alternative archaeology: has it happened?', in R.J. Wallis and K.J. Lymer (eds) *A Permeability of Boundaries?: New Approaches to the Archaeology of Art, Religion and Folklore*, Oxford: British Archaeological Reports.

Simek, R. (1993) *A Dictionary of Northern Mythology*, Bury St. Edmunds: St. Edmundsbury Press.

Sparkes, B.A. (1998) 'Sex in Classical Athens', in B.A. Sparkes (ed.) *Greek Civilisations: An Introduction*, Oxford: Blackwell.

Starhawk. (1989) *The Spiral Dance*, San Francisco: Harper & Row.

Taussig, M. (1987) *Shamanism, Colonialism and the Wild Man: A Study in Terror and Healing*, Chicago: University of Chicago Press.

—— (1989) 'The nervous system: homesickness and Dada', *Stanford Humanities Review* 1(1): 44–81.

Thompson, B. (1998) 'Cliff Richard is a Pagan', *The Independent Weekend Review*, 24.10.98: p. 12.

Ucko, P.J. (1990) 'Foreword', in P. Gathercole and D. Lowenthal (eds) *The Politics of the Past*, London: Unwin Hyman.

Wallis, R.J. (2000) 'Queer shamans: autoarchaeology and neo-shamanism', *World Archaeology* 32(2): 251–61.

—— (In press) 'Return to the source: neo-shamanism and shamanism in Central Asia and Siberia', in T.A. Dowson, M.M. Kośko and A. Rozwadowski (eds) *Rock Art, Shamanism and Central Asia: Discussions of Relations*. International Rock Art Monographs 2. Oxford: British Archaeological Reports.

Whitehead, H. (1993) 'The bow and the burden strap: a new look at institutionalised homosexuality in Native North America', in H. Abelove, M.A. Barde and D.M. Halperin (eds) *The Lesbian and Gay s tudies Reader*, London: Routledge.

Wilson, D. (1992) *Anglo-Saxon Paganism*, London: Routledge.

Young, D.E. and Goulet, J.-G. (eds) (1994) *Being Changed: The Anthropology of Extraordinary Experience*, Peterborough, Ontario: Broadview Press.

Index

Note: page numbers in italics denote illustrations
or figures